Love, Sex and Marriage

Love, Sex and Marriage

Insights from Judaism, Christianity and Islam

Dan Cohn-Sherbok
George D. Chryssides
Dawoud El Alami

scm press

© Dan Cohn-Sherbok, George D. Chryssides and
Dawoud El Alami 2013

Published in 2013 by SCM Press
Editorial office
3rd Floor
Invicta House
108–114 Golden Lane
London
EC1Y OTG

SCM Press is an imprint of Hymns Ancient & Modern Ltd
(a registered charity)
13A Hellesdon Park Road
Norwich NR6 5DR, UK

www.scmpress.co.uk

All rights reserved. No part of this publication may be reproduced,
stored in a retrieval system, or transmitted,
in any form or by any means, electronic, mechanical,
photocopying or otherwise, without the prior permission of
the publisher, SCM Press.

The Authors have asserted their right under the Copyright, Designs and
Patents Act, 1988, to be identified as the Authors of this Work

British Library Cataloguing in Publication data

A catalogue record for this book is available
from the British Library

978-0-334-04405-5

Typeset by Regent Typesetting, London
Printed and bound by
CPI Group (UK) Ltd, Croydon

Contents

The Authors	vii
Introduction: The Historical Background	xi

Part 1 Themes — 1
1 Sex Law — 3
2 Marriage — 48
3 Family Life — 91
4 Divorce — 132

Part 2 Trialogue — 175
5 Sex before Marriage — 177
6 Marriage — 184
7 Sex within Marriage — 191
8 Homosexuality — 198
9 Polygamy — 205
10 Intermarriage — 212
11 Abortion — 219
12 Assisted Reproduction and Adoption — 226
13 Family Life — 233
14 Divorce — 239

Glossary	245
Further Reading	251
Index	255

For Kate, Lavinia and Margaret

The Authors

Dan Cohn-Sherbok

My great-grandfathers were immigrants to the United States from Hungary at the end of the nineteenth century. Initially the family lived on the East Side of New York City; one of my great-grandfathers was a kosher butcher, and I have a photograph of him standing in front of his shop. After my maternal grandmother married my grandfather, who worked initially as a cigar-roller, they moved to Denver, Colorado. My mother grew up in a modern Orthodox synagogue, where she was confirmed. My father, who was an orthopaedic surgeon, came to do medical research at the National Jewish Hospital in Denver and met and married my mother. They joined the large Reform Temple, where I had a *bar mitzvah* and was confirmed. I went to a typical American high school and then studied philosophy at a small all-male liberal arts college, Williams College in Massachusetts. From a young age I wanted to be a rabbi, and I subsequently was a student at the Hebrew Union College, the main American rabbinical seminary for Reform Judaism. During my studies I served as a Reform rabbi at various congregations in the United States. I then was a rabbi in Australia, England and South Africa. I came to realize that the rabbinate was not for me – some time ago I wrote an autobiographical memoir, *Not a Job for a Nice Jewish Boy*, explaining why. In 1971 I enrolled as a PhD student at Cambridge University, and several years later became a lecturer in theology at the University of Kent. Subsequently I became Professor of Judaism at the University of Wales, where I am now Emeritus Professor. I am also an Honorary Professor at Aberystwyth University and Visiting Professor at St Mary's University College and York St

John University. Over the years I have been particularly interested in interfaith dialogue and have published a number of books dealing with Judaism and other faiths.

George D. Chryssides

I was brought up in the Church of Scotland. The minister in the Glasgow congregation we attended was an evangelical fundamentalist, but although I came to believe in a much more liberal form of Christianity, he generated enthusiasm, inspiring me to train for the ministry in the Church of Scotland. In order to do this I completed philosophy and theology degrees at the University of Glasgow. Having gained a first-class honours in both subjects, I decided to embark on an academic career instead of a church one and went to the University of Oxford, where I completed my doctoral thesis in 1974.

My first teaching post was at Plymouth Polytechnic, later to become the University of Plymouth. Around that time the Open University was starting up, and I became a tutor on its pioneering Religious Quest course. Many of the tutors, myself included, had limited knowledge of other faiths in the late 1970s and had a steep learning curve ahead. The university encouraged taking students on visits, which brought me into contact with Jews, Muslims, Hindus and Buddhists, whom I came to know as people rather than ideas in books. Being in England, I joined a local United Reformed Church and came to serve on its national Other Faiths Committee, where interfaith dialogue was an important interest. My first book, *The Path of Buddhism*, was the result of some of these conversations and was the first of several single-authored and edited works.

In 1992 I moved to the University of Wolverhampton, becoming Head of Religious Studies in 2001. On taking early retirement in 2008, I joined the University of Birmingham as an honorary research fellow. Having married an Anglican, I subsequently joined the Church of England and currently attend Lichfield Cathedral. I have a son and a daughter, both of whom have long since become adults, and I have two grandchildren.

THE AUTHORS

Dawoud El-Alami

My family are Palestinian but I was brought up in Egypt. I am the youngest of nine and the only one born after 1948. My father studied law at Montpellier in the 1920s but did not practise as a lawyer, devoting himself to managing his property. My parents were keen, however, that I should follow his profession.

My first degree was the *Licence en Droit* from the University of Cairo in 1978, and I started my career as a lawyer in Egypt. My particular interest was in family law, and in 1986 I commenced my doctoral studies at the University of Glasgow on the marriage contract in the Shari'a and the Personal Status laws of Egypt and Morocco. Over the next few years I worked at the University of Kent on a project analysing marriage and divorce records from a Libyan civil archive, and then in the early 1990s at Oxford University on a project investigating the way in which Arab Muslim communities in the UK apply Islamic family law within the framework of UK law. I was Chair of the Higher Studies Institute during the inaugural year of Al al-Bayt University in Jordan, and then moved to Wales in 1995, where for 16 years I taught Islamic Studies at the University of Wales Lampeter. This was a unique community of staff and students of all faiths, and it is where I met Dan Cohn-Sherbok. After a brief spell as Director of Research at Al Maktoum Institute in Dundee, I briefly took early retirement in 2012, but have now taken up a post as part-time Senior Teaching Fellow at the University of Aberdeen.

My wife is English. We have been married for 26 years and have three grown-up children, the eldest of whom is herself about to set out on the journey of marriage.

Introduction

The Historical Background

Judaism

BCE

1900–1600	Age of the Patriarchs
1250–1300	Exodus from Egypt
1030–930	United Monarchy
930	Division of the Kingdom
722	Destruction of the Northern Kingdom by the Assyrians
586	Destruction of the Southern Kingdom by the Babylonians
538	Return of the Exiles
450	End of Prophecy
146–400 CE	Roman period
100–200 CE	Mishnaic period

CE

70	Conquest of Jerusalem by the Romans
200	Mishnah compiled
c.200–600	Talmudic period
Sixth century CE	Babylonian Talmud
900–1000	Golden Age of Spain
1096	First Crusade
1230	Establishment of the Inquisition
1492	Expulsion of the Jews from Spain
1700–1800	Rise of Hasidism
1750–1800	Beginning of the Haskalah (Jewish Enlightenment)
c.1850	Reform Judaism founded

1897	First Zionist Congress
c.1905	Modern Orthodoxy Founded
1942–5	Holocaust
1948	Founding of the State of Israel
1967	Six Day War
1973	Yom Kippur War
1982	Israeli advance into Southern Lebanon
1992	Labour Party engages in dialogue with the PLO

Love, sex and marriage are key themes of Scripture at the beginning of the Genesis narrative. According to Genesis 1, God created Adam out of the dust of the ground and breathed into his nostrils the breath of life. He was then placed in the Garden of Eden. Yet God declared that it was not good for him to be alone, and created Eve out of one of his ribs. Eventually they were expelled from the Garden because they broke God's law about eating of the fruit of the tree of the knowledge of good and evil. Recognizing they were naked, they covered themselves with garments made of fig leaves. Subsequently they produced two sons.

The biblical narrative continues with an account of the Flood and later with the patriarchal narratives. According to the book of Genesis, Abraham was the first Jew. Living in a polytheistic culture in Babylonia, Abraham was called by God to be his servant and promised that his descendants would be as numerous as the stars in heaven. His progeny settled in the land of Canaan, but due to a famine migrated to Egypt, where the Hebrew clan grew in numbers. In time they were enslaved by Pharaoh; hearing their cries of suffering, God sent Moses to deliver them from their oppressors. After crossing the Red Sea they wandered for 40 years in the desert. During this period Moses received a revelation from God on Mount Sinai. According to tradition, he received the entire Torah (Five Books of Moses) there. The commandments contained in these books relate to all aspects of Jewish life, including regulations regarding sex and marriage.

After Moses' death the ancient Israelites conquered the land of Canaan under Joshua's leadership and established a united kingdom, ruled over first by judges and then by kings. In the tenth

INTRODUCTION

century BCE, however, the kingdom divided into two: Israel in the north and Judah in the south. During the first millennium BCE the Jews watched their country emerge as a powerful state, only to see it sink into spiritual and moral decay. Following the Babylonian conquest in 586 BCE the Temple lay in ruins, Jerusalem was demolished and the Jews despaired of their fate. Yet despite defeat and exile, the nation rose from the ashes of the two kingdoms. In the centuries that followed, the Jewish people continued their religious traditions and communal life. Under Roman rule, however, the Jewish population rebelled. In 70 CE the Temple was destroyed and thousands of Jews were deported. Such devastation did not quell the Jewish hope of ridding the Holy Land of its Roman oppressors. In the second century a messianic rebellion led by Simeon Bar Kokhba was crushed. Yet despite this defeat, the Pharisees carried on the Jewish tradition through teaching and study.

From the first century CE, Palestinian rabbinic scholars engaged in the interoperation of Scripture. The most important scholar of the early rabbinic period was Judah ha-Nasi, the head of the Sanhedrin, whose main achievement was the redaction of the Mishnah – a compendium of oral Torah – in the second century. This was followed by the redaction of the Palestinian Talmud in the fourth century and the Babylonian Talmud about two centuries later. These two multi-volume works contain the teachings of generations of rabbinic scholars, focusing on all aspects of Jewish law, including regulations regarding sex and marriage. By the sixth century the Jews had become a largely diaspora people. Despite the loss of a homeland, they were unified by a common heritage: law, liturgy and shared traditions. Within the Islamic world, Jews along with Christians were recognized as 'people of the Book' and were guaranteed religious freedom. In Christian lands, however, they were frequently subject to persecution.

By the end of the fourteenth century, political instability in Christian Europe led to the massacre of many Jewish communities. At the beginning of the fifteenth century, Spanish rulers introduced the Castilian laws, which segregated Jews from their Christian neighbours. In 1492, the entire Jewish community was expelled from Spain. In the next century the Inquisition was established in Portugal. To escape such persecution, many Spanish and Portuguese Marranos sought refuge in various parts of the Ottoman Empire. During the early modern period, Poland became a great centre of scholarship: in Polish academies, scholars collected together the legal interpretations of previous authorities and composed commentaries on the *Code of Jewish Law*, which had been compiled in the sixteenth century by Joseph Caro. In the seventeenth century, Jewish life became increasingly insecure due to political instability; nonetheless the Jewish community increased in size considerably during the eighteenth century. Despite such growth, Polish Jewry was subject to repeated onslaughts. Elsewhere in Europe this period witnessed Jewish persecution and oppression.

By the middle of the eighteenth century the Jewish community had suffered numerous waves of hostility and was deeply dispirited by the conversion of the seventeenth-century false Messiah Shabbetai Zevi. In this environment the Hasidic movement – grounded in Kabbalah – sought to revitalize Jewish life. Within this environment, Jewish emancipation gathered force. At the end of the eighteenth century, Moses Mendelssohn advocated the modernization of Jewish life. Later reformers pressed for the reformulation of the Jewish tradition. At the beginning of the nineteenth century, Israel Jacobson initiated a programme of reform. In the middle of the century the first Reform Synod took place in Germany. In the United States, Reform Judaism became an important force in Jewish life. Similarly, Conservative Judaism sought to modify the tradition in accord with historical change and development. After the pogroms of 1881–2 in Russia, many Jewish people emigrated to the United States, but a significant number were drawn to Palestine.

By the late 1880s the idea of a Jewish homeland had spread throughout Europe. At the first Zionist Congress in 1887, Theodor Herzl called for a national home based on international law. After establishing the basic institutions of the Zionist movement, Herzl embarked on a range of diplomatic negotiations. By the 1920s, Labour Zionism had become the dominant force in Palestinian life; in 1930 various socialist and Labour groups joined together in the Israel Labour Party. As Zionism gathered

INTRODUCTION

force in Europe and elsewhere, the Nazi onslaught engulfed Jewry in the Holocaust. Following this event, the United Nations approved the creation of a Jewish homeland in Palestine in 1948. In the following decades Israel was besieged by neighbouring countries. Despite a series of devastating wars, Jewish life continues to flourish in the Holy Land and the diaspora.

Christianity

c.4 BCE	Birth of Jesus of Nazareth
c.27 CE	Jesus' preaching ministry begins
c.30 CE	Jesus' crucifixion
c.30 CE	Day of Pentecost marks the beginning of the Christian Church
c.35 CE	Conversion of Paul (formerly Saul of Tarsus)
c.45–62	Paul's missionary journeys
70 CE	Fall of Jerusalem
325	Council of Nicaea defines the Creed of Nicaea
367	Letter of Bishop Athanasius defines the canon of Scripture
386	Conversion of Augustine of Hippo
451	Council of Chalcedon defines the Nicene Creed in its final form
1054	Great Schism, separating the Eastern and Western Churches
1517	Martin Luther defines his '95 Theses'
1534	Henry VIII's Act of Supremacy establishes his authority over the Church of England
1545–63	Council of Trent introduces reforms as part of the Roman Catholic Counter-Reformation
1611	The King James Version of the Bible is published
1869	First Vatican Council. The Council formally defines the doctrine of papal infallibility the following year
1910	Great Missionary Conference in Edinburgh marks the beginning of the ecumenical movement
1948	World Council of Churches formed
1962–5	Second Vatican Council

The Christian faith traces its origins to Jesus of Nazareth and also to the apostle Paul (formerly Saul) of Tarsus, who adapted its teachings to the Gentile world. As far as we know, both these leaders were unmarried, although their teachings contained much about human relationships and about love, sex and marriage.

Few non-Christian historical sources refer to Jesus, whose identity has been much debated by modern scholars. The Gospels state that he was a Jewish rabbi, and in its early years the Christians were part of the Jewish community, accepting and studying the Hebrew Scriptures. In contrast with the Jews, however, the Christians interpreted Jewish prophecy as pointing to Jesus as the expected Messiah, who fulfilled the promises made to Abraham and the other patriarchs and who is the culmination of Jewish law and prophecy.

The Christians added their own writings to those of the Jews, which included four Gospels (accounts of Jesus' life and work), letters of Paul and a few other early leaders, and the book of Revelation – a somewhat enigmatic apocalyptic work. The final corpus of Christian writing was not finally decided until the fourth century CE. The Gospels tell of Jesus' birth and ministry, in which he proclaimed the coming kingdom of God and the hope of salvation for his followers. The precise charges leading to Jesus' crucifixion remain unclear, but traditionally Christians have held that his death was an atoning sacrifice for sin, and that he rose from the dead three days later. Sunday, being the day of Christ's resurrection, became the principal day of worship for the majority of Christians, in preference to the Jewish sabbath.

A number of controversies about the person of Christ led to the formation of Christian creeds, the most important being the Nicene Creed, which affirms Jesus' full humanity and full divinity. Mainstream Christians regard Jesus Christ as one of three persons of a Trinity: Father, Son and Holy Spirit.

Christians attach importance to two principal rites – baptism and Holy Communion (also known as the Eucharist, or in the Roman Catholic tradition as the Mass). The former is the means of initiation into the Church while the latter is a symbolic re-enactment of Jesus' last meal with his disciples. Christians observe a number of festivals relating to the life of Jesus and the Church, the most important of which are Christmas and Easter. In common with other religions, Christians mark rites of passage within the context of their faith: this includes marriage, and family life is the most common lifestyle for Christians. Christianity is the only one of the Abrahamic faiths to have monastic orders, but these were not favoured among Protestants.

As Christianity developed, it introduced a hierarchy of priests and bishops, with two principal seats of authority in Rome and Constantinople (now Istanbul). A dispute about the nature of the Trinity in 1054 caused the Eastern and Western churches to split, and this event is known as the Great Schism, giving rise to the Eastern Orthodox and Roman Catholic churches respectively. In the sixteenth century a further major split occurred with the Protestant Reformation, the origins of which are usually attributed to Martin Luther (1483–1546), a scholar and a priest at Wittenberg, Germany. Luther and subsequent Protestant leaders regarded the Bible as the supreme source of authority, in contrast with the traditional Roman Catholic view that authority lies principally in the Church. Luther taught that salvation came through faith rather than works, and that divine grace could be obtained directly from God rather than through the saints and the Virgin Mary or the Church's priesthood. The Reformers introduced changes to the Mass, making worship available in the language of the people rather than in Latin – the traditional language used in the Church's liturgy.

The European Enlightenment of the eighteenth and nineteenth centuries caused Christianity to come to terms with modern science and scholarship. Darwin's theory of evolution proved particularly divisive in Protestant circles. Some became open to questioning the literal veracity of the creation story, while others aligned themselves with the emergent fundamentalist movement. Many Christians continue to accept the inerrancy of their Scriptures, while others perceive them as emanating from ancient worldviews that cannot be literally accepted in the modern world, but that nonetheless bear important spiritual truth.

Recent years have witnessed greater harmony between the Church's different traditions, with the rise of ecumenism. The World Council of Churches was set up in 1948, and in 1965 the

Roman Catholic and Orthodox churches revoked their mutual excommunications. The Second Vatican Council (1962–5), convened by Pope John XXIII, enabled the Roman Catholic Mass to be celebrated in the vernacular, in common with Protestant and Eastern Orthodox churches. Although Christianity has traditionally been a missionary religion, the increased presence of other faiths in the United States and Europe has brought many Christians into closer contact with other world religions and fostered greater tolerance and respect.

Islam

570 CE	Birth of the Prophet Muhammad
595	Muhammad's marriage to Khadija
610	Beginning of the Revelation of the Qur'an
620	Death of Khadija
622	Hijra – Emigration of the Muslims to Madina
630	Conquest of Mecca
632	Death of the Prophet – succeeded by Abu Bakr al-Siddiq (father of Aisha, favourite wife of Muhammad after the death of Khadija)
634	Death of Abu Bakr – succeeded by Umar ibn al-Khattab (father of Hafsa, wife of Muhammad who held and preserved a transcription of the Qur'an)
644	Death of Umar – succeeded by Uthman ibn Affan
656	Assassination of Uthman – succeeded by Ali ibn Abi Talib
656	Battle of the Camel – unsuccessful revolt against Ali by supporters of Uthman disappointed with Ali's failure to pursue his killers
657	Battle of Siffin between supporters of Ali and Mu'awiyya – ended in arbitration
661	Murder of Ali – succeeded briefly by his son al-Hasan, who abdicated the same year in favour of Mu'awiyya ibn Abi Sufyan, founder of Umayyad dynasty
680	Battle of Karbala – revolt against Mu'awiyya by

INTRODUCTION

	Al-Hussain, son of Ali and grandson of Muhammad. Martyrdom of Al-Hussain – key formative event in the history and doctrine of the Shi'a
711	Beginning of conquest of Iberian Peninsula
c.750–850	Foundation of the main Sunni schools of jurisprudence
765	Death of Ja'far al-Sadiq, sixth Shi'i Imam, leading to dispute over succession and schism between Shi'i denominations: Isma'ilis and Twelvers
c.768	First written biography of the Prophet Muhammad by Ibn Ishaq
c.850–875	Collection of the *hadith* and compilation of the first authoritative collections
970	Founding of Al-Azhar in Cairo – one of the first great centres of Islamic learning which retains its authority to the present day
1095–9	First Crusade – capture of Jerusalem by Christians
1145	Second Crusade – Muslims successfully defend Damascus
1187	Third Crusade launched after Muslims recapture Jerusalem
1229	Jerusalem returned to Christian control by Sultan Al-Malik Al-Kamil, who formed an alliance with the Christians
1245	Jerusalem recaptured by Muslims
1258	Mongol invasions
1300	Rise of Ottoman Empire
1492	End of Kingdom of Granada – last area of Islamic rule in Spain
1501–1723	Foundation of Safavid Empire with Isma'ili Shi'ism as official religion
1750	Rise of the Wahhabi movement
1922	Fall of the Ottoman Empire
1928	Formation of the Muslim Brotherhood
1932	Creation of the Kingdom of Saudi Arabia
1947	Foundation of Pakistan
1979	Islamic Revolution in Iran

LOVE, SEX AND MARRIAGE

Islam arose in the early seventh century in the city of Mecca in the Arabian Peninsula as, in the belief of Muslims, the culmination of the great monotheistic tradition of Judaism and Christianity. The received history of the life of the Prophet Muhammad and the early years of Islam is central to the belief of Muslims worldwide. Muhammad was born around 570 CE in Mecca, which was an important commercial centre at the crossroads of trade routes across the Arabian Peninsula, and a place of pilgrimage for the pagan Arabs. There were also significant Jewish and Christian populations and considerable interaction with merchants from southern Arabia, India, Syria and the Levant, and even Egypt and East Africa.

The heart of Mecca was the Kaaba, a cube-shaped building that Muslims believed was built by Abraham and his son, Isma'il, but by the time of Muhammad was filled with idols.

Around 610 CE Muhammad began to receive revelations through Jibril (the Angel Gabriel). The main message that he was to convey was that there was only One God and that he, Muhammad, was the last of His Prophets. The revelations were memorized by the early believers and recorded piecemeal, and later collated as the Qur'an, the literal word of God.

The Islamic calendar dates from 622 CE, when the early Muslim community fled Meccan persecution to the oasis town of Madina, where the population were looking for a leader to resolve local tribal disputes. Until this time the revelations, which continued throughout Muhammad's lifetime, had been largely concerned with principles of faith, monotheism, the evils of idolatry and reward and punishment in the hereafter. Now they started to deal with practical issues for a new community, such as marriage and divorce, care of children, inheritance, ethical conduct and honesty in trade. The Muslims conquered Mecca in 630 CE. Muhammad died in 632 CE, leaving the whole of the Arabian Peninsula under Muslim control. Under his first four successors, the Rightly Guided Caliphs, Islam expanded into Mesopotamia, the Levant and Persia.

The great theological schism between Sunna and Shi'a arose only about 30 years after the death of Muhammad with the rise of the Shi'a, whose founding belief is the divine right to the Caliphate

INTRODUCTION

in the line of the Prophet through his cousin Ali, who was married to Muhammad's daughter Fatima.

Following the first four Caliphs, the Sunni Umayyad dynasty (660–750) took Egypt, North Africa, the Iberian Peninsula and parts of Central Asia. It was swept away by the Shi'i Abbasids, who ruled the Muslim world as various sub-dynasties from Baghdad for the next 500 years. This is often referred to as Islam's Golden Age. Under Caliph Haroun Al-Rashid (786–809) and his successors, Baghdad became the cultural centre of the Islamic world, and during this period many of the great works of science, literature and philosophy were translated from Greek into Arabic and thereby preserved for the world. The most important early works of jurisprudence were written during this period by the scholars after whom the four main Sunni schools of jurisprudence are named, and the great collections of *hadith*, the narrative reports of the Prophet's words and deeds, were collected, collated and scrutinized to provide the second main source of law after the Qur'an.

Central Abbasid government was undermined to some extent by the existence of semi-autonomous Abbasid petty dynasties throughout the Islamic Empire. This allowed the Crusaders to make inroads into the Islamic territories from the late eleventh century. They established control of a number of cities in greater Syria, but their main aim was to take the city of Jerusalem from the Muslims, which they did in 1099.

Abbasid power was broken by the Mongol conquests in the mid thirteenth century as progressively they took all of the eastern provinces before defeating the Abbasid Caliphate in Iraq and advancing into Syria. They were only stopped in Palestine by Mamluk armies dispatched from Egypt and Syria. The Mamluks were also responsible for driving the last of the Crusaders out of the Levant.

Meanwhile a new power was emerging in Turkey. From the fourteenth century the Ottomans began their expansion into Greece, Italy and the Balkans, and in the sixteenth century they conquered Syria and Egypt and transferred the Caliphate to Istanbul. At the height of its power, the Ottoman Caliphate controlled Turkey, parts of Eastern Europe and Central Asia,

Iraq, Syria, Egypt and the Arabian peninsula. The Ottoman Empire began a slow decline from the seventeenth century as the influence of the European countries grew, fuelled particularly by the capitulations or trading monopolies granted by the Caliph, which undermined the economy of the Empire, and partly by the corruption and mismanagement that was inevitable in a complex centralized bureaucracy.

By the late nineteenth century the Caliphate in Istanbul, having lost most of its territories, was in irrecoverable decline and was challenged from within by Turkish and Arab nationalism. The Caliphate as the last vestige of a central Islamic authority was officially abolished in 1924.

Nationalism characterized the governments of many Muslim countries throughout the mid twentieth century, but since the 1970s there has been an Islamic resurgence in response to dictatorship and corruption, failure of governments to resolve long-standing political issues such as the Palestinian question, Western political and military involvement and the failure of governments to deliver economic prosperity for all.

Part 1

Themes

I

Sex Law

Judaism

The historical background

Modern attitudes towards sex are based on the biblical tradition: in order to understand sexuality in Judaism it is necessary to survey what the Hebrew Bible teaches. According to Scripture, in about the thirteenth century BCE the ancient Israelites escaped from Egyptian bondage. Led by Joshua, they conquered the Canaanites and became a nation. Living in farming communities, these early settlers had a relatively simple view of sexual matters. A smooth and comfortable relationship between the sexes was regarded as the basis for family life. Both men and women were mutually interdependent, and marriage was believed indispensable to a healthy existence. The purpose of sexuality was to create a family, which was perceived as the foundation of a humane society.

This is the context for understanding biblical legislation regarding sexual behaviour. Sexual intercourse was to be enjoyed at regular intervals and was a basic right of the husband and wife. Unlike the ascetic tradition that existed much later in Christianity, there was no trace of a negative attitude towards sex. As might be expected in a patriarchal society, men had more rights than women. Only men, for example, could initiate divorce. Yet adultery was considered to be a major sin whether committed by the husband or wife: there was no question of permitting the husband to mitigate or cancel the punishment. Rape and other forcible sexual relationships were similarly regarded as serious transgressions. Homosexuality was likewise prohibited, and according to Leviticus, could be punished by death.

This view of the relationship between men and women continued for centuries. However, in 720 BCE the Northern Kingdom (Israel) was conquered by the Assyrians, and nearly two centuries later, in 586 BCE, the Southern Kingdom (Judah) was vanquished by the Babylonians, and many of its inhabitants were taken to Babylonia. At the end of the sixth century BCE, King Cyrus of Persia, who had conquered the Babylonians, permitted Jews to return from exile, and the Temple was restored. These catastrophic events had a profound impact on Jewish life. The contact with foreign peoples and the movement of the population from rural areas to urban centres produced a profound change in Jewish attitudes. The simple peasant life of earlier times was transformed into a commercial city-dwelling community. Urban centres in Judaea (the Roman name for Judah), as well as cities where there were large Jewish populations (such as Alexandria in Egypt), became centres of immorality and turbulence. In such a context a new conception of human nature emerged. Men were conceived as weak, helpless creatures, heirs to inborn evil inclinations. Women, on the other hand, were perceived as sources of temptation. This changed understanding was accompanied by an increasing emphasis on asceticism as well as a strict code of sexual morality. Numerous restrictions relating to social contact came into place.

Such a negative conception of men and women during the period of the second commonwealth (sixth century BCE to first century CE) lessened during the early rabbinic period. The rabbis of the Talmud regarded women as less dangerous than had been considered previously. In their view, moderate discipline of women should be the norm. According to rabbinic theology, the evil inclination (*yetzer ha-ra*), which in part was understood as the sexual drive, was viewed as the source of energy for properly sublimated activities. The goods of the physical world were to be enjoyed but only in moderation, in accordance with the numerous laws formulated during this period. In this context marriage was considered to be a fundamental institution of society, and a Jew who was unmarried was viewed as living without joy or blessing.

During the post-Talmudic period such a moderate view of marriage was influenced by other cultures, which introduced an ascetic strain into Jewish life. During the Middle Ages, for example, the body was viewed as evil and the soul as good. Hence human beings were regarded as animal and divine. Sexual appetites were seen as the animal element of human nature; the soul, on the other hand, was divine – the beast within each person was to be subdued by wise rule and mastery of the soul. Without such restraint, humans would become slaves to their passions. By contrast, satisfaction of the soul and the higher ideals would lead to contentment. Medieval Jewish philosophers, such as the twelfth-century thinker Moses Maimonides, argued that the exercise of the intellectual faculties is the highest human activity. Nonetheless, it was recognized that the needs of the body must be fulfilled.

During the medieval period there also emerged a mystical (Kabbalistic) view of sexual activity, which regarded sexual relations as holy and divine. It was believed that when a man cleaves to his wife, the divine is present – the human body and its physical needs were perceived as bound up with holiness. In this light, human beings were seen as an expression of the universal union of the physical and the spiritual. As such, human action was regarded as having cosmic significance. For the Kabbalist, the sexual impulse was not simply a physical passion but a holy urge.

Through these different periods of Jewish history there persisted a view of sexuality as a human good. Despite the emphases that emerged at different times, there was a general recognition that sex must be socialized to fit with the needs of the community. Through biblical and rabbinic legislation, sexual life was regulated and governed by rules and restrictions. Adultery, rape, harlotry and homosexuality were condemned. Sexual activity was prohibited outside of marriage. A man was forbidden even to pass by the house of a harlot within a specified distance. If he were seen too often about the house of a woman of ill-repute, disciplinarily flogging was prescribed. Masturbation was considered a wasting of the seed and prohibited. The first commandment in Scripture – be fruitful and multiply – was viewed as of fundamental importance. In modern times the legal restrictions of the past have been substantially modified, yet across the religious spectrum marriage continues to be regarded as fundamental to Jewish life.

Sex in marriage

In the earliest sections of the Bible there is a simple code of sexual morality. Marriage laws and the prohibition of adultery are linked to penalties for acts not connected to marriage, including rape, seduction, prostitution, buggery, wearing the attire of the opposite sex, copulation between two men and exposing a father's nakedness in the presence of his sons. The standards of sexual morality were radically changed during the period of the Second Temple. As we have seen, the naivety of the older period gave way to worldly suspicion. This worldliness was the result of the new setting in which Jews found themselves in the post-exilic period. Men were conceived as helpless creatures, heirs to inborn evil tendencies inherited from Adam; constantly, they were lured by evil. Taking advantage of such inherent weakness, Satan employs women as his tool to entice and corrupt his victims. Such pessimism led inevitably to asceticism, which engendered a negative view of sex. Some of these morbid teachings concerning human sexuality continued in the Talmudic period and shaped rabbinic legislation.

The Jewish view of sexual morality involves strict discipline, as is evident in the *Code of Jewish Law*, a compilation of earlier teachings composed by Joseph Caro in the sixteenth century, which has served as the framework for Jewish existence until modern times. In the sections dealing with the laws of marriage, prescriptions concerning legitimate sexual behaviour are described in detail. These laws begin with the injunction to marry:

> It is the duty of every man to take a wife to himself in order to fulfill the precept of propagation. This precept becomes obligatory on a man as he reaches the age of eighteen. At any rate, no man should pass his twentieth year without taking a wife. Only in the event when one is deeply engrossed in the study of the Torah, and he is afraid that marriage might interfere with his studies, may he delay marrying, providing he is not lustful. (*Code of Jewish Law*, vol. 4, ch. 150, 1)

Here the injunction to marry is paramount. Today it is rare even in Orthodox circles for marriage to take place at such an early stage. Yet among the strictly Orthodox, marriages of relatively young couples are frequently arranged by watchful parents. Once a marriage has taken place, sexual relations are strictly regulated. The *Code of Jewish Law* continues with laws of chastity within marriage. How should the husband conduct himself?

> A man should accustom himself to be in a mood of supreme holiness and to have pure thoughts, when having intercourse. He should not indulge in levity with his wife, nor defile his mouth with indecent jests, even in private conversation with her. He should not converse with her either at copulation or immediately before it, excepting about matter directly needed for the act. (*Code of Jewish Law*, vol. 4, ch. 150, 1)

The *Code* goes on to describe the proper mode of intercourse:

> The intercourse should be in the most possible modest manner. He underneath and she above him, is considered an impudent act; both at the same level is considered a pervert act ... When having intercourse, one should think of some subjects of the Torah, or of some other sacred subjects; and although it is forbidden during this act to utter holy words, yet thinking is permissible, even meritorious (*Code of Jewish Law*, vol. 2, ch. 150, 1,2)

According to Jewish law there are numerous prohibitions connected with the sexual act:

- It is forbidden to have intercourse by a light.
- It is forbidden to have intercourse in the presence of any person.
- It is forbidden for a man to look at the genital organ of his wife.
- It is forbidden to have intercourse in a room where a *sefer torah* (Torah scroll) is found. (*Code of Jewish Law*, vol. 4, ch. 150, 3,4,5,6)

Other laws specify the attitude of the husband towards his wife when performing his marital duty:

LOVE, SEX AND MARRIAGE

- A person must not be unduly familiar with his wife, excepting at the regular time appointed for the performance of his marital duty.
- When having intercourse, his intention should not be to satisfy his personal desire, but to fulfil his obligation to perform his marital duty ... and to comply with the command of his Creator and that he may have many children engaged in the study of the Torah and the practice of its precepts. (*Code of Jewish Law*, vol. 4, ch. 150, 7,9)

In the Jewish tradition, marriage is seen as a sacred act. At the marriage ceremony, seven blessings are recited expressing the joy of married life:

Blessed are you, O Lord Our God, King of the Universe who creates the fruit of the vine ...
Who has created all things to your glory ... Creator of man.
Who has made man in your image, after your likeness ...
made she who was barren (Zion) be glad and
exult when her children are gathered within her
in joy. Blessed are you, O Lord, who makes
Zion joyful through her children.
O make these loved companions greatly to rejoice, even as of old you did gladden your creatures in the Garden of Eden. Blessed are you, O Lord, who makes bridegroom and bride to rejoice.
... Who has created joy and gladness,
bridegroom and bride, mirth and exultation,
pleasure and delight, love, brotherhood, peace
and fellowship. Soon may there be heard in the cities
of Judah and in the streets of Jerusalem,
the voice of joy and gladness, the voice of the
bridegroom and the bride, the happy
sound of bridegrooms from their
canopies, and of youths from their feasts
of song. Blessed are you, O Lord, who makes the
bridegroom to rejoice with the bride.

Sexual modesty

Within the Jewish tradition, sexual morality extends to all aspects of human life. Exposure of the body, for example, constitutes a violation of God's decree. In the biblical period the priests who ministered in the Temple were cautious not to uncover any part of their bodies: for this reason trousers and a cap were worn. Even a lay person committed a grievous transgression if he came into the sanctuary with garments torn in such a manner that his chest was uncovered. Later, during the early rabbinic period, a woman with an uncovered head was considered partly naked. In this context it was considered an offence to observe the nakedness of one's father. For this reason it was forbidden for a man to go to the bath house with his father, father-in-law or brother-in-law. Of pre-eminent importance were the regulations forbidding a woman's body to be exposed. Female nurses, for example, were permitted to attend patients suffering from intestinal disorders, even though seeing a patient's private parts was involved. Yet a male nurse was not allowed to attend a female patient with such a condition.

In the early and later rabbinic period it was also considered sinful to look at a woman's hair. Among the sages of the second century CE there is a view recorded in the name of R. Judah that despite the fact that the Bible requires uncovering the head of the woman charged with adultery, this should not be done if the woman has beautiful hair, because it might undermine the morals of the young priests. Following such rabbinic legislation it is customary for married Orthodox women to cover their hair or to wear a wig (*sheitel*). This substitution for the head cover is widely practised and is regarded as an expression of modesty. Some traditional authorities, however, did not regard the veiling of the head or donning a *sheitel* as sufficient; in addition they demanded that married women have their hair cut or shaven. Accordingly, a special ceremony was arranged, either immediately before the nuptials or soon after, of cutting the bride's hair.

Such attitudes of female modesty have persisted into modern times. The eminent eighteenth-century scholar Jonathan Eibeschutz, for example, bemoaned the sinfulness of non-Jewish fashions. 'In our sinful generation,' he wrote, 'they (the women) have learned from the gentile manner of dress to bare their necks ... I warn you, cease this evil thing, for the woman whose neck is uncovered is destined eventually to be drawn unto the slaughter by the angel of death ... for she is wicked and causes sin to others' (*Ya'arot Debash* I, 12, ed. Warsaw, 1889, p. 30a).

The proper use of ornaments and cosmetics by women was also a subject of public morality. In traditional circles it has been felt that too extravagant a display takes on the character of coquetry and vulgarity, suggesting an attitude of seeking to attract men in the manner of harlots. Loud ornaments and cosmetics were regarded as offensive and indicative of a lack of refinement. A further reason for restraint was that the display of expensive ornaments could create envy in the hearts of Gentiles. In the Middle Ages a series of sumptuary laws were enacted by Jewish courts and communities, restricting women and men as well to simplicity in dress and ornamentation.

Sexual morality also extended to prescriptions about social segregation. Rabbinic sages were determined to regulate the mingling of the sexes. Through the centuries it was considered dangerous for women to be out in public. Rabbinic law also provided firm guidelines for social relationships between men and women. In this regard the *Code of Jewish Law* stipulates a range of restrictions:

- One must not be alone with any woman, whether she is young or old, a Jewess or a non-Jewess, or whether she is related to him or not, with the exception of a father who is permitted to be alone with his daughter, a mother with her son, and a husband with his wife.
- If one is accompanied by his wife, he may also be alone with another woman, because his wife watches him.
- One woman may be alone with two virtuous men, but only in a town and in the daytime; but in the field or at night even in a town, there must be at least three virtuous men.
- A woman should never be alone with immoral men, even if there are many, unless their wives are with them (*Code of Jewish Law*, vol. 4, ch. 152, 1,2,3).

Such suspicion of lustful conduct extends into all spheres of daily living. Even in the lavatory, men must be careful to avoid lascivious thoughts. Thus the *Code of Jewish Law* states:

- A man must exercise modesty when in the lavatory; he should not expose himself before he sits down, and should not expose his body more than is actually necessary. While in the lavatory, it is forbidden to think of sacred matters; it is, therefore, best to concentrate there upon one's business affairs and accounts, so that one may not be led to think either of holy matters or, God forbid, indulge in sinful thoughts (*Code of Jewish Law*, vol. 1, ch. 4, 2).
- One is forbidden to bring on an erection or to think about women. If lascivious thoughts come to one spontaneously, he should divert his attention to a subject of the Torah.
- A man should be extremely careful to avoid an erection. Therefore, he should not sleep on his back with his face upward, or on his belly with his face downward, but sleep on his side in order to avoid it.
- It is forbidden to hold the penis while urinating. If one is married and his wife is in town and she is clean, it does not matter, for since he has the possibility, he will not indulge in lustful thoughts or become stimulated.
- It is forbidden to discharge semen in vain. This is a graver sin than any other mentioned in the Torah. Those who practice masturbation and cause the issue of semen in vain, not only do they commit a grave sin, but they are under a ban, concerning whom it is said (Isa. 1.15): 'your hands are full of blood' (*Code of Jewish Law*, vol. 4, ch. 151, 1,2,3).

Natural and unnatural sexual conduct

As previously noted, biblical and rabbinic law stipulates that a variety of acts should be regarded as sexual perversions. Hence Leviticus prohibits buggery:

> If a man lies with a beast, he shall be put to death; and you shall kill the beast. If a woman approaches any beast and lies with

it, you shall kill the woman and the beast; they shall be put to death, their blood is upon them. (Lev. 20.15-16)

Together with other unnatural connections, this perversion is regarded as belonging to the various abominations of heathens, particularly the former inhabitants of Canaan. In post-biblical times it appears that such perverse acts were uncommon among Jewry. Hence when the second-century sage R. Judah b. Illai wanted to prohibit young unmarried Israelites from engaging in shepherding out of fear they might commit buggery with animals under their care, his colleagues protested: 'Israelites are above suspicion of buggery' (Kid. 82a).

Basing themselves on biblical law, rabbinic scholars argued that the death penalty for sexual contact with a beast is stoning for both the offender and the animal. The execution for the animal, however, presented a problem since if a female animal were attacked by a man, the animal would not have sinned since it is under no moral code. Nonetheless, they believed the law was justified in executing the beast because it served as the tool for the downfall of a human being. The Talmud regards the moral injunction against copulation with beasts as binding on all human beings – in the view of rabbinic sages it is one of the seven moral laws (Noachide Laws) that are obligatory for non-Jews. Thus a heathen who is under Jewish jurisdiction committing the crime of buggery should suffer the death penalty by the hand of a Jewish court.

Sodomy (copulation between two males) was similarly regarded as an evil practice and belonged to the same category of perversion. The prevalence of this act is illustrated in the biblical stories of the atrocities of Sodom and those of the town of Gibeah, in which it appears the mob demanded to be given the visiting strangers for male copulation (Gen. 19.5). Leviticus explicitly forbids such sexuality: 'If a man lies with a male as with a woman, both of them have committed an abomination; they shall be put to death, their blood is upon them' (Lev. 20.13). For the ancient Israelites the practice of sacred sodomy among the Canaanites was regarded as hateful; nonetheless, under King Rehoboam in the ninth century BCE, idolatry became rampant in Judaea and 'there were also male cult prostitutes in the land' (1 Kings 14.24). His grandson, Asa, tried to cleanse the Temple in Jerusalem of the practice, and a further effort was made by his great-grandson Jehoshaphat. Even so, sodomy in the Temple was not eradicated until the reforms of King Josiah in the seventh century BCE. Later, the prohibition against sodomy was seen not simply as a sexual crime but as a form of idolatry.

In rabbinic times the law forbidding sodomy was viewed as a prohibition for all human beings. Yet it was widely perceived that the standards of sexual morality were much more lax in Roman circles. Hence according to the first-century historian Josephus, Herod refused to send his young brother-in-law Aristobulus to the Roman court at the request of Anthony because he did not think it safe for him to send one so handsome in the prime of his life (Josephus, *Antiq.*, XV.2, 6). It was recognized that women could also engage in homosexual practice, but the law did not treat lesbianism so severely. R. Huna, a Babylonian sage, declared that a woman who indulged in such acts was unfit for marriage with a priest. The twelfth-century Jewish philosopher and legalist Maimonides argued that women should suffer flagellation and be separated from other women if they committed such acts.

As we have seen, the purpose of sexual intercourse is procreation: hence Jewish law stipulates that spilling semen in vain is an immoral act. The Bible records such an act of wickedness in relation to Onan, who married his deceased brother's wife:

> But Onan knew that the offspring would not be his; so when he went in to his brother's wife he spilled the semen on the ground, lest he should give offspring to his brother. (Gen. 38.9)

In this light, masturbation was viewed as a serious offence. Hence R. Ishmael taught that the command 'Thou shalt not commit adultery' includes lewdness by means of the hand as well (Nid 13b). Another early rabbinic scholar applied to those who practise self-abuse the biblical phrase 'Your hands are full of blood' (Nid 13b). More explicit was the Palestinian scholar R. Johanna, who states that such a person is guilty of a capital crime (Nid 13a). The medieval mystical work, the Zohar, states that such a sexual act is the most severe sin recorded in Scripture. Further, post-Talmudic ethical literature continually stresses the severity of this sin and exhorts its avoidance, pointing out its dangers to health.

Because procreation is fundamental to Jewish life, marrying a woman who is unable to bear children is to be avoided. According to some authorities, marrying a barren woman involves wasting semen. The first-century Jewish philosopher Philo considers this a violation of Jewish law and argues that such cohabitation is lustful indulgence (Philo, *de spec. leg.*, iii.36). As a consequence, he argues that marriage with a barren woman should be prohibited. The rabbis, on the other hand, do not entirely agree, although they too believe that Jewish men should marry women who are capable of producing offspring. Regarding contraception, the law specifies that men are not permitted to use contraceptive devices (such as condoms) because of the waste of semen. Nonetheless, the Talmud permits the insertion of a pessary in the vaginal canal when the wife is too young, or in a condition of pregnancy, or if she is a nursing mother. In such cases if the woman or her child is at risk of serious complications, the use of such contraception is allowed. Post-Talmudic law is lenient on the question of female contraceptives for medicinal purposes. Yet when there is no medical purpose for such contraceptives, the law is more rigorous. Within Jewish law there are two main approaches. The first declares that both men and women are prohibited from wasting nature: unless there is medical necessity, any artifice calculated to make the seed unproductive is prohibited. The other view is that a woman is not included in the prohibition of waste of nature. As a result, female contraception (such as the use of IUD or a contraceptive pill) is permitted for a wide range of reasons.

Modern Jewish attitudes

From the foregoing it might be assumed that Jews today would feel obliged to embrace the many restrictions regarding sexual morality that we have surveyed. This, however, is not the case. Across the religious spectrum, Jews have largely abandoned the vast corpus of biblical and rabbinic law. Only among the strictly

Orthodox does the *Code of Jewish Law* have binding authority. The Jewish tradition affirms that God revealed 613 commandments to Moses on Mount Sinai. According to the rabbis, the expositions and elaborations of the law were also given to Moses; subsequently they were passed from generation to generation, and through this process additional legislation was incorporated. This process is referred to as the Oral Torah. Thus traditional Judaism affirms that God's revelation was two-fold and obligatory for all time.

For the strictly Orthodox what this means in practice is that the entire *Code of Jewish Law* must be followed because it is God's will for his chosen people. In the various non-Orthodox movements (Conservative Judaism, Reform Judaism, Liberal Judaism, Reconstructionist Judaism, Humanistic Judaism), however, there has been a rejection of this fundamental belief. Instead there has been a general acceptance of the findings of biblical scholarship, which asserts that the Pentateuch is a composite work, reflecting the views of the ancient Hebrews over centuries of development. Further, the rabbinic interpretations of biblical law are understood as human inventions rather than expressions of the divine will. Such a view rules out the traditional belief in the infallibility of Scripture as well as the rabbinic chain of tradition, and thereby provides a rationale for changing the law in the light of contemporary knowledge. In the modern period, therefore, there has been a shift away from the legal fundamentalism of the past. As a result, non-Orthodox Jews – who comprise the vast majority of Jews throughout the world – do not feel obliged to follow traditional Jewish teaching about sexual morality.

Yet despite such a reorientation of Jewish life, there is a general acceptance of the centrality of marriage. Both Orthodox and non-Orthodox Jews regard marriage as God's plan for humanity: it is viewed as both a sacred bond and a means to personal fulfilment. The purpose of marriage is to build a home, create a family and thereby perpetuate society. In this light, many of the laws regarding sexual behaviour continue to be relevant in contemporary society. Due to the sacred nature of marriage, sexual relations outside marriage are regarded as undermining this fundamental feature of Jewish life. However, the stringent regulations of the past concerning the relationship between men and women have been abandoned. No longer are men and women rigorously separated for fear of arousing lust. Instead, Jewish men and women mingle freely in all social situations. Rather than being kept separate, it is universally accepted – except among the strictly Orthodox – that young Jewish men and women will go out together and engage in various degrees of sexual activity before marriage. Instead of marrying at an early age, it is not unusual for couples to get engaged in their late twenties or later, many living together before becoming husband and wife.

There has also been a major shift away from traditional teaching about homosexuality and lesbianism. In the past such behaviour was regarded as perverse and abhorrent. Today, however, same-sex relations are perceived in a completely different light. The Reform movement, for example, has officially recognized the validity of same-sex relationships and has called for civil same-sex marriages for many years. The CCAR (Central Conference of American Rabbis), the professional association of Reform Rabbis, passed a resolution in 1996 opposing governmental efforts to ban gay and lesbian marriage. The Union of American Hebrew Congregations, the congregational arm of the Reform movement, followed suit in 1997, resolving to support secular efforts to promote legislation that would provide civil marriage and equal opportunity for gay men and lesbians.

The Reconstructionist movement has also expressed its support for the full inclusion of gay men and lesbians in all aspects of Jewish life in its 1992 Report of the Reconstructionist Commission on Homosexuality. The report affirmed the holiness of homosexual relationships and the need to affirm them in a Jewish context. The Reconstructionist movement today also fully endorses efforts to legalize civil same-sex marriages and grant homosexual couples equal benefits.

Turning to the issue of women's status, there has been a major shift away from the numerous restrictions relating to women's role in the community. In the various non-orthodox branches of Judaism there is a universal acceptance that women should have an equal role in all aspects of religious life. In Conservative, Reform, Reconstructionist and Humanistic Judaism, women are ordained as rabbis and officiate as cantors. It is only among the Orthodox that legislation curtailing women's rights remains. Today the vast majority of Jewish women have embraced the principles of feminism, insisting that women should play a full part in Jewish life.

In *The American Jew: Voices from an American Jewish Community*, a committed feminist expressed her disenchantment with traditional Orthodoxy:

> Judaism is a patriarchal religion: obviously it's institutionalized sexism. It's role-based; it's gender based ... I know that Orthodox Judaism suits the traditional family. It attracts those who want to live in this manner and it is a growing area of Judaism. I certainly see its attractions for men ... You have your wife waiting on you hand and foot. You're the king of the roost, and you have all these wonderful rituals. Honestly! For me it's deplorable. I will not support that kind of organization with one cent of my money. I'm not going to give my paltry little contribution from my paltry little salary to any organization that does not conform with my beliefs ... I'm much more interested in the positive side. Reinforcing and listening to Jewish women who have done something significant, resurrecting Jewish heroines, encouraging Jewish women's accomplishments.[1]

Christianity

Christian ethics: the basics

> They do not inhabit separate cities of their own, or speak a strange dialect, or follow some outlandish way of life. Their teaching is not based upon reveries inspired by the curiosity of men. Unlike some other people, they champion no purely human doctrine. With

---

1 Dan and Lavinia Cohn-Sherbok, *The American Jew: Voices from an American Jewish Community*, London: HarperCollins, 1994, pp. 259–60.

> regard to dress, food and manner of life in general, they follow the customs of whatever city they happen to be living in, whether it is Greek or foreign.
>
> And yet there is something extraordinary about their lives. They live in their own countries as though they were only passing through. They play their full role as citizens, but labour under all the disabilities of aliens. Any country can be their homeland, but for them their homeland, wherever it may be, is a foreign country. Like others, they marry and have children, but they do not expose them. They share their meals, but not their wives.
>
> They live in the flesh, but they are not governed by the desires of the flesh. They pass their days upon earth, but they are citizens of heaven.
>
> (Letter to Diognetus from an unknown author, second or third century CE)

Christianity has an estimated 2.1 billion followers and possibly around 40,000 different denominations; around 350 alone belong to the World Council of Churches. It is therefore unreasonable to expect to find an agreed view on sexual morality, apart from a few fundamentals. It is often difficult, too, to distinguish liberalizing tendencies from sheer bad practice. One of my students put on his online university profile that he was an evangelical Christian and, after declaring several of his interests, added, 'and likes sleeping around'! Much of the time Christian teaching does not differ significantly from that of secular forms of morality. As the writer to Diognetus explained (above), Christians do not seek to stand out as being noticeably different from others but rather to act in accordance with prevailing social customs while stimulating others to behave as they should. Western secular morality has of course been deeply influenced by Christian history, and Christian teaching in turn owes much to its roots in the Jewish faith.

Christians may not feel quite at home with the phrase 'sex law'. Although Christianity took its rise in first-century Judaism, St Paul taught that the Christian is 'not under law, but under grace' (Rom. 6.14). In order to make sense of the Christian position on sexual morality – its preferred term to 'sex law' – it is important to look at its sources of authority. Christianity has three main traditions: Eastern Orthodoxy, Roman Catholicism and Protestantism. All three traditions share a common set of Scriptures, albeit with some minor differences (for example, the Roman Catholic Church accepts the Apocrypha as authoritative while Orthodox and Protestant Christians do not). The Protestant tradition regards the Scriptures as the fundamental although not necessarily infallible source of authority; the leaders of the Protestant Reformation, such as Martin Luther and John Calvin, affirmed the principle of *sola scriptura*, meaning that 'scripture alone' was all that was needed to gain religious truth and to find salvation.

Roman Catholicism, by contrast, holds that the tradition of the Church is the seat of authority. While Protestants contend that it is Scripture that recounts the story of the Church's beginnings and early progress, the Catholic Church points out that it was the Church that defined the canon of Scripture and hence is primordial. While not rejecting the authority of Scripture, Roman Catholics hold that Scripture is the secondary source of authority and that the Church is the custodian of its interpretation and application.

While affirming the authority of the Bible, Eastern Orthodoxy tends not to disseminate it in much detail. The average homily in an Orthodox church tends to be very short – perhaps around five minutes or even less – and often simply retells the Gospel reading, commending its import to the congregation.

For the Roman Catholic, the Church's teachings on all matters of faith and morals can be found in its canon law. This consists of the decisions of the Church's Councils and teachings of the Magisterium (the bishops, archbishops and cardinals collectively), which are expressed in their canons or summed up by papal authority in pronouncements or encyclical letters, the most significant of which for our present purposes are *Casti connubii* (Of Chaste Marriage, 1930) and *Humanae vitae* (Of Human Life, 1968). Although the full text of such documents can be accessed on the Vatican website, most Catholics are familiar with the Church's position through nurture and through dissemination via its clergy. The most definitive reference work on Church doctrine and practice is the *Catechism of the Catholic Church* (1994), which provides a distillation of the Church's teachings on most matters, cross-referenced to its official pronouncements.

The Orthodox position is that teachings on matters of faith and morals should reflect 'the mind of the Church' – that is to say, the whole Church. The Eastern and Western Churches separated at the Great Schism of 1054, and hence considerable importance is attached to the pronouncements of ecumenical councils and to the canons of the Church that pre-date 1054, since such decisions reflect a more united Christendom. Considerable weight is therefore attached to the teachings of the early Church Fathers and to Scripture, since the canon of Scripture was defined by Bishop Athanasius in 367 CE. The emphasis on the early Church's teachings tends to give a conservative bias to Orthodox teaching, possibly more so than in the other two traditions.

It may be helpful to identify my own stance. I was brought up in the Protestant tradition in the Church of Scotland but, since moving to England, decided to join the Church of England. Although the Anglicans were an important part of the Protestant Reformation, they are not always considered to be fully Protestant and sometimes describe themselves as 'catholic and reformed'. Christianity is complicated, and that is another story that I have written about elsewhere. In what follows I have attempted to present the positions of all three traditions. If I seem to have given undue prominence to Roman Catholicism, this is because it has defined its position in more detail than other traditions and because it is possibly the most controversial.

Law or grace?

> They made her stand before the group and said to Jesus, 'Teacher, this woman was caught in the act of adultery. In the Law Moses commanded us to stone such women. Now what do you say?' They were using this question as a trap, in order to have a basis for accusing him. But Jesus bent down and started to write on

> the ground with his finger. When they kept on questioning him he straightened up and said to them, 'Let any one of you who is without sin be the first to throw a stone at her.' Again he stooped down and wrote on the ground. At this, those who heard began to go away one at a time, the older ones first, until only Jesus was left, with the woman still standing there. Jesus straightened up and asked her, 'Woman, where are they? Has no one condemned you?' 'No one, sir,' she said. 'Then neither do I condemn you,' Jesus declared. 'Go now and leave your life of sin.'
>
> (John 8.3–11, NIV)

One important consequence of the Protestant Reformation, which began in the sixteenth century, was that Protestant Christians were no longer subject to papal authority or to the Church of Rome's canon law. Of course, this did not entail a rejection of everything the Church had taught on moral matters, although in England King Henry VIII's dispute with the Pope was about marriage and annulment. What the Protestant churches had lost was the basis of authority in moral matters. This caused Protestant Christians to fall back on Scripture as the ultimate source of authority in faith and morals.

For Christian fundamentalists, belief in the authority of the Bible amounts to regarding it as inerrant in all matters, whether historical, scientific, theological or ethical. Belief in scriptural inerrancy incurs obvious problems, however, not least of which is the relationship between the Christian and the Jewish Scriptures. Christians chose to adopt the scriptures of their Jewish ancestry, as well as their own new ones, and Christian fundamentalists have not fully resolved the question of the relationship between the two 'testaments' or 'covenants'. If the Bible is an infallible book, and includes the Old as well as the New Testament, then why are Christians not stoning adulterers, insisting that women are confined during menstruation or that men observe purification rites after semen ejaculation?

When asked why we do not observe these ancient Israelite laws, Christians will frequently echo Paul's words that they are 'not under law, but under grace' (Rom. 6.14). As Paul says, 'All who rely on the works of the law are under a curse' (Gal. 3.10), and the writer of Ephesians (whom some scholars believe may not have been Paul) says, 'For it is by grace you have been saved, through faith ... not by works, so that no one can boast' (Eph. 2.8–9). Jesus' famous Sermon on the Mount (Matt. 5—7) is popularly taken to mean that Jesus' teachings supersede the Law of Moses and that Jesus was setting himself up as 'worthy of greater honour than Moses' (Heb. 3.3). While it is true that Christians ascribe a higher status to Jesus Christ, it should be remembered that Jesus was a Jewish rabbi interpreting the Law and, despite the fact that he appears to contrast his own teachings with those of Moses, he makes the somewhat puzzling statement that 'not the smallest letter, not the least stroke of a pen, will by any means disappear from the Law until everything is accomplished' (Matt. 5.18).

At a popular level, Christians tend to ignore the question of the uneasy relationship between the Old and New Testaments, viewing the New Testament has having greater authority than the Old and frequently making oversimplified contrasts like 'law' and 'gospel'. Some Christians, particularly in the Adventist tradition, continue to observe the Jewish dietary laws and observe the period from Friday evening to Saturday at dusk as the sabbath and day of worship. Perhaps the clearest stance on matters of Jewish law is that taken by the Jehovah's Witnesses, namely that only those commandments in Hebrew Scripture are binding if they are reinforced by a similar injunction in the New Testament.

Christians who are more liberal tend to view the Bible more as a record of God's dealings with his people, how he has dealt with them through history and how he has brought them progressively towards a greater understanding of his will and nearer to salvation. Many of the insights of the authors of ancient Scripture still hold good. No Christian would disagree with the Ten Commandments, including its prohibitions on adultery and on coveting one's neighbour's spouse. Other biblical injunctions no doubt reflect a partial understanding of the divine plan at various points in human history. They may have originated as tribal taboos, such as the perception of menstruation and semen ejaculation as polluting, while others may have made better sense in times when standards of hygiene and social care were inferior to those of today. The liberal Christian therefore perceives God's law as dynamic rather than static, to be reappraised according to one's time and place.

One incident in the Gospels that highlights Jesus' relationship with the teachers of the Jewish law is the story of the woman who was caught in the act of committing adultery (John 8.1–11, above). Although the incident leaves unresolved the question of whether stoning is an appropriate punishment for adultery, the passage makes two important points. First, Jesus does not contradict the law against adultery. It is still to be regarded as sinful, and the adulteress is enjoined to mend her ways. Second, there remains the question of who can appropriately take the moral high ground and actually administer the punishment. God's commandments should not cause Christians to condemn others but rather to examine their own lives to determine whether they also have the vestiges of the sin that they are prone to condemn. In connection with adultery, Jesus teaches in his Sermon on the Mount that 'anyone who looks at a woman lustfully has already committed adultery with her in his heart' (Matt. 5.28). As the Lutheran scholar Rudolf Bultmann observed, Jesus' distinctive interpretation of the Torah is that it must apply to one's thoughts as well as one's actions. Most Christians stand condemned by this somewhat disconcerting saying.

Conscience

> Indeed, when Gentiles, who do not have the law, do by nature things required by the law, they are a law for themselves, even though they do not have the law. They show that the requirements of the law are written on their hearts, their consciences also bearing witness, and their thoughts sometimes accusing, and at other times even defending them.
>
> (Romans 2.14–15)

> God alone is Lord of the conscience, and hath left it free from the doctrines and commandments of men which are in any thing contrary to his word, or beside it, in matters of faith or worship.
>
> (Westminster Confession of Faith, XX, ii)
>
> Deep within his conscience man discovers a law which he has not laid upon himself but which he must obey. Its voice, ever calling him to love and to do what is good and to avoid evil, sounds in his heart at the right moment ... For man has in his heart a law inscribed by God ... His conscience is man's most secret core and his sanctuary. There he is alone with God whose voice echoes in his depths.
>
> (Catechism of the Catholic Church 1776)

In addition to Scripture and tradition there is another important source of authority in moral matters: conscience. Regarding the Gentiles, Paul claims that 'the requirements of the law are written on their hearts, their consciences also bearing witness' (Rom. 2.15). It is in this passage in Romans that Paul uses the well-known expression, 'a law unto themselves', as the Authorized Version puts it. At a popular level the expression refers to those who do as they please, but Paul is here making a plea for moral behaviour rather than the opposite. Paul's point is that the Gentiles, who have lacked prior acquaintance with the law, have no excuse for immoral acts since they have an 'inner voice' that prompts them to discern right from wrong, without recourse to the intricacies of the Jewish law. Conscience is particularly important within the Protestant tradition, which jettisoned the Roman Catholic system of canon law, but it features in all three Christian traditions. Resorting to conscience as the arbiter of right and wrong might seem to invite subjectivity and arbitrariness, as different Christians make different judgements on moral matters while using their conscience. The *Catechism of the Catholic Church* acknowledges that conscience can be ignorant, in error or dulled through habitual wrongdoing (*Catechism* 1970). For this reason conscience needs training, through acquaintance with the Christian faith and through prayer and devotion.

Associated with the concept of conscience is the notion that the rightness and wrongness of moral decisions may vary according to the context. One theory that has attracted much attention is 'situation ethics', expounded by Joseph Fletcher in his book bearing that title. Fletcher's contention is that there are no 'absolutes' in ethics that cannot, at least in theory, admit of exceptions, depending on the circumstances. One example he cites, which is relevant to the present study, is that of Mrs Bergmeier during the Second World War. Mrs Bergmeier had been captured by Russian soldiers and taken to a prison camp in the Ukraine. Knowing that her family needed her and were trying desperately to find her, she realized that her only way of being released to return to Germany was to become pregnant. After much deliberation, she persuaded one of the guards to have sex with her and to impregnate her. Her plan succeeded and she was sent home to be reunited with her husband and three children. Fletcher views her decision sympathetically: perhaps we should not view even God's commandments as being written in tablets of stone.

Fletcher concludes, in line with the Christian tradition, that there is only one law that is absolute, admitting of no exceptions: the law of love. When Jesus was asked to identify the most important commandment in the Jewish law, his reply was 'Love the Lord your God with all your heart and with all your soul and with all your mind and with all your strength', followed closely by 'Love your neighbour as yourself' (Mark 12.30–31). This was not an innovation on Jesus' part: it was an answer typically given by first-century rabbis, including the famous Rabbi Hillel. Christian ethics does not seek to innovate or to recommend an ethic that differs from that of those who are concerned to live a life of integrity, whether they belong to the Christian faith, another faith or have no faith at all.

Some comment on the concept of love is appropriate here. The popular Christian author C. S. Lewis once wrote a book entitled *The Four Loves*. In this he distinguished between four Greek words that are capable of being translated as 'love'. The first is *storgē*, which might be translated as 'affection' and describes the relationship between family members, who have commitments to each other and are willing to make sacrifices for one another. The second is *philia*, meaning friendship or 'Platonic love'. Third, there is *erōs* (from which the English word 'erotic' is derived), which connotes romantic or sexual love and even lust. This is a feeling or emotion that we tend to find ourselves experiencing rather than voluntarily eliciting. We speak, for example, of 'falling in love', indicating that it is something that happens to us rather than being actively chosen. Finally, there is *agapē*, which is the type of love to which Jesus and the exponents of the Jewish law were referring. In a famous passage Paul enumerates the virtues that comprise a loving person: love is patient, kind, not envious, boastful, proud, rude or self-seeking. It does not keep a score of wrongs, it rejoices in the truth, protects, trusts, hopes, and perseveres (1 Cor. 13.4–7).

Procreation or pleasure?

> Marriage and conjugal love are by their nature ordained toward the begetting and educating of children. Children are really the supreme gift of marriage and contribute very substantially to the welfare of their parents. The God Himself Who said, 'it is not good for man to be alone' (Gen. 2.18) and 'Who made man from the beginning male and female' (Matt. 19.4), wishing to share with man a certain special participation in His own creative work, blessed male and female, saying: 'Increase and multiply' (Gen. 1.28). Hence, while not making the other purposes of matrimony of less account, the true practice of conjugal love, and the whole meaning of the family life which results from it, have this aim: that the couple be ready with stout hearts to cooperate with the love of the Creator and the Savior. Who through them will enlarge and enrich His own family day by day.
>
> (*Gaudium et spes*, 1965)

Much of the diversity of views among Christians about sexual morality stems from the issue of whether sex is predominantly for procreation or whether – or in what circumstances – it can be enjoyed as pleasure. At an early stage in its history Christianity fell under the influence of Greek philosophical thought, which understood the human self in terms of a distinction between mind (or soul) and body. Both Plato and Aristotle had taught that the soul was the true self, the seat of one's true identity that would live eternally after death. The body, by contrast, was compared to a garment that grew old and threadbare and finally was cast off at death. It was this ephemeral body that enjoyed life's pleasures: eating, drinking, watching entertainments, performing one's bodily functions and, of course, sex. The early Christians, believing that Jesus Christ had been raised from the dead in bodily form, taught the doctrine of the resurrection of the body, which the Church continues to affirm in its ancient creeds, which many believers recite at public worship.

Christians do not necessarily believe that the physical body will be resuscitated at the resurrection, although eminent theologians like Augustine (354–430 CE) taught this. The Bible speaks of a 'spiritual body', the nature of which is unclear but involves some kind of transformation of one's earthly body, which will live with Christ eternally in the kingdom of heaven (1 Cor. 15.35–56). Although this idea is different from resuscitating dead bodies, it caused Paul some difficulty when he tried to persuade the Athenian philosophers (Acts 17.16–32). Paul discouraged speculation about the precise nature of a 'resurrection body', however, claiming that this was beyond human imagination. Christianity therefore has not committed itself to any definitive teaching about the nature of the resurrection, resulting in a diversity of positions. Some Christians believe in a fairly literal physical resurrection while other theologians appropriated the Greek philosophical idea that the soul leaves the body behind on death, and other Christians may believe that in some way the soul and the body are reunited in the after-life.

Whatever the precise mechanics of the resurrection, Christianity embraced the notion of two worlds: the spiritual and the physical. God is a spiritual being, 'without body, parts or passions', as the Church of England's Thirty-Nine Articles puts it. Hence if we want to become God-like we must cultivate spiritual, God-like virtues and shun the pleasures of the flesh. This notion of the God–world relationship draws on the Platonic notion of the world of the 'Forms' – the perfect archetypal world, of which the physical world is only a shadowy and very imperfect reflection. The soul is the seat of the virtues, the most important being 'righteousness' (often translated as 'justice'), which keeps in check other physical desires, particularly appetite. The idea of becoming God-like is particularly emphasized in Eastern Orthodoxy, where the supreme spiritual goal is *theosis* – literally, becoming divine. In Protestantism, the Puritans stressed the importance of spiritual practice – prayer, studying Scripture and Sunday observance – to the minimization of earthly pleasures. As far as sex was concerned, the observance of chastity, even within marriage, was extolled as a virtue to be pursued. When Augustine, centuries earlier, described the celestial City of God, he declared that men and women would retain their gender after the resurrection but that they would no longer arouse sexual desires.

> And the sex of woman is not a vice, but nature. It shall then indeed be superior to carnal intercourse and child-bearing; nevertheless the female members shall remain adapted not to the old uses, but to a new beauty, which, so far from provoking lust, now extinct, shall excite praise to the wisdom and clemency of God, who both made what was not and delivered from corruption what He made.
>
> (*City of God*, IV, 22.17; accessible at www.ccel.org/ccel/schaff/npnf102.iv.XXII.17.html)

At least on this side of death, the vast majority of people find sex pleasurable and it would be difficult, if not impossible, for any religion to teach that it should be practised without being enjoyed. However, enjoyment is only one aspect of sexual activity: the other obvious function of sex is reproduction. The human race, the pinnacle of God's creation, would die out if sexual activity ceased, and God would be left without creatures who have been made in his image and are capable of knowing and worshipping him. If God's creation is ultimately for human dominion and enjoyment, the extinction of humanity would leave the earth and the rest of creation without purpose.

There is a third, less obvious function of sex. Commenting on the relationship between husband and wife, the author of the book of Genesis says, 'they become one flesh' (Gen. 2.24) – a verse later quoted by Jesus (Mark 10.8; Matt. 19.5). There is an incompleteness of one gender in isolation. Humans are not like those elementary ungendered life forms that reproduce by bifurcation: each individual requires a partner of the opposite sex for reproduction, and this process involves an intimacy between couples that neither the man nor the woman would normally be prepared to extend to any other human being. It thus becomes an expression of love and commitment, which casual sex cannot be.

In view of these different functions of sex, controversy among Christians is not about whether it should be enjoyed but whether its prime purpose is enjoyment. The Roman Catholic view is that the primary purpose of sex is procreation, and therefore sexual intercourse should always leave open the possibility of conception. This is not the same as holding that one should only have sex with the explicit intention of having children, but recognizes God's role as the giver of life. The 'rhythm method', which Roman Catholicism permits, ensures that the chances of pregnancy are minimized without resorting to 'unnatural' forms of contraception. Since God is the ultimate source of life, natural forms of contraception enable God to determine whether a new life is to begin or not. The use of contraceptive pills, condoms and vaginal caps is forbidden since they are designed to prevent life beginning as a result of sexual intercourse. Some other forms of contraception, such as the inter-uterine device (IUD) and the so-called 'morning after' pill, are viewed even less favourably, since they are abortificents, allowing life to be created, albeit for a very short period, and then destroyed. Recourse to surgery is also forbidden: sterilization for women and vasectomies for men are viewed as mutilations of the human body, and interference with the body's integrity can only be justified for therapeutic purposes. Not all Roman Catholics by any means comply with the Church's teachings on sexual morality, and a recent survey showed that only 15 per cent of Mass-going Catholics accepted the Pope's teachings on sex.[2] When the Pope wrote his encyclical letter *Humanae vitae* in 1969, many hoped that the Church's stance on sex would become more liberal. They were disappointed, however, since the papal letter merely reaffirmed existing Church teaching on the subject. Protestantism is more liberal, and leaves the issue of contraception to the individual conscience.

Sex outside marriage

> Our vision is to see a world where people are free from exploitation, and where those involved in prostitution have the option to pursue genuine alternatives, free from constraints such as drug use, abusive relationships and poverty.
>
> The sex industry is an ever expanding arena for sexual exploitation. Street prostitution, off-street prostitution, sex tourism, strip clubs, lap dancing, international and domestic trafficking and pornography are some of the venues where sexual exploitation against women, children and men happen every day. We are working towards seeing an end to the sexual exploitation of those in prostitution, many of whom have been trafficked. We believe that sex trafficking and prostitution overlap in fundamental ways and that there is an inequality of social and economic power between those exploited and those who exploit. The sex industry is a theatre for gender power dynamics to take the stage.
>
> It is unknown how many people are working in prostitution in the UK – but what we do know is that it affects people in every town and city in the UK.
>
> (Beyond the Streets – formerly the National Christian Alliance on Prostitution, www.beyondthestreets.org.uk)

In common with most faiths, all forms of Christianity concur in holding that sexual relationships should be between consenting adults, ideally in the context of marriage. Sexual relationships

---

2 George D. Chryssides and Margaret Z. Wilkins, *Christians in the Twenty-first Century*, London: Equinox, 2011, p. 324.

that are non-consensual, that cause harm or distress or that are exploitative are to be avoided. Christians are well aware of the dangers of sexually transmitted diseases, the risks of unwanted pregnancies (many of which cause the expectant mother to resort to abortion), the distress involved on discovering that one's partner has been unfaithful and the trauma caused to one's children when parents get divorced. Like many other religions, the Church is opposed to the commodification of sex and has done much to oppose the sex industry. The Church of Christ in Thailand, together with the Roman Catholic Church, co-operated on an ecumenical project in the country to counter prostitution and sex tourism, and in particular to prevent children embarking on a life in which their bodies are offered for sale. Pope John Paul II explicitly denounced the industry in his *Ecclesia in Asia*:

> Tourism also warrants special attention. Though a legitimate industry with its own cultural and educational values, tourism has in some cases a devastating influence upon the moral and physical landscape of many Asian countries, manifested in the degradation of young women and even children through prostitution. (n.7)

Christianity has typically condemned all forms of sexual activity that are enacted outside of marriage, including pornography, prostitution, rape, fornication and masturbation. The last of these merits some comment. The Roman Catholic Church has described masturbation as a 'grave moral disorder', being extramarital and lustful. The masturbator often entertains mental fantasies, and Jesus taught that one's thoughts are subject to the law, not merely one's actions. The Orthodox churches regard it as 'self-pollution', a distortion of sexuality, demonstrating a lack of self-control and requiring confession to a priest. Many Protestants are similarly condemnatory, although there are few, if any, references to it in the Bible. Masturbation is sometimes called onanism, and the story of Onan is sometimes cited as an example of God's displeasure at the practice. However, Onan's misdeed was not in fact masturbation but coitus interruptus, with the purpose of avoiding having progeny to his sister-in-law (Gen. 38.7–9). Referring to semen emission, the book of Leviticus does not state that it is sinful but rather that the man incurs ritual impurity, just as a woman's menstruation makes her ritually impure (Lev. 15.16–23).

Although historically the Church's three traditions have expressed displeasure at the practice, numerous liberal Christians have reappraised the subject. Against the traditional view, they would argue that the practice does no harm: it causes no unwanted pregnancies and cannot incur STDs. Contrary to myths about it making its practitioners blind, insane or depressed, there is some medical support for the belief that it can help to relieve depression, can induce sleep and may prevent some illnesses, notably prostate cancer. It is certainly not abnormal, unless one equates 'normal' sexual practice with potentially procreative sex. Kinsey's surveys in the 1950s showed that 92 per cent of men and 62 per cent of women had masturbated at some point in their lives, and subsequent surveys have had similar findings.[3] Far from exhibiting a lack of restraint, it could be argued that masturbation is actually a means of self-control, reducing the need for other forms of sexual expression with a member of the opposite sex that could have unwanted consequences. A few churches have gone so far as to express approval of masturbation, notably the Lutheran Churches in Germany, Scandinavia and Iceland, and the United Church of Christ in the United States.

Modern technology has made possible new forms of sexual activity that were not open to previous generations. The late twentieth century witnessed the advent first of phone sex and then of cyber-sex, sometimes known as netsex or mudsex. (MUD is the acronym for 'multi-user defined' and is not a pejorative term for the practice: the term indicates that the material on such websites is contributed by a multiplicity of users.) Cyber-sex can take a variety of forms, ranging from a pair of (often anonymous) web users using chat-line or messenger services to send each other erotic messages. The use of web cams and services such as Skype can enable users to add images of genitalia or other erogenous body parts. Many Christians view such activities as pornographic

---

3 The Kinsey Institute for Research in Sex, Gender, and Reproduction, Inc. (1996–2012). Data from Alfred Kinsey's studies: www.kinseyinstitute.org/research/ak-data.html. Accessed 6 October 2012.

and, especially if the Christian is married, they could be construed as adulterous.

Some liberal Christians take a positive view of these forms of sex, pointing out that they incur no physical harm and simply encourage sexual role play with no strings attached. Apparently, some novelists have made use of such facilities in order to enhance their creativity. Erotic phoning and 'cybering' need not be confined to anonymous strangers: they can help lovers and married couples maintain their intimacy if they are separated by distance. Some Christians – and others – may have more pragmatic objections to these uses of modern technology. Phone sex can be expensive, frequently using premium-rate numbers or credit card payment – and would we really be comfortable with an online sex worker having our credit card details?

The Christian faith finds itself set amid a world of societal and technological change. While there are some Christians who believe that looking at Jesus' teaching and example will provide the answers to today's moral questions, there can be no certainty about how Christianity's founder-leader would have reacted to the large changes in the world over the last two millennia. For the Christian, it is no easy matter to find acceptable answers to many of these issues.

Islam

Background to the Law

> So he [Satan] made them fall, through deception. And when they tasted of the tree, their private parts became apparent to them, and they began to fasten together over themselves from the leaves of Paradise. And their Lord called to them, 'Did I not forbid you from that tree and tell you that Satan is to you a clear enemy?' They said, 'Our Lord, we have wronged ourselves, and if You do not forgive us and have mercy upon us, we will surely be among the losers.' [Allah] said, 'Descend, being to one another enemies. And for you on the earth is a place of settlement and

> enjoyment for a time.' He said, 'Therein you will live, and therein you will die, and from it you will be brought forth.' O children of Adam, We have bestowed upon you clothing to conceal your private parts and as adornment. But the clothing of righteousness – that is best. That is from the signs of Allah that perhaps they will remember.
>
> (Qur'an 7.22–6)

Islam does not hold Eve responsible for mankind's banishment from Paradise. According to the Qur'an both Adam and Eve ate of the forbidden fruit, and there is no suggestion that Eve persuaded Adam to partake of it. The Islamic view is that God forgave both of them and placed them on Earth as His representatives. Men and women are equal in their religious and moral duties.

For Muslims, the Shari'a is God's law – God is the law-giver and man's duty is to understand it and obey its divine provisions. The Shari'a governs all aspects of life and every field of law – constitutional, international, criminal, civil and commercial – but family law is at its very heart.

For Sunni Muslims the Shari'a is derived from two main sources. The first and most important source is the Qur'an, which Muslims believe to be the literal and infallible word of God revealed to the Prophet Muhammad through Jibril (the Angel Gabriel) over a period of some 23 years from around 610 CE.

The Qur'an is not a book of law and does not present a codified or comprehensive body of legislation; it is, for the greater part, a collection of narratives and injunctions to belief and right behaviour framed mostly in general or rhetorical terms. It does, however, contain a significant number of clear and explicit provisions, and the area that is most comprehensively and clearly regulated is marriage and the treatment of spouses.

The second main source is the Sunna or practice of the Prophet Muhammad, being his words, deeds and tacit acceptance of certain actions as reported in the collections of *hadith* (individual reports) that were collected, collated, assessed for authenticity and categorized by *hadith* scholars in the eighth and ninth centuries CE, resulting in six main authoritative collections. The categories of *hadith* cover all aspects of human activity both public and private. There are many *hadith* referring to the Prophet's own relationships with his wives as well as his responses to questions from the community.

At the time of the Prophet, the law would have been limited to these elements. Following his death, however, and with the rapid spread of Islam and the requirement to provide for the infinitely varied needs of an expanding civilization, it was necessary to establish methods of regulation and adjudication. The religious scholars developed tools and methods for deriving rulings in specific cases using a set of principles of jurisprudence: *ijtihad* (independent reasoning); *ijma'* (consensus); *qiyas* (analogy); *istihsan* (choosing the most preferable); *masalih mursalah* (the public benefit) and *'urf* (custom or practice). The division of the jurists into various 'schools' began during the Umayyad Caliphate (661–750 CE) and developed further during the Abbasid Caliphate that succeeded it. Sunni Islam recognizes the mutual orthodoxy of its four main schools – the Hanafi, Maliki, Shafi'i and Hanbali schools, named after their most important scholars. Other schools arose but did not attain the same prominence, although the Zahiri school produced many important opinions.

The Shi'a are divided into two main denominations and numerous smaller groupings. The Shi'a accept a more limited range of *hadith* as a basis for rulings – they recognize only those that can be traced to the Prophet and his immediate family – and a more limited range of tools of jurisprudence.

It is estimated that there are approximately one and a half billion Muslims worldwide. Islamic societies and cultures are ethnically and culturally diverse and there are unbridgeable sectarian and political divides, but they share certain fundamental and unchanging principles, including codes of sexual morality.

Sex and marriage

> And of His signs is that He created for you from yourselves mates that you may find tranquillity in them; and He placed between you affection and mercy. Indeed in that are signs for a people who give thought.
>
> (Qur'an 30.21)

The Shari'a as it applies to marriage and the family, including sexual morality, is untouchable. Marriage and the family are the core of Islam and the notion that a person should be single or celibate by choice is completely alien to Islamic culture in any of its regional or ethnic manifestations. There are numerous references to marriage in the Qur'an, and the Prophet is reported to have said that if a Muslim marries then he has completed half of his religion and that piety makes up the other half.

There is no virtue in deliberate abstinence from legitimate sexual relations and no tradition of monasticism in the same form as in Christianity.

There is a *hadith* of the Prophet that describes how a group of three men came to the houses of the wives of the Prophet asking how the Prophet worshipped (Allah), and when they were informed about that, they considered their worship insufficient and said, 'Where are we compared with the Prophet as his past and future sins have been forgiven?' Then one of them said, 'I will offer the prayer throughout the night forever.' The other said, 'I will fast throughout the year and will not break my fast.' The third said, 'I will keep away from the women and will not marry forever.' Allah's Apostle came to them and said, 'Are you the same people who said so-and-so? By Allah, I am more submissive to Allah and more afraid of Him than you; yet I fast and break my fast, I do sleep and I also marry women. So he who does not follow my tradition in religion, is not from me (not one of my followers).'

One of the two main words for marriage in Arabic, and the one that appears in this *hadith*, is *nikah*, which also means sex. Sex

SEX LAW

is something to be enjoyed by both men and women, but Islam is clear that the only permissible context for sexual relations is within marriage. Unlawful sexual intercourse is not merely a sin; it is a crime entailing specific punishment.

The Qur'an states with regard to chastity:

> And come not near unto fornication. Lo! it is an abomination and an evil way. (Qur'an 17.32)

> The woman or man found guilty of adultery or fornication – lash each one of them with a hundred lashes, and do not be taken by pity for them in the religion of Allah, if you should believe in Allah and the Last Day. And let a group of the believers witness their punishment. (Qur'an 24.2)

The Qur'an itself does not differentiate between fornication (intercourse between unmarried people) and adultery (intercourse between a married person and someone other than his or her spouse). Although it has been incorporated into the Shari'a by the jurists, the punishment of death by stoning appears only in the *hadith*. In one instance the Prophet is said to have ordered the stoning of a Jewish man and woman brought before him by a member of their own community, but under the provisions of the Torah not of Islam. In another case, a married Muslim man confessed to adultery, bearing witness against himself four times, and was ordered to be put to death by stoning. The *hadith* scholars admit, however, that there is no evidence to suggest that the incidents reported in the *hadith* occurred after the revelation of the verse prescribing flogging. Those who argue against the death penalty for adultery – which is only in the legislation of a limited number of Muslim countries – claim that the Prophet would not have countermanded the clear injunctions of the Qur'an and that the Qur'anic prescription of flogging must, therefore, have been revealed after these events as the definitive ruling. Where there is a contradiction between a Qur'anic ruling and the *hadith*, the Qur'an takes precedence.

The threshold of proof of adultery or fornication is high: four competent adult male witness or three men and two women are required to prove adultery, unless there is a confession. They must be eyewitness to the act of adultery. Hearsay or assumption are not admissible as evidence. As reprehensible as fornication or adultery is the slandering of virtuous women: 'And those who accuse chaste women and then do not produce four witnesses – lash them with eighty lashes and do not accept from them testimony ever after. And those are the defiantly disobedient' (Qur'an 24.4).

Verses relating to slander are believed to have been revealed to the Prophet in response to allegations of adultery against his wife Aisha, who used to accompany him on campaigns. In the 'story of the necklace', in the very early morning Aisha went to look for a necklace she had lost, but before she could return to her camel, the caravan departed leaving her behind. Her absence from her *howdaj*, the enclosed saddle, went unnoticed. She sat down at the spot where the camp had been, expecting the party to return to find her, and fell asleep. She was found by a young tribesman named Safwan, who was on his way to catch up with the party. He put her on his camel and walked alongside to complete the journey to Madina.

This created a scandal and Muhammad sent Aisha home to her father Abu Bakr. Not knowing what to do, Muhammad eventually went to Aisha to hear her version of events. He is then said to have gone into a prophetic trance where he received parts of Sura 24 (*al-Nur*):

> Indeed, those who came with falsehood are a group among you. Do not think it bad for you; rather it is good for you. For every person among them is what [punishment] he has earned from the sin, and he who took upon himself the greater portion thereof – for him is a great punishment. Why, when you heard it, did not the believing men and believing women think good of one another and say, 'This is an obvious falsehood'? Why did they [who slandered] not produce for it four witnesses? And when they do not produce the witnesses, then it is they, in the sight of Allah, who are the liars. And if it had not been for the favour of Allah upon you and His mercy in this world and the Hereafter, you would have been touched for that [lie] in which you were involved by a great punishment. (Qur'an 24.11–14)

The Sura goes on to describe the punishment for this in the Hereafter:

> Indeed, those who [falsely] accuse chaste, unaware and believing women are cursed in this world and the Hereafter; and they will have a great punishment. On a Day when their tongues, their hands and their feet will bear witness against them as to what they used to do. That Day, Allah will pay them in full their deserved recompense, and they will know that it is Allah who is the perfect in justice. Evil words are for evil men, and evil men are [subjected] to evil words. And good words are for good men, and good men are [an object] of good words. Those [good people] are declared innocent of what the slanderers say. For them is forgiveness and noble provision. (Qur'an 24.23–6)

In a process known as *li'an* or mutual imprecation, if a man accuses his wife of adultery but cannot produce witnesses, he may swear four times that she is guilty and on the fifth time invoke God's wrath upon himself if he is untruthful. His wife may then avert punishment by swearing four times that she is innocent and on the fifth time invoke God's wrath upon herself if she is untruthful.

> And those who accuse their wives [of adultery] and have no witnesses except themselves – then the witness of one of them [shall be] four testimonies [swearing] by Allah that indeed, he is of the truthful. And the fifth [oath will be] that the curse of Allah be upon him if he should be among the liars. But it will prevent punishment from her if she gives four testimonies [swearing] by Allah that indeed, he is of the liars. And the fifth [oath will be] that the wrath of Allah be upon her if he was of the truthful. (Qur'an 24.6–7)

In this case, the jurists agree that their marriage is then dissolved and they are prohibited permanently from remarrying.

Previously unmarried women are expected to be virgins upon their marriage, and this is a matter of honour for their families. In some traditional communities, blood-stained bed sheets are displayed with pride after the wedding night to the family of the groom and even to the wider community to prove the virginity of the bride. Where virginity cannot be proved, the consequences can be catastrophic for the bride: at the least, she may be rejected by her husband and the marriage annulled, and she may be ostracized by her family and community, and at worst in very traditional societies she may even face death at the hands of the husband or of her own family.

Traditional Islamic culture does not permit socialization between men and women. Women are to be protected and not exposed to the humiliation of male attention. Women keep company with women and men with men, there being no reason why a respectable woman should want to socialize with men outside her immediate family. In traditional households, certain areas (referred to as the 'harem' – literally 'forbidden', to express their protected status) would be reserved for the women and children. Here the women would not have to worry about veiling as they would not be exposed to people in whose company they would normally have to be covered, that is, those outside the degrees of relationship to them that would prohibit marriage.

In modern urban society it is normal for women to mix with men in education and the workplace, but it remains unacceptable and relatively uncommon for men and women to socialize outside these contexts. It is not acceptable for a man and woman who are not married to each other to be alone in each other's company. This can raise issues in educational environments and medical care and other situations where it may be necessary for women to be chaperoned. In Saudi Arabia this has led to the prohibition in law of women driving because of the possibility that a woman might find herself – or choose to be – alone in a vehicle with a man. At all levels of society, families will be more protective of their daughters and other female family members than of their sons. Unmarried women in particular will have limited independence and will be considered to be under the protection of their families until they pass to the protection of their husbands.

Dress and veiling

> Say to the believing men that they should lower their gaze and guard their private parts: that will make for greater purity for them: And Allah is well acquainted with all that they do.
>
> And say to the believing women that they should lower their gaze and guard their private parts; that they should not display their beauty and ornaments except what (must ordinarily) appear thereof; that they should draw their veils over their bosoms and not display their beauty except to their husbands, their fathers, their husbands' fathers, their sons, their husbands' sons, their brothers or their brothers' sons, or their sisters' sons, or their women, or the slaves whom their right hands possess, or male servants free of physical needs (eunuchs), or small children who have no awareness of shame; and that they should not strike their feet in order to draw attention to their hidden ornaments (referring to anklets). And O ye Believers! turn ye all together towards Allah, that ye may attain Bliss.
>
> (Qur'an 24.30–1)

Islamic custom requires modesty of dress for both men and women. The ordinary word for the veil in Arabic is *hijab*, which may mean a cover, curtain or screen. The word *muhajjaba* or 'veiled (f)' carries a sense not just of physical covering but of having assumed a way of living in which interaction with men outside a woman's immediate family is strictly regulated. There are no specific or detailed Qur'anic injunctions with regard to veiling but there are general commandments such as those in Sura 24.30–1 (*al-Nur*) addressed to men and women respectively.

The verses do not prescribe a specific dress code but require a certain modesty and decorum. There is an expectation of both men and women that they should not expose their bodies unnecessarily or look at each other in such a way as to indicate or invite sexual attraction. In terms of dress, it is usually understood that as a minimum a man should be covered between the navel and the knees. Other than in a sporting environment and perhaps certain occupational contexts, however, it would be considered improper for a man to be bare-chested in public.

For women, outside the home and the immediate family environment, clothing should not expose or accentuate their figures in such a way as to attract attention. This means that clothing should be loose fitting and should cover the arms and legs. The head veil may take a variety of forms and styles but where it is worn it should cover the hair completely as this is one of the attractive features of a woman. In some cultures, a more complete covering is worn, such as the *burqa* in Afghanistan, which is a complete covering for the head, face and body with a mesh over the face to allow the wearer to see, or the *niqab*, which covers the face leaving only a small gap to see through. Those women who by custom or by choice wear the full covering will normally also wear gloves and shoes or stockings that conceal their feet and ankles (not open-toed footwear). A woman whose face and hands are not covered should not wear make-up or nail polish and women should not wear perfume in public.

A woman need not be covered in the presence of her husband, father, sons, brothers or uncles (those categories of men to whom she is permanently prohibited in marriage), small children or in all-female company. She must be covered in the presence of male cousins as they are not prohibited in marriage.

In many societies and communities dress is a matter of custom, but in modern urban society it may be a matter of choice or of fashion. A commonly worn form of contemporary Islamic dress is a floor-length coat with long sleeves, which may simply be worn over ordinary clothing and accompanied by a scarf.

Until the early part of the twentieth century it was the norm for Muslim women in Islamic countries to be veiled and to a great extent segregated. There were a number of early pioneers of women's emancipation, notably in Egypt, among whom the most famous is Hoda al-Shaarawi, who was the first to remove her veil in public as a political act in 1923 on her return from a women's conference in Rome (it may be noted that privileged Muslim, Christian and Jewish women in Egypt were also veiled and segregated at this time). Throughout the middle decades of the twentieth century, it became normal for middle-class Muslim women in Egypt and the Levant to adopt western dress, and films of this period mostly depict middle-class women in this way, although their servants, women in the poorer quarters and rural women remain covered.

Since the 1970s there has been a gradual return to the wearing of the *hijab*, accompanying the rise of political Islam that has taken place over the last four decades or so. Many young women whose mothers and grandmothers were unveiled are now adopting the *hijab* as part of their Muslim identity.

Sexual propriety

Marriage is the keystone of society and is ordained for the formation of a family and the rearing of children in a safe, stable and wholesome environment. It is recognized that sexual desire is natural in both men and women, and a healthy sexual relationship is at the core of a marriage. The Qur'an stipulates: 'Your wives are a tilth for you, so come to your place of cultivation however you wish and put forth [righteousness] for yourselves' (Qur'an 2.223). This is interpreted in different ways by the commentators. Some have suggested that it simply means that a man should enjoy a sexual relationship freely with his wife. Some have focused on the words 'however you wish' to suggest that this means that intercourse may be in any position and even include sodomy, while others have focused on the word 'tilth' to suggest that this means intercourse that may result in pregnancy, which must therefore imply normal vaginal intercourse.

Men should not approach their wives during menstruation. In Sura 2 we find:

> They ask thee concerning women's courses. Say: They are a hurt and a pollution: So keep away from women in their courses, and do not approach them until they are clean. But when they have purified themselves, you may approach them as ordained for you by God. For God loves those who turn to Him constantly and He loves those who keep themselves pure and clean. (Qur'an 2.222)

It may be noted also that women are not permitted to pray or touch, read or recite the Qur'an during menstruation as they are not able to perform the ablution necessary for prayer and for reading the Qur'an. They are not allowed to fast during this time as fasting itself has to be combined with prayer.

Intercourse is not permitted during the 40 days following childbirth and during the hours of fasting in the month of Ramadan, that is, between the first light of dawn and sunset, when Muslims may neither eat, drink nor smoke.

> It has been made permissible for you the night preceding fasting to go to your wives [for sexual relations]. They are clothing for you and you are clothing for them. Allah knows that you used to deceive yourselves, so He accepted your repentance and forgave you. So now, have relations with them and seek that which Allah has decreed for you. And eat and drink until the white thread of dawn becomes distinct to you from the black thread [of night]. Then complete the fast until the sunset. And do not have relations with them as long as you are staying for worship in the mosques. These are the limits [set by] Allah, so do not approach them. Thus does Allah make clear His ordinances to the people that they may become righteous. (Qur'an 2.87)

It is also prohibited during the Hajj or pilgrimage.

Following sexual intercourse, both men and women must perform full ablution before they may pray or touch or read the Qur'an.

Homosexuality and 'unnatural' practices

Homosexuality is prohibited in Islam. This is an absolute and there is no room for any argument for it to be permitted. Under Islamic law there can be no same-sex marriage or civil partnership. The Qur'an refers in several places to the destruction of the people of Sodom, and the only specific offence for which it is indicated that they incurred God's wrath and punishment is homosexuality.

> And [We had sent] Lot when he said to his people, 'Do you commit such immorality as no one has preceded you with from among the worlds? Indeed, you approach men with desire, instead of women. Rather, you are a transgressing people.' But the answer of his people was only that they said, 'Evict them from your city! Indeed, they are men who keep themselves pure.' So We saved him and his family, except for his wife; she was of those who remained [with the evildoers]. And We rained upon them a rain [of stones]. Then see how was the end of the criminals.
>
> (Qur'an 7.80–4)
>
> And [mention] Lot, when he said to his people, 'Do you commit immorality while you are seeing? Do you indeed approach men with desire instead of women? Rather, you are a people behaving ignorantly.' But the answer of his people was not except that they said, 'Expel the family of Lot from your city. Indeed, they are people who keep themselves pure.' And We rained upon them a rain [of stones], and evil was the rain of those who were warned.
>
> (Qur'an 27.55–8)

Not only is homosexuality considered sinful in itself, but as marriage can only be between a man and a woman, homosexual acts are by definition adulterous and therefore attract the penalties prescribed for adultery. Opinion is divided on the form of punishment: some scholars, including the Hanafi school of jurisprudence, consider that the punishment should be by flogging, while the Shafi'is and Malikis believe it should be death by stoning on the basis of a report in the *hadith* that the Prophet said: 'If you find anyone doing as Lot's people did, kill the one who does it and the one to whom it is done.' The same degree of evidence is required for proof of an act of homosexuality as is required for heterosexual adultery or fornication. Four witnesses must be produced and they must testify to actual witnessing of the act.

References to homosexuality in the legal sources generally refer to relationships between two men. There is little mention of relationships between women but generally it is considered that they attract *ta'zeer* (discretionary) punishment for indecency rather than the prescribed punishments applicable to acts of male homosexuality.

Homosexuality is illegal in most Islamic countries. In Iran, for example, it is dealt with by the penal code, which prescribes flogging or the death penalty according to the circumstances. In March 2008, the BBC reported that more than 4,000 homosexuals had been executed by the regime since the revolution.[4] In Egypt there is no specific prohibition but homosexuality falls under the laws of public morality, and the legal authorities have taken a strong line against it in recent years. Syrian law provides for a jail sentence of up to three years for 'carnal relations against the order of nature'. Homosexuality has been decriminalized in Iraq, although it is included with adultery in the grounds on which divorce may be sought. There have been reports of vigilante groups persecuting and torturing male homosexuals in Iraq in the last five years, including tracking them down via social networking websites.

Attitudes towards transsexualism vary between governments. While the Iranian government is intolerant of homosexuality, it permits gender re-assignment on medical grounds, including change of legal status, and even contributes to the cost. There have been reports of families pressuring their children into gender re-assignment operations to avoid the consequences of accusation of homosexuality. The first legal sex-change operation in Egypt took place in the early 1990s and was a high-profile case, but was never accepted by the Egyptian religious authorities, and the Muslim Brotherhood-dominated medical union has imposed severe restrictions on gender re-assignment surgery. Irrespective of the legal position, transgender people suffer serious discrimination and ostracism in Muslim communities.

There is no reference to intercourse with animals in the Qur'an but there is a report in the *hadith* that the Prophet ordered that a man who had intercourse with an animal should be killed and that the animal, though deemed blameless, should also be killed. The Hanafi school along with the Maliki and Zahiri jurists indicate that the punishment should be flogging and that the flesh

---

4 http://news.bbc.co.uk/1/hi/world/europe/7294908.stm 13 March 2008.

of the animal may lawfully be eaten, but the Shafi'i school prescribes death for the perpetrator and rules that the animal should be killed and its meat destroyed.

There are few references to masturbation but it is generally considered to be prohibited on the basis of the Qur'anic injunctions to chastity and the guarding of a person's private parts. There is no prescribed punishment, but there are references in the *hadith* to punishment in the hereafter, in which a person who masturbates habitually will find his hand pregnant. As with any other sexual act, however, a person who has masturbated must perform the ablution required before praying, otherwise his or her prayers will not be accepted.

The crime of rape falls under the category of *hiraba* (assault and robbery) rather than under sexual offences, but in reality in some traditional societies it is often treated under the *zina* laws. As *hiraba* the normal forms of evidence in crimes of violence may be used, and if found guilty the rapist will be liable to pay compensation, usually in the amount of the dower of the woman. If it is treated as adultery, however, it is notoriously difficult to prove because, like adultery, it requires four adult male witnesses. There have been reports from Bangladesh and Pakistan, mostly from tribal communities, that women who have brought accusations of rape but have been unable to prove them with witnesses have themselves been punished for adultery while their attackers have escaped punishment, or in some cases have been forced to marry their rapists to save the family honour, thereby removing the punishment from the rapist. In Egypt the law that allowed a rapist to avoid punishment by marrying his victim was only repealed in 1999. Being a victim of rape carries great social stigma in Muslim society and greatly reduces a woman's marriage prospects. It is still often the case in some communities that families will pressure their daughters into marriage to avoid this shame.

2

Marriage

Judaism

The traditional practice

According to tradition, marriage is God's plan for humanity, as illustrated by the story of Adam and Eve in the book of Genesis. In the Jewish faith it is viewed as a sacred bond as well as a means to personal fulfilment. It is more than a legal contract, rather an institution with cosmic significance, legitimized through divine authority. The purpose of marriage is to build a home, create a family and thereby perpetuate society. Initially Jews were allowed to have more than one wife, but this was banned in Ashkenazic countries by a decree of Rabbenu Gershom in 1000 CE. In modern society, all Jewish communities – Ashkenazic as well as Sephardic – follow this ruling.

In the Bible, marriages were arranged by fathers: Abraham, for example, sent his servant to find a wife for Isaac (Gen. 24.10–53), and Judah arranged the marriage of his firstborn son (Gen. 38.6). When the proposal of marriage was accepted by the girl's father (or elder brother in his absence), the nature and amount of the *mohar* (payment by the groom) was agreed. By Second Temple times there was a degree of choice in the selection of the bride – on 15 of Av and the Day of Atonement, young men could select their brides from among the girls dancing in the vineyards.

Traditionally a period of engagement preceded marriage itself. The ceremony was a seven-day occasion for celebration, during which love songs were sung in praise of the bride. In the Talmudic period a major development occurred concerning the *mohar* – since it could be used by the father of the bride, a wife could become penniless if her husband divorced or predeceased her. As a result the *mohar* evolved into the formulation of a marriage document (*ketubah*), which gave protection to the bride. In addition the act of marriage changed from being a personal civil procedure to a public religious ceremony, which required the presence of a *minyan* (quorum) and the recitation of prayers.

In biblical and Talmudic times, marriage occurred in two stages: betrothal and *nissuin*.

Betrothal

The concept of betrothal has two stages: first, the commitment of a couple to marry as well as the terms of the financial obligations (*shiddukhin*); second, a ceremony establishing a nuptial relationship independent of the wedding ceremony (*kiddushin* or *erusin*). An early instance of *shiddukhin* is found in Genesis 34, where the term *mohar* is used for a sum of money the father of the groom is to pay the father of the bride. During the Talmudic period this term is not used; instead the Talmud stipulates that negotiations should take place between the respective parents concerning financial obligations. The term for such negotiations is *shiddukhin* (an Aramaic word meaning 'tranquillity'). The terms agreed upon were written in a document called a *shetar pesikta*; the amount given to the son was called *nedunyah*. From the medieval period to the present, the prenuptial agreement was itself divided into two stages: a verbal understanding (*vort*) was made, followed by a ceremony (*kinyan*) symbolizing the acceptance of the obligation to marry. This normally occurred at a meal; the act of accepting was accomplished by taking an object (usually the corner of a handkerchief). The second stage involved the writing in a document (*tenaim*) of the terms undertaken. In addition, the *tenaim* designated the date and place of the nuptial ceremony. The ceremony of the *tenaim* concludes with the mothers of the bride and groom breaking a pottery dish. This ceremony is frequently celebrated with a dinner, and during the following period the bride and groom exchange gifts.

In the Bible the betrothal or nuptial ceremony that takes place prior to the wedding is referred to as *erusin*: in the rabbinic period the sages who outlined this procedure called it *kiddushin* to indicate that the bride is forbidden to all men except her husband. According to the Mishnah, the bride could be acquired in marriage in three ways: by money, deed or sexual intercourse. Traditionally the method involved placing a ring on the bride's finger. At this stage the groom declared: 'Behold, you are consecrated unto me with this ring according to the Law of Moses and of Israel.' Then the blessing over wine was recited:

> Blessed are you, O Lord our God, King of the Universe, who has hallowed us by your commandments, and has commanded us concerning forbidden marriages; who has forbidden unto us those who are betrothed, but has sanctioned unto us such as are wedded unto us by the rite of the nuptial canopy and the sacred covenant of wedlock.

After this ceremony the bride continued to remain in her father's house until the stage of *nissuin*.

Nissuin

During this second stage of the procedure for marriage, the seven blessings (*sheva berachot*) are recited.

> Blessed are You, Lord our God, sovereign of the universe, who creates the fruit of the vine.
> Blessed are You, Lord, our God, sovereign of the universe, who created everything for his glory.
> Blessed are you, Lord, our God, sovereign of the universe, who creates man.
> Blessed are You, Lord our God, sovereign of the universe, who creates man in your image, fashioning perpetuated life. Blessed are you, Lord, creator of man.
> Blessed are you, Lord, who gladden Zion with her children.
> Grant perfect joy to these loving companions, as you did your creations in the Garden of Eden. Blessed are you, Lord, who grants the joy of groom and bride.

Blessed are you, Lord, our God, sovereign of the universe, who created joy and gladness, groom and bride, mirth, song, delight and rejoicing, love and harmony and peace and companionship. Lord our God, may there ever be heard in the cities of Judah and in the streets of Jerusalem voices of joy and gladness, voices of groom and bride, the jubilant voices of those joined in marriage under the bridal canopy, the voices of young people feasting and singing. Blessed are you, Lord, who causes the groom to rejoice with his bride.

Ketubah

In ancient times rabbinic sages insisted on the marriage couple entering into the *ketubah* as a protection for the wife. The *ketubah* served as a replacement of the bridal *mohar*, the price paid by the groom to the bride or her parents. Subsequently the *ketubah* became a mechanism by which the amount due to the wife (the bride price) came to be paid in the event of the cessation of marriage either through the death of her husband or divorce. An important function of the *ketubah* was to discourage the husband from contemplating divorce since he would need to have the amount to be able to pay his wife.

The content of the *ketubah* is in essence a one-way contract that formalizes the various requirements of *halakah* to a wife. The Jewish husband takes on the obligation in the *ketubah* of providing clothing, food and conjugal relations. It is also expected that he will guarantee his bride a pre-specified amount of money in the case of divorce. Hence the content of the *ketubah* provides a basis for security and protection of the woman and her rights in marriage. In Conservative synagogues it is common for the *ketubah* to contain an additional paragraph that stipulates that divorce will be adjudicated by a modern rabbinical court in order to prevent the creation of an *agunah* – a wife unable to remarry because she has not obtained a *get* (bill of divorce).

The text of a *ketubah* is written in Aramaic rather than Hebrew. In modern times many *ketubot* have been translated into English or other vernacular languages. Many Conservative Jews and other non-Orthodox Jews use *ketubot* written in Hebrew rather than

Aramaic; others use Aramaic *ketubot* but also have an official version in Hebrew. Contemporary *ketubot* have become available in various formats as well as the traditional Aramaic text used by the Orthodox community. It is common for Jewish couples to hang their *ketubah* in the home as a daily reminder of their vows and responsibilities to each other. However, in some communities the *ketubah* is either displayed in a private section of the home or not at all. This is due to the belief that a prominent display may invite jealousy or fears of the evil eye. According to Jewish law, spouses are prohibited from engaging in marital relations if the *ketubah* is lost – in such cases a second *ketubah* is made, which states that it is a substitute for the original *ketubah*.

Currently there are several versions of the *ketubah*. The Orthodox version is the traditional form. The Conservative version is identical to the Orthodox version with the addition of the 'Liberman clause', which states that either the husband or wife may invoke the authority of the Bet Din (rabbinical court) in the event of a civil dissolution of the marriage. The added clause provides for equal legal recourse for the husband and wife. The Reform version features contemporary sentiments and promises that the bride and groom express to one another.

Orthodox ketubah

On the _____ day of the week, the _____ day of the month of _____, in the year five thousand seven hundred _____, as we reckon time here in _____, the groom _____ son of _____ said to the bride _____ daughter of _____ 'Be my wife according to the statutes of Moses and Israel. And I will work for, esteem, feed, and support you as is the custom of Jewish men who work for, feed and support their wives faithfully. And I will give you _____ zuzim and I will provide you food and clothing and necessities and your conjugal rights according to accepted custom.' And the bride _____ agreed to become his wife. And

MARRIAGE

this dowry that she brought from her _____ house, whether in silver, gold, jewellery, clothing, furnishings or bedding, the groom _____ accepted responsibility for all in the sum of _____ *zuzim*, and agreed to add to this amount from his own assets the sum of _____, for a total of _____ *zuzim*. The groom said: 'The obligations of this *ketubah*, the dowry and additional sum, I accept upon myself and my heirs after me, to be paid from all the best part of my property that I now possess or may hereafter acquire, real and personal. From this day forward, all my property, even the shirt on my back, shall be mortgaged and licensed for the payment of this dowry and additional sum, whether during my lifetime or thereafter.' The obligation of this *ketubah*, this dowry and this additional sum, was accepted by _____ the groom with the strictness established for *ketubot* and additional sums customary for the daughters of Israel, in accordance with the decrees by our sages of blessed memory. This *ketubah* is not to be regarded as a formality or as a perfunctory legal form. We have established the acceptance on the part _____ son of _____ the groom to _____ daughter of _____ the bride, of this contract, all of which is stated and specified above, with an article fit for that purpose. And all shall be valid and binding.

Liberman clause

And both together agreed that if this marriage shall ever be dissolved under civil law, then either husband or wife may invoke the authority of the Bet Din of the Rabbinical Assembly and the Jewish Theological Seminary of America or its duly authorized representatives, to decide what action by either spouse is then appropriate under Jewish matrimonial law; and if either spouse shall fail to honour the demand of the other or to carry out the decision of the Bet Din or its representative, then the other spouse may invoke any and all remedies under civil law and equity to enforce compliance with the Bet Din's decision and this solemn obligation.

> ### Reform ketubah
>
> On the _____ day of the week, the _____ day of _____ in year _____, corresponding to the _____ day of _____, in the year _____, _____ son of _____, and _____ daughter of _____, join each other in _____, before family and friends to make a mutual covenant as husband and wife, partners in marriage. The groom _____, promises _____ the bride: 'You are my wife according to the tradition of Moses and Israel. I shall cherish you and honour you as is customary among the sons of Israel who have cherished and honoured their wives in faithfulness and in integrity.' The bride _____, promises _____, the groom: 'You are my husband according to the tradition of Moses and Israel. I shall cherish you and honour you as is customary among the daughters of Israel who have cherished and honoured their husbands in faithfulness and in integrity.' 'We, as beloveds and friends, promise each other to strive throughout our lives together to achieve an openness which will enable us to share our thoughts, our feelings, and our experiences. We promise to try always to bring out in ourselves and in each other qualities of forgiveness, compassion and integrity. We, as beloved and friends, will cherish each other's uniqueness, comfort and challenge each other through life's sorrow and joy; share our intuition and insight with one another; and above all do everything within our power to permit each of us to become the persons we are yet to be. All this we take upon ourselves to uphold to the best of our abilities.' All is valid and binding.
>
> Bride _____ Groom _____
> Witness _____ Witness _____
> Rabbi _____

The Jewish wedding

Although Jewish wedding ceremonies vary, common features include a *ketubah*, which is signed by witnesses, a wedding canopy (*huppah*), a ring owned by the groom that is given to the bride under the *huppah*, and the breaking of the glass. As indicated previously, the Jewish wedding process has two distinct stages: *kiddushin* (betrothal) and *nissuin* (marriage). The first stage prohibits the wife from any other man, requiring a religious divorce (*get*) to dissolve the union, and the final stage allows the couple to each other. The ceremony that accomplishes *nissuin* is known as *huppah*. In modern times, *nissuin/kiddushin* takes place when the groom gives the bride a ring or other object of value with the intent of creating a marriage. There are different views as to which part of the ceremony constitutes *nissuin/huppah* – they include standing under the canopy (which is referred to as a *huppah*) and being alone together in a room (*yichud*). While historically these two events could take place as much as a year apart, they are now commonly combined into one ceremony.

Before the wedding ceremony takes place the *ketubah* is signed in the presence of two witnesses. As we noted, the traditional *ketubah* details the husband's obligations to his wife, among which are food, clothing and marital relations. Non-Orthodox *ketubot* omit these financial aspects of the *ketubah* and focus instead on the couple's relationship. The *ketubah* is often written as an illuminated manuscript, which is framed and displayed in the home. Under the *huppah* it is customary to read the signed *ketubah* aloud, usually in Aramaic or in translation. In non-Orthodox weddings this practice varies.

The wedding itself takes place under the *huppah*, symbolizing the new home being built by the couple when they are husband and wife. Prior to the ceremony, Ashkenazi Jews have the custom of covering the face of the bride (usually with a veil), and a prayer is often said for her based on the words spoken by Rebecca in Genesis 24.60. The veiling ritual is known in Yiddish as *badeken*. Various reasons are given for this practice. In Sephardic communities this ritual does not take place. In many countries the groom is led under the *huppah* by the two fathers and the bride by the two mothers (known as *untefirers* – 'one who leads under').

The bride traditionally walks around the groom three or seven times when she arrives at the *huppah*. This practice may derive from Jeremiah 31.22 ('A woman shall surround a man'). The three circuits possibly represent the three virtues of marriage: righteousness, justice and loving kindness (Hos. 2.21). Seven circuits derive from the biblical concept that seven denotes perfection or completeness. Sephardic Jews do not perform this ceremony. In non-Orthodox marriages it is sometimes the case that both the husband and the wife walk around each other, symbolizing equality in marriage. In traditional weddings two blessings are recited before betrothal: a blessing over wine and the betrothal blessing that is specified in the Talmud. The wine is then tasted by the couple. The groom then gives the bride a ring, traditionally a plain wedding band. He then recites the declaration: 'Behold you are consecrated to me with this ring according to the Law of Moses and Israel.' The groom then places the ring on the bride's right index finger. According to traditional Jewish law, two valid witnesses must see him place the ring. In some egalitarian weddings the bride will also present a ring to the groom, frequently with a quote from the Song of Songs: 'I am my beloved's and my beloved is mine', which may also be inscribed on the ring itself.

The *sheva berachot* (seven blessings) are then recited by the *hazzan* or rabbi, or by select guests who are called up individually. Being called on to recite one of these blessings is an honour. The groom is then given the cup of wine to drink from after the seven blessings. The bride also drinks the wine: in some cases the cup will be held to the lips of the groom by his new father-in-law and to the lips of the bride by her new mother-in-law. Traditions vary as to whether additional songs are sung before the seven blessings.

After the bride has been given the ring, or at the end of the ceremony, the groom breaks a glass, crushing it with his right foot. The guests then shout 'Mazel Tov' (congratulations). At some modern weddings a light bulb may be substituted for the glass because it is easier to break. The origin of this practice is unknown, although various explanations have been given. The primary reason is that joy should be tempered. This is based on two accounts in the Talmud, where rabbis, seeing that their son's wedding celebration was getting out of hand, broke a glass to calm the proceedings. Another explanation is that it is a reminder that despite the joy of the marriage celebration, Jews still mourn the destruction of the Temple in Jerusalem.

Yichud (togetherness) refers to the Ashkenazi practice of leaving the bride and groom alone for about 10–20 minutes after the ceremony. The reason for this practice is that according to several authorities, standing under the *huppah* does not constitute *huppah* and seclusion, which is necessary to complete the wedding ceremony. Sephardic Jews do not follow this custom.

Following the ceremony it is customary for guests to dance in front of the seated couple and entertain them. Traditional dances include the *krenzl*, in which the bride's mother is crowned with a wreath of flowers as the daughters dance around her; the *mizinke*, a dance for parents of the bride or groom when their last child is wed; the *horah*, an Israeli dance; the gladdening of the bride in which guests dance around the bride; the *mitzvah tantz*, in which family members and honoured rabbis are invited to dance in front of the bride.

After the meal, the *Birkat Hamazon* (Grace after Meals) is recited, followed by the *sheva berachot*. At the wedding banquet the wording of the blessings preceding the *Birkat Hamazon* is slightly different from the everyday version. Prayer booklets are frequently given to guests. After these prayers the blessing over the wine is recited, with two glasses of wine poured together into a third; this symbolizes the creation of a new life together. In modern times several branches of Judaism in the United States as well as in Israel and the United Kingdom have developed prenuptial agreements that are designed to prevent a man from withholding a *get* from his wife, should she desire to have one.

Intermarriage

In the Bible, intermarriage with a Canaanite was prohibited on the basis that it might lead to a son being brought up to follow the Canaanite religion (Deut. 7.4). Nonetheless, in the Hebrew Bible there are instances where intermarriage seems to have taken place: King David is described as having married the daughter of the King of Gusher, and Bathsheba is depicted as having married Uriah the Hittite. Further, the book of Deuteronomy implies that intermarriage to Edomites or Egyptians is acceptable by permitting the grandchildren of such couples to be treated as

Israelites. Yet after the Babylonian captivity in the sixth century BCE, intermarriages were censured. The book of Malachi states that intermarriages that had taken place are profanity, and several Jewish leaders eventually made a complaint to Ezra about these unions. Ezra extended the law against intermarriage to forbid marriages between a Jew and any non-Jew, and excommunicated those who refused to divorce their foreign spouses.

Even though most rabbis in the Talmud considered the Deuteronomic law to refer only to marriages to Canaanites, they viewed all religious intermarriage as illegitimate. Nonetheless traditional Judaism does not regard marriage between a Jew by birth and a convert as an intermarriage. Hence all biblical passages that appear to support intermarriages, such as that of Joseph to Asenath and of Ruth to Boaz, were regarded by the rabbis as having occurred only after the foreign spouses had converted to Judaism. The Talmud and later classical sources of Jewish law are thus clear that the institution of Jewish marriage (*kiddushin*) can only be effected between Jews.

In the modern world, however, the more liberal Jewish movements do not generally regard this traditional ruling as binding. Reform Judaism, for example, has no firm prohibition against intermarriage. According to a survey of rabbis conducted in 1985, more than 87 per cent of Reconstructionist rabbis were willing to officiate at interfaith marriages. In 2003 at least 50 per cent of Reform rabbis were willing to perform interfaith marriages. The Central Conference of American Rabbis (CCAR), the Reform rabbinical association in North America and the largest Progressive rabbinical association, consistently opposed intermarriage at least until the 1980s. Yet today intermarriage has become a common feature of modern Jewish life, and non-Jewish spouses are generally welcomed as members of Reform congregations. However, regardless of their personal attitude to intermarriage, most Reform rabbis do still try to persuade intermarried couples to raise their children as Jews.

> **Reform Judaism and intermarriage**
>
> Rabbinic officiation at interfaith weddings is indeed a challenging and emotionally charged issue. Clearly, the weight of Jewish tradition falls on the side of non-officiation, while some [Reform] rabbis base their position upon individual conscience and their belief that interfaith officiation benefits the Jewish people. The official stance of the Reform rabbinate is articulated in this 1973 resolution of the Central Conference of American Rabbis:
>
>> The Central Conference of American Rabbis, recalling its stand adopted in 1909 that mixed marriage is contrary to the Jewish tradition and should be discouraged, now declares its opposition to participation by its members in any ceremony which solemnizes a mixed marriage. The Central Conference of American Rabbis recognizes that historically its members have held and continue to hold divergent interpretations of Jewish tradition.
>
> Thus, rabbinic officiation is discouraged, with latitude granted to rabbis to apply their own interpretation to the mandates of the Jewish tradition. This is the brilliance of the Reform Movement and its rabbinate, that autonomy is granted to each of us to wrestle with the claims of God and Torah upon our lives. And it has led some Reform rabbis to perform interfaith marriages, but almost always with a set of standards and conditions. These conditions vary, but can often include a requirement to raise children exclusively within the Jewish faith, or ritual modifications of the wedding ceremony, or even a condition that the ceremony take place outside of a synagogue setting.
>
> (From the website of the Union for Reform Judaism, www.urj.org/ask/questions/intermarried/)

All branches of Orthodox Judaism follow the historical attitudes to intermarriage and therefore refuse to accept that intermarriages have any legitimacy and strictly forbid sexual intercourse between a Jew and a non-Jew. Orthodox rabbis refuse to officiate at interfaith weddings, and also try to avoid assisting them in any way. Secular intermarriage is viewed as a deliberate rejection of Judaism, and an intermarried person is effectively cut off from the Orthodox community (even though Chabad-Lubavitch and modern Orthodox Jews do reach out to intermarried Jewish couples).

The Conservative movement does not sanction or recognize the Jewish validity of intermarriage; instead it encourages the acceptance of the non-Jewish spouse within the family, hoping that such acceptance will lead to the spouse's conversion to Judaism. The Rabbinical Assembly Standards of Rabbinic Practice prohibits Conservative rabbis from officiating at intermarriages.

> **Conservative Judaism and intermarriage**
>
> While Conservative Judaism discourages intermarriage, its understanding and approach to intermarriage is more open than that of Orthodox Judaism. According to the Conservative Movement's Joint Commission on Response to Intermarriage, '[i]n the past intermarriage ... was viewed as an act of rebellion, a rejection of Judaism. Jews who intermarried were essentially excommunicated. But now, intermarriage is often the result of living in an open society ... If our children end up marrying non-Jews, we should not reject them. We should continue to give our love and by that retain a measure of influence in their lives, Jewishly and otherwise. Life consists of constant growth and our adult children may reach a stage when Judaism has new meaning for them. However, the marriage between a Jew and a non-Jew is not a celebration for the Jewish community. We therefore reach out to the couple with the hope that the non-Jewish partner will move closer to Judaism and ultimately choose to convert.'
>
> (www.judaism.about.com/od/interfaithfamilies/a/intermarr_jew.htm)

These various attitudes to intermarriage within the Jewish world reflect the growing importance of this issue. In the early nineteenth century, in some modernized religions of the world, intermarriage was extremely rare. Even in the early twentieth century intermarriage was infrequent. In contemporary society, however, rates of intermarriage have risen substantially. The US National Jewish Population Survey reported that in the United States between 1986 and 2001, nearly half (47 per cent) of Jews who had married during that period had married non-Jewish partners. Such statistics have caused great alarm within the Jewish establishment. Most Jewish leaders across the Jewish religious spectrum believe that such a development constitutes a major threat to Jewish life. In the view of some rabbis, the phenomenon of intermarriage is perceived as a silent holocaust. As a result there is a concerted effort to reach out to descendants of intermarried parents to bring them back into the fold.

Same-sex marriage

As we have seen, homosexuality is condemned in Jewish sources. As a result same-sex marriage is regarded as anathema by the Orthodox. The Union of Orthodox Jewish Congregations of America, for example, has publicly rejected civil and same-sex marriage. A December 1996 declaration explained its position: 'While the Orthodox Jewish community in no way condones discrimination against individuals on the basis of their private conduct, we believe that America's moral values and traditions, of which traditional Judaism is a fountainhead, clearly asserts that the unique status of marriage is reserved for the sacred union of a man and a woman in a loving relationship.'

Yet within the Jewish world, particularly in the United States, the issue of gay marriage has recently been debated. For Jewish communities there are two primary questions. First, should the government legalize same-sex marriage, offering couples the same legal rights as married, heterosexual couples? Second, should rabbis perform same-sex wedding ceremonies? If so, should such ceremonies be regarded as *kiddushin* (the term for a holy union)? If such a practice were acceptable, this would give such ceremonies the same status as heterosexual marriages. The Reform, Reconstructionist and Conservative movements have been grappling with these questions for over a decade.

The Reconstructionist movement has expressed its support for the full inclusion of gay men and lesbians in all aspects of

Jewish life in its 1992 Report of the Reconstructionist Commission on Homosexuality. This document affirmed the holiness of homosexual relationships in a Jewish context: 'As we celebrate the love between heterosexual couples, so too we celebrate the love between gay or lesbian Jews. The Reconstructionist movement today also fully endorses efforts to legalize civil same-sex marriages and grant homosexual couples equal benefits.'

The Reform movement has called for civil same-sex marriage for many years. The CCAR, the professional association of Reform rabbis, passed a resolution in 1996 opposing governmental efforts to ban gay and lesbian marriage. The Union of American Hebrew Congregations, the congregational arm of the Reform movement, similarly resolved in 1997 to support secular efforts to promote legislation that would provide civil marriage equal opportunity for men and lesbians.

In a December 1996 statement commending the decision of the Circuit Court of Hawaii to recognize same-sex marriages, the Associate Director of the Religious Action Centre of Reform Judaism declared that God calls us to the love that binds two people together in a loving and devoted commitment; it is accessible to all of God's creatures. Gay and lesbian couples should thus have the legal right, as heterosexual couples do, to form such lasting partnerships.

The issue of gay and lesbian Jewish wedding ceremonies, however, has been a subject of controversy in the Reform movement. In 1997 the CCAR Committee on Response voted by a majority that homosexual relationships do not fit within the Jewish legal category of *kiddushin*. It further stated that Jewish marriage does not exist apart from *kiddushin*. In other words, although the Reform movement supports same-sex civil marriage, it rejects the notion of same-sex Jewish marriage.

Nevertheless, in March 2000 a different conclusion was reached by the CCAR itself, which voted to support colleagues who choose to perform same-sex ceremonies. Their Resolution on Same Sex Gender Officiation states that the relationship of a Jewish, same-gender couple is worthy of affirmation through appropriate Jewish ritual. However, the final text of the resolution permitted individual rabbis to choose not to perform such ceremonies. Further, it avoided the term *kiddushin*, leaving open the question of the exact form or Jewish status of the ceremonies. It also called for the development of sample ceremonies to be used as a resource for rabbis who are willing to perform such weddings.

Within Conservative Judaism, same-sex marriage as well as other gay and lesbian topics met with little consensus. The standing ruling of its Committee on Jewish Law and Standards, which determines the official positions of the movement, is that Jewish law prohibits homosexuality; therefore Jewish same-sex marriage is not appropriate. However, a number of influential Conservative rabbis disagree with the Committee's interpretation of Jewish law and call for the support of civil and Jewish same-sex marriage, and there are a small number of Conservative rabbis who perform same-sex marriages.

Christianity

The nature of marriage

Marriage vows

I, N, take you, N,
to be my wife,
to have and to hold
from this day forward;
for better, for worse,
for richer, for poorer,
in sickness and in health,
to love and to cherish,
till death us do part;
according to God's holy law.
In the presence of God I make this vow.

(Church of England, Marriage Service)

It is a normal expectation, although not an obligation, for Christian men and women to marry. Christian marriage shares the functions of secular marriage: it is an expression of affection, enabling companionship, sexual gratification and the procreation of children. It has the pragmatic function of conferring rights of property, allowing a widowed partner to utilize his or her spouse's property and enabling rights of inheritance. It allows a distribution and division of labour, although feminists will point out that the apportioning of tasks tends to favour the husband rather than the wife. The Church's role in conducting marriage seems to have gone back at least to the second generation of Christians: the Church Father Polycarp (c.69–c.155) mentions that marriage partners require the approval of the bishop, and throughout its history the Church has continually offered itself as the facilitator of marriages.

Different Christian traditions have had different views on whether the Church controls the institution of marriage. Traditional Catholicism harks back to Polycarp's belief not merely that marriage should be conducted by an appropriately authorized religious specialist such as a priest but that no relationship can count as a true marriage unless it has its origin within the Catholic Church. The Church's control was signified by the fact that its officials conducted the marriage ceremony, that it held the records of marriages and that the Church alone had the power to dissolve a marriage in accordance with its own ecclesiastical laws on annulment. The Protestant Reformers saw matters differently: Martin Luther described marriage as a 'worldly affair', and John Calvin published his Marriage Ordinance of Geneva, requiring both Church and state involvement in validating a marriage. In 1563, as part of the Counter-Reformation, the Roman Catholic Church reaffirmed its view at the Council of Trent that a marriage may only be enacted by one of its priests, with two witnesses present.

In all traditions, however, the Church would wish to ensure that marriages were civilly as well as religiously valid, and would insist that couples complied with civil law. In many countries, including Canada, the United States, the United Kingdom and Ireland, a church wedding incorporates the features that are needed to make it civilly valid – the taking of vows and the signing of a marriage register. In countries where the religious ceremony lacks civil validity, for example in Belgium, France and the Netherlands, the couple are required to fulfil the civil requirements before proceeding with the Church ceremony.

The Roman Catholic and the Orthodox traditions name seven 'sacraments' (Orthodoxy often prefers to call them 'mysteries'), of which marriage is one. A sacrament is defined as a celebration that bestows Christ's power and offers means of grace. The best known of these are baptism, the Eucharist (Holy Communion) and confirmation (which will be dealt with in Chapter 4); matrimony – sometimes prefixed with the adjective 'holy' – is another. However, the Protestant Reformers disputed the number of sacraments, defining baptism and the Eucharist as the only two on the grounds that rites such as marriage were not instituted by Christ. Jesus instructed his disciples to baptize (Matt. 28.19) and to celebrate his last meal in his memory (Matt. 26.26–7), but not to marry. Jesus himself appears to have been unmarried, and only one of his disciples – Peter – is recorded as having a wife (Mark 1.30). This does not mean that Protestants attach less importance to marriage than the other traditions: the difference is a technicality about what constitutes a sacrament. On the contrary, since most Protestant denominations do not have celibate holy orders, marriage is the most common lifestyle. In a Protestant marriage ceremony the rite typically draws attention to the presence of Jesus and his mother Mary at a wedding at Cana at which, according to John, Jesus performed his first miracle, reportedly turning 150 gallons of water into wine (John 2.1–11). Marriage is indeed something to be celebrated!

In all three Christian traditions, the wedding ceremony is typically a religious one, conducted by an appropriately licensed officiant, on church premises. In countries where the law of the land requires civil registration of a marriage, Christians will comply, but it would be unusual for a Christian couple merely to have a civil wedding.

Fundamentalist and liberal views

> Marriage is the uniting of one man and one woman in covenant commitment for a lifetime. It is God's unique gift to reveal the union between Christ and His church and to provide for the man and the woman in marriage the framework for intimate companionship, the channel of sexual expression according to biblical standards, and the means for procreation of the human race.
>
> The husband and wife are of equal worth before God, since both are created in God's image. The marriage relationship models the way God relates to His people. A husband is to love his wife as Christ loved the church. He has the God-given responsibility to provide for, to protect, and to lead his family. A wife is to submit herself graciously to the servant leadership of her husband even as the church willingly submits to the headship of Christ. She, being in the image of God as is her husband and thus equal to him, has the God-given responsibility to respect her husband and to serve as his helper in managing the household and nurturing the next generation.
>
> (Southern Baptist Convention, statement on Family, at www.sbc.net/bfm/bfm2000.asp#xviii)

In any household, decisions have to be taken about how relationships work. Traditionally the husband has been the bread-winner and the wife the home-keeper, the husband holding the pursestrings and exercising a leadership role. Western society has changed, however: labour-saving devices enable wives to be no longer subjected to endless household chores, and modern technology and improved education have made it possible for women to perform tasks typically done by men, despite being on average physically less strong. The modern feminist movement has empowered women and encouraged them to seek equality economically, politically, socially and financially. In numerous Protestant denominations, women are increasingly attaining equality ecclesiastically as the movement for women's ordination has progressed.

Christians are divided on the issue of whether women should attain equality with men or remain subservient. The Bible teaches that Adam was created first, that God made Eve to be 'helper' to Adam (Gen. 2.18) and that Eve was the first to transgress God's law by yielding to the serpent in the Garden of Eden (Gen. 3.1–19). Writing to the Corinthians some centuries later, Paul (or someone writing in Paul's name) reminds them of these details (1 Cor. 11.3–16), adding that women should be submissive and respectful to their husbands (Eph. 5.22, 33) and that they should not hold any teaching role within the Church but should sit silently through the worship, dressed modestly with their heads always covered (1 Tim. 2.9–15). The husband is the head of the household, including being head over the wife, just as Christ is the head of the Church. The woman should be willing to learn, but her main role is child-bearing and bringing up children in the faith.

Many conservative Christians take such statements literally, particularly in the US Bible Belt. The Southern Baptist Convention (the largest US Protestant denomination) formally subscribes to this view of women, and a number of other fundamentalist denominations, such as the Brethren, endorse these values. This view of the subjection of women does not mean that they are to be downtrodden. On the contrary, the Bible teaches that the husband is to love his wife, offer her protection, and – employing the analogy of the Christ–Church relationship – since the Church is Christ's body, the wife is to be regarded as an extension of the husband's body and therefore treated with respect. Accordingly the husband should not be a tyrant but he should not be a wimp who allows the wife to wear the trousers and do the decision-making.

On this view the wife should still be submissive to her husband, even if he is not a Christian. Even though a non-believing partner does not acknowledge the biblical standard of having Christ as his head, the husband's authority is an integral part of the husband–wife relationship. The woman must still obey him, unless he exceeds his authority by demanding of her behaviour contrary to her Christian faith – for example, if he forbade her to attend church. The wife should bear witness to her faith through her deeds, while continuing to obey. She should certainly not engage in 'strike action' by refusing to cook, do household chores or have sexual relationships with her husband.

More liberal Christians tend not to take Paul so literally and would argue that he was writing as a man of his time and that Christians cannot subscribe to all the social mores of first-century Mediterranean culture. Liberal Christians will often refer to biblical passages that suggest a more egalitarian relationship between men and women. One much-cited passage is: 'There is neither Jew nor Gentile, neither slave nor free, nor is there male and female, for you are all one in Christ Jesus' (Gal. 3.28). Although much of the Bible's imagery is patriarchal, feminist Christians can point out that it is both male and female who are made in God's image, not just the male (Gen. 1.27), and that Jesus had at least one female disciple in Mary, the sister of Lazarus (Luke 10.39). Women have leadership roles in the Bible (for example, Miriam, Deborah, Esther) and they are portrayed as the first witnesses to Christ's resurrection, despite the fact that in Jewish law a woman's testimony was regarded as inferior (Luke 24.10).

Seeking a partner

For the Christian the ideal marriage partner is another Christian. Paul wrote, 'Do not be yoked together with unbelievers' (2 Cor. 6.14). Marrying outside one's faith has obvious drawbacks, although not necessarily insuperable difficulties. Bringing up children is also less problematic where both partners are agreed about passing on their faith to their offspring and ensuring that they receive consistent and appropriate nurture and guidance for life. Even to marry outside one's own tradition can be problematic, particularly where there are acrimonious rivalries between traditions, such as Protestants and Catholics in Northern Ireland. Although the Roman Catholic Church permits 'mixed marriages' and will even allow a church wedding to partners of different traditions, it requires their children to be brought up in the Catholic faith and not any other form of Christianity.

Finding a partner tends to be one's own responsibility, at least in the West, and arranged marriages are not favoured. In one's own congregation the range of potential partners that might be suited to a young single person is likely to be limited. Even in a thriving congregation there are unlikely to be more than 20 members of the opposite sex of similar age. Some of these are no doubt already in relationships, have educational or social divergences or are simply 'not one's type'. Increasing educational equality of the sexes now increases the likelihood of one's lifelong partner being found at university or college. Although specific subjects still remain male- and female-dominated, chaplaincies and societies such as the Christian Union and the Student Christian Movement have an important role in facilitating relationships between the sexes. However, women are renowned for having more interest in religion than men, as any visitor to a typical church service will readily observe. A recent US survey indicated that 14 per cent more women than men reported that religion was important in their lives.[1] This gender imbalance among practising Christians inevitably gives rise to many partnerships between Christians and non-Christians, most of the latter being uncommitted to any religion. There is no evidence to show that such relationships do not work in terms of marital harmony and stability: the husband will simply remain at home or pursue his own interests, perhaps occasionally attending social events at church and perhaps the occasional celebration, such as a special Christmas service or rites of passage such as a family member's baptism, a friend's wedding or a funeral.

Many Christians now expand their options by using online dating services, many of which are specifically for Christians. A number of organizations offer holidays aimed at Christian singles, and many Christians also make use of secular dating and singles services. Although people were once reluctant to admit making use of dating agencies, their popularity has become more widespread and I have heard no objections to Christians using such facilities.

---

1 Pew Research Center (2008), 'The Stronger Sex – Spiritually Speaking': www.pewforum.org/The-Stronger-Sex----Spiritually-Speaking.aspx. Accessed 6 October 2012.

Sex within marriage

> Joy Wilson went looking for something to spice up her marriage without compromising her Christian beliefs. Finding nothing, she founded her own 'sin-free' sex toy business. Book22.com caters to the Christian community with books, toys and occasional advice. The name refers to the Song of Solomon, the extended love poem that forms the 22nd book of the Bible.
>
> Wilson says that after the birth of her first child, she had trouble rekindling her desire for intimacy ... She and her husband talked it over and decided that there must be a way for conservative people to add a spark to their romantic lives. She says their site steers clear of certain types of sexual activity that they believe are unholy. And they carefully consider which new products to add.
>
> 'We pray about things before we add them to our site', she says. 'We live our lives very openly in front of Jesus, so we just kind of pray for direction about which way he would have us go, and I have to be honest with you – he's really surprised us ... Almost our whole entire 'special order' page has come about from that.'
>
> ('The Joy of Christian Sex Toys', 21 March 2008: www.npr.org/templates/story/story.php?storyId=18975616)

Marriage is the institution that legitimizes sexual relationships. All three Christian traditions have affirmed throughout their history that sex outside marriage is a grave sin. However, does this entail that all types of sexual relationship between husband and wife are permitted? What does Christianity teach about oral sex, anal sex, the use of sex toys, the use of role play and fantasy in sex, the use of pornography for sexual stimulation or sex while the woman is menstruating? One Christian web author has likened sex to a playground with a fence around it. It is pleasurable but it has its boundaries, and the difficult question is deciding where they lie. Catholic and Orthodox teaching on sex has traditionally taught that since the primary purpose of sex is human reproduction, any sexual activity that does not serve this function is sinful. It therefore follows that at least some methods of sexual stimulation that constitute part of foreplay are allowable since they lead on to sex that is potentially reproductive. Other forms of eroticism that are practised after intercourse, or in place of it, cannot serve the real purpose of sex and hence are prohibited.

The Protestant tradition is more liberal. The comic Monty Python film *The Meaning of Life* portrays a Protestant couple looking out of their window at some Roman Catholic families. The Protestant husband comments: 'When Martin Luther nailed his protest up to the church door in 1517, he may not have realized the full significance of what he was doing, but four hundred years later, thanks to him, my dear, I can wear whatever I want on my John Thomas. And Protestantism doesn't stop at the simple condom. Oh, no! I can wear French Ticklers if I want.' He had a point. There is nothing in the Bible that dictates what may or may not happen in the marriage bed. One Christian author has even seen approval of oral sex in the Song of Solomon:

> Like an apple tree among the trees of the forest
> is my beloved among the young men.
> I delight to sit in his shade,
> and his fruit is sweet to my taste. (2.3)

This is not to imply that Protestants are enthusiastic about the products of sex shops. On the contrary, they have frequently objected to planning applications for such businesses, and many object to the way in which sex receives such a high profile in the media and in the world of advertising and marketing. The blank fronts of 'private shops' give them a somewhat sleazy appearance, making sex a furtive activity, encouraging the sex industry rather than enhancing sex within marriage. There are exceptions: a few 'Christian' sex stores exist, usually online, such as Book22.com (mentioned above).

For the Protestant these issues are matters for conscience, and decisions about how to 'spice up one's sex life' are no doubt subject to a number of biblical ground rules. Regarding sexual morality, Paul reminds the church at Corinth that 'your bodies are temples of the Holy Spirit' (1 Cor. 6.19) – a text that is much quoted by Protestant Christians in connection with matters that affect one's body.

Gay and lesbian issues

> Therefore God gave them over in the sinful desires of their hearts to sexual impurity for the degrading of their bodies with one another. They exchanged the truth about God for a lie, and worshipped and served created things rather than the Creator – who is forever praised. Amen.
> Because of this, God gave them over to shameful lusts. Even their women exchanged natural sexual relations for unnatural ones. In the same way the men also abandoned natural relations with women and were inflamed with lust for one another. Men committed shameful acts with other men, and received in themselves the due penalty for their error.
>
> (Rom. 1.24–7)

Not everyone feels sexually attracted to the opposite sex, and Christians are divided on lesbian and gay issues. Conservative Christians, especially fundamentalists, hold that homosexual relationships are wrong. Particularly in the Protestant tradition the practice of homosexuality is perceived as contrary to Scripture: the book of Leviticus condemns same-sex relationships, and at the beginning of his letter to the Romans, Paul includes 'shameful acts with other men' as being among the 'shameful lusts' that he condemns (Lev. 18.22; Romans 1.24–7). Further, if the purpose of sex is procreation, sexual activity between same-sex partners cannot result in the birth of children and appears to run counter to God's initial purpose of creating men and women to 'be fruitful and multiply'. The official Catholic stance is the same. It acknowledges that homosexuality is a deep-seated psychological trait and urges other Christians to treat homosexuals with respect and sensitivity and not to discriminate against them unfairly. It nonetheless insists that homosexual acts are 'acts of grave depravity'. Homosexuals are therefore called upon to live a life of chastity, drawing on prayer and the Church's sacraments to achieve self-mastery. Some Christians have gone so far as to contend that homosexuality is an ailment for which there is a 'cure', and a number of conservative Christian organizations, such as Operation U-Turn, claim to have reversed homosexuals' tendencies, enabling them to live as heterosexual people.

Liberal Christians, and especially those who are themselves gay or lesbian, do not accept such judgements, holding that one's sexuality is something that is God-given. Some have attempted to reinterpret Paul, who states that 'men committed shameful acts with other men' (Rom. 1.27, above); some have suggested that Paul was condemning excessive sexual urges; others that Paul was condemning the widespread sexual exploitation of Roman slaves; while other scholars have pointed out that Paul goes on to write, 'You, therefore, have no excuse, you who pass judgment on someone else' (Rom. 2.1), possibly implying that these were accusations the early Roman Christians were making about their society and calling on them to examine their own lives.

Many Christians would hold that God's law is not to be understood through determining the meaning of single biblical verses. A broader view might be obtained, for instance, by looking at the example of Jesus. He was certainly not the father in the stereotypical household with a wife and 2.4 children. Although some authors have claimed that Jesus had a sexual relationship with Mary Magdalene and that she gave birth to a family of holy children, such theories are sheer speculation and certainly not part of the biblical story, on which Christians draw. Conversely there are those who have speculated that Jesus may himself have been gay, perhaps suggesting that John's references to a 'disciple whom Jesus loved' might indicate more than a special spiritual relationship. Even if Jesus was not gay, some gay and lesbian Christians have suggested that same-sex partnerships might have existed between other biblical characters: David and Jonathan, Ruth and Naomi, Aquila and Priscilla (who both have names with apparently feminine endings).

Whatever the truth or falsity of such speculations, many gay Christians believe that they have been the victims of prejudice.

A great deal of criticism surrounded the appointment of the Revd Gene Robinson as the Anglican Bishop of New Hampshire in 2003, and five years later in England the Bishop of Oxford decided not to proceed with the ordination of the Revd Jeffrey John as the Suffragan Bishop of Reading, following criticism of his involvement in a (celibate) long-term relationship with another man. Many gay and lesbian Christians have challenged such prejudices, forming their own special interest groups, such as the Gay Christian Network and the Evangelical Fellowship for Lesbian and Gay Christians. Some have set up their own denominations, for example the Metropolitan Community Church, founded by Troy Perry in 1968, which is attended predominantly by gay, lesbian and transgendered Christians who can be sure they will find acceptance within their congregations.

There is a further step beyond accepting the possibility of being Christian and gay. Many gay and lesbian Christians, like their non-religious counterparts, have entered into relationships in which they live together as partners in a household with the same kind of affection for each other as exists between a husband and wife. When a gay partner dies, one's feeling of loss is comparable to that of a marriage partner, and gay couples have often seen the need for civil partnerships, which ensure that one's same-sex partner receives due entitlements to their shared finances, goods and chattels. Should not the Church take the step of recognizing such relationships not merely by accepting same-sex couples in congregations but by enabling them to have a rite of passage that celebrates their decision to live together with the same commitments as heterosexual partners? Traditional conservative Christians emphatically disapprove of such suggestions, believing that the Church would be officially sanctioning sin. Fundamentalist organizations like Christian Voice who deplore civil partnerships – legalized in Britain in 2005 – find it abhorrent that some sectors of the Church are complicit in sanctioning same-sex partnerships.

Most Christians would acknowledge that a couple who have cemented a heterosexual union exclusively by a civil ceremony make similar commitments to each other as those who marry in church: they agree to share their lives and possessions and their commitment is to lifelong fidelity. This being the case, why should the Church refuse to celebrate a same-sex union in a religious way? Further, if a country allows same-sex marriages in law, then unless the Church permits same-sex marriage in church, gay and lesbian partners will be forced to have a civil rather than religious ceremony, with the implication that the Church views their relationship as inferior to that of heterosexuals and allows homosexuals to continue to be stigmatized.

One compromise is for gay couples to have a civil ceremony followed by a blessing of their partnership in church (or simply a blessing ceremony if the state makes no provision for civil partnerships). Such blessings are currently available in several denominations, for example the Metropolitan Community Church and some Unitarian churches, particularly in the United States. Although some lesbian, gay, bisexual and transgender (LGBT) Christians may think this is sufficient it is nonetheless a compromise, and their relationship still cannot be given the same religious legitimation as that of a traditional marriage between husband and wife. It is therefore understandable that many gay and lesbian Christians would like their relationships to be given full recognition by 'gay marriage' – sometimes called 'homogamous marriage'. Already some churches offer this option, for example the Church of Sweden, where same-sex marriage is fully recognized in law. The Roman Catholic Church finds such a proposal quite unacceptable – as do many Christians from other traditions – on account of the sacramental nature of marriage. For a rite to be a sacrament, certain conditions must be satisfied, of which the coming together of one male and one female partner is one. Not only would such a rite lack any validity and not be a proper marriage; it would be an affront, just as a celebration of a Black Mass would be an affront to a practising Christian.

Certainly homogamous marriage requires some shift of the traditional understanding of Christian marriage. Such an innovation cannot draw on the stories of Adam and Eve and the Cana wedding, and such marriage cannot be said to be for the procreation of children. The ceremony could not be couched in biblical language that implied that male and female were each incomplete and complementary, and indeed the liturgy could not differentiate the partners by gender. There would be no 'giving away' of the bride, and it is debatable whether such a homogamous marriage ceremony would make reference to bodily union or pronounce the couple as 'one flesh', although the ritual could certainly make reference to lifelong commitment, 'for better, for worse, in sickness and in health', to loving and cherishing and forsaking all others. All this discussion is not to imply that homogamous marriage is not possible but merely to highlight some of the issues that are currently being thought through. There are further dimensions: if the marriage liturgy were to be rewritten for gay partnerships, would the new, presumably genderless liturgy also be used for traditional male–female weddings? This might be less popular with heterosexual couples, but the use of different ceremonies could be construed as discriminatory. Couples might be allowed to choose the form of liturgy – indeed, there are already choices that can be made regarding the traditional ceremony's wording.

Conservative Christians claim that the Church is yielding to the standards of the world in contemplating such innovations, while the liberals contend that the Church must find a place for gay and lesbian Christians without their having to feel second-rate or spiritually inferior. Inevitably, Christian ecumenical issues feature in the debate. If one denomination moves too radically on such a contentious issue, it places itself further out of reach in attempts to secure mutual interdenominational acceptance. There is also the risk of schism: the Church of England has been continually restrained by the Anglican churches in Africa, who are fiercely opposed to homosexuality and have threatened to secede.

The United Methodist Church has described its deliberations on gay and lesbian partnerships as a 'pilgrimage of faith', meaning that Christians have embarked on a difficult journey that takes them into new territory. After much debate in its Annual Conventions, it was decided not to allow its clergy to bless same-sex unions. Some clergy have defied the ban, risking disciplinary action. In discussing the topic with various other Christians, I have encountered a wide spectrum of opinion. Some are fiercely condemnatory, others approving and quite a few people uncertain about whether their thinking should move on or whether it is important to defend values the Church has affirmed through the centuries.

Islam

Definitions of marriage and prelude to the contract

The Qur'an uses two terms to refer to marriage: *nikah* and *zawaj*. *Nikah* is the more commonly used term. There is some disagreement as to whether its principal meaning is the marriage contract or the act of sexual intercourse, but the classical jurists define the marriage contract essentially in terms of the husband's right to sexual enjoyment of his wife. The term *zawaj* causes no such disagreement: its linguistic root refers to pairing and the jurists define it as a contract encompassing all aspects of marriage.

Contemporary jurists have tried to produce new definitions to encompass all aspects of marriage, and the legislatures of several Muslim countries have produced definitions of it.

> Moroccan law states:
>
> Article 4: Marriage is a legal contract by which a man and a woman mutually consent to unite in a common and enduring conjugal life. Its purpose is fidelity, virtue and the creation of a stable family, under the supervision of both spouses according to the provisions of this Code.
>
> (*Mudawwanat al-Ahwal al-Shakhsiyya al-Maghribiyya* – Moroccan Personal Status Code)

Although an Imam may oversee the conclusion of the contract, there is no religious ceremony as such. Nonetheless marriages are at the centre of family and community life and weddings are a cause for celebration. And in any community, although the contract is the key element there are customs and conventions surrounding the process of getting married.

Any contract must be preceded by some initial agreement or expression of intention to form a contract. In the case of marriage this is engagement or betrothal, in Arabic *khutba*. There are certain conditions for the propriety of betrothal; the parties may not become engaged unless they are free to marry immediately and without impediment. A man may not propose marriage to any of the categories of women who are forbidden to him in marriage, including those with regard to whom the prohibition is temporary, which means that he may not propose to a married woman or one who is observing the prescribed waiting period after being widowed or divorced (this will be discussed below). He may not propose to the sister, aunt or niece of his wife, unless he first divorces her, as it is prohibited to be married to two sisters or an aunt and niece at the same time. It is also generally agreed that in the case where a suitor has proposed marriage to a woman, it is not permitted for another to do so unless the woman has rejected the first.

Although engagement or betrothal is a promise to marry, it is not legally binding and entails no contractual responsibility. Either party may terminate the engagement. The jurists are generally in agreement that any gifts – other than consumables – given to a woman by her suitor should be returned to him if the engagement is terminated, particularly if it is she who has broken it off, although the Maliki school holds that return of gifts is not obligatory unless required by prevailing custom.

The *hadith* offers guidance in the selection of a marriage partner, recommending piety and good character as a sounder basis for marriage than other characteristics.

> Narrated Abu Huraira:
>
> The Prophet said, 'A woman is married for four things: her wealth, her family status, her beauty and her religion. So you should marry the religious woman, (otherwise) you will be the losers.'

Customs in relation to betrothal vary greatly. In modern urban society and among professional classes, people often meet their marriage partners at university or in the working environment, but it remains the norm for a formal approach to be made by the suitor's family to the family of the woman to whom he wishes to propose. Both families will make inquiries about the background, character and reputation of the other. In some cultures there is an understanding among families that their children will marry in the future. In others, families may seek a marriage partner for their child through family and community and in some cases through matchmakers. For Muslims who do not have networks to turn to, including converts and Muslims in non-Muslim countries, there has been a proliferation of matchmaking websites.

The marriage contract

As with any other legal contract, the essential elements of the marriage contract are offer (*ijab*) and acceptance (*qubul*). These should take place in a single session or meeting with no significant interruption. The offer may originate from either of the parties and the acceptance must correspond with it.

It is generally held that offer and acceptance should take place in the immediately understood spoken language of the two parties. The marriage contract is essentially a verbal contract. There is no requirement for it to be written in order for it to be valid according to the Shari'a, although contracts are generally recorded in writing for purposes of registration and many Muslim countries require this. The most important factor is that the wording should be a clear and definite indication of the establishment of the contract of marriage with genuine intention and valid consent. A typical formula might be: Bride: 'I marry myself to you upon the dower of [amount].' Groom: 'I have accepted the marriage upon the dower specified.' In many cases the offer may be pronounced by the guardian of the bride (this will be discussed below) in a form such as: 'I marry my daughter [name] to you upon the dower of [amount]', to which the groom will respond: 'I have accepted your daughter [name] in marriage at the dower specified.'

Certain conditions are required in the parties to the marriage. First and foremost they must be a man and a woman. This is an absolute and there is no scope for consideration of the possibility of same-sex marriage. The parties to the marriage should be of sound mind and of an age suitable for marriage. Although this is not stipulated in the source texts, most Muslim countries stipulate a minimum age for marriage, and in the majority of these it is 16 or 18 years. The parties should be freely consenting; it is, however, a reality that in some communities marriages are arranged and in many cases forced, or there may be no realistic option of refusal.

The parties to the contract should be free of impediment. This includes permanent impediment that causes the parties to be forbidden to each other permanently due to some factor that cannot be changed, and temporary impediments where certain factors prevent marriage so long as they remain unchanged.

Marriage is prohibited between certain close blood relations and in-laws:

> Prohibited to you are your mothers, your daughters, your sisters, your fathers' sisters, your mothers' sisters, your brothers' daughters, your sisters' daughters, your mothers who nursed you, your sisters through nursing, your wives' mothers and the daughters of your wives with whom you have consummated marriage, but if you have not consummated the marriage then there is no sin upon you. Also [prohibited to you are] the wives of your sons who are from your loins, two sisters simultaneously except for what has already occurred. (Qur'an 4.23)

The blood relationships are categorized by the jurists as follows:

- Women from whom the man is descended, 'how high so-ever'. It is forbidden for a man to marry his mother or either his paternal or maternal grandmothers or great-grandmothers.
- Women descended from the man, 'how low so-ever'. It is forbidden for a man to marry his daughter or the daughters of his sons, daughters or grandchildren.
- Women descended from the parents of the man, 'how low so-ever', that is, his sisters or the daughters of his brothers or sisters or of his nieces or nephews.
- Women descended from the grandparents of the man in the first generation, that is, his paternal or maternal aunts. Women in the succeeding generations, that is, cousins, are not forbidden: 'and the daughters of your paternal uncles, the daughters of your paternal aunts, the daughters of your maternal uncles and the daughters of you maternal aunts' (Qur'an 33.50).

It may be noted that in many Muslim communities cousin marriage has been a preferred pairing, and this remains the case in many traditional Muslim cultures. Cousin marriage accounts for significant proportions of all marriages in many Middle Eastern countries.

The in-law or step-parent/child relationship or *musahara* is the second major impediment to marriage. There are two categories of in-law relationship that preclude marriage. The first of these is temporary, and an example is that it is not permitted for a man to marry the sister or the aunt or niece of a woman to whom he is already married so long as he remains married to her. Other in-law relationships result in permanent prohibition, and specifically a man is not permitted to marry his father's widow or divorcee or his wife's mother or grandmothers, as these are of comparable status to his mother, the widow or divorcee of his son, or his stepdaughter or granddaughters in the case where he has consummated his marriage to her mother as they would be like his own daughter, but if the marriage in the latter case is unconsummated, then the prohibition does not apply as it is as if the marriage had never existed.

Again the jurists provide definitions of these categories:

- Women from whom the wife is descended, 'how high so-ever'. This means the mother of the wife and her maternal and paternal grandmothers and all preceding generations. This prohibition applies even if only the contract has been concluded, but consummation has not taken place.
- The female descendants of the wife, 'how low so-ever'. This includes the daughters of the wife and the daughters of her sons and daughters and so on. A condition of this prohibition is that the marriage to the mother has been consummated.
- The wives of the men from whom the man is descended, 'how high so-ever'. This comprises the wives of his father and grandfathers.
- The wives of the descendants of the man, 'how low so-ever'. This comprises the wives of his sons and of his grandsons via the male or female line. It is specified that this refers to biological offspring, thereby excluding adopted sons.

The third factor that precludes marriage is suckling. In pre-Islamic Arabia and in the early Islamic period, the practice of wet-nursing was widespread, particularly among affluent families. Throughout history it has been common in many cultures and communities and remains so. The basis for this prohibition is that a child suckled and nurtured within a family other than his or her own biological family becomes like a member of that family, and it is unthinkable that they could then be considered as marriage partners. There is also a sense that by absorbing nourishment from a woman who is not his or her natural mother, the child somehow becomes biologically linked to her and thereby to her family. In Islamic societies the risk of creating such an impediment has always been a consideration when choosing a wet nurse, although it has often been the case that more affluent families have given their children to poorer families to be nursed so any union thereby precluded would not have been considered in the first place. The degrees of relationship by suckling are complex, but essentially reflect the degrees of natural and in-law relationship that preclude marriage. The jurists agree that for suckling to result in prohibition it should take place during the first two years of infancy, and there are opinions that the prohibition is not created by a single suckling but only by a minimum number of feeds (variously suggested as five or ten feeds), whereby a relationship is created between the woman and child.

It is forbidden for a Muslim man to marry a woman who does not belong to the 'People of the Book', the Abrahamic (monotheistic) faiths: Islam, Judaism and Christianity. This prohibition is found in the Qur'an:

> And do not marry polytheistic women until they believe; a believing slave woman is better than a polytheist, even though she might please you ...

> And do not marry polytheistic men [to your women] until they believe; a believing slave is better than a polytheist, even though he might please you. (Qur'an 2.221)

> O you who have believed, when the believing women come to you as emigrants, examine them. Allah is most knowing as to

their faith. And if you know them to be believers, then do not return them to the disbelievers; they are not lawful [wives] for them ... (Qur'an 60.10)

On the basis of these two verses and reports in the *hadith* that Umar separated a couple in the case of a Christian man whose wife embraced Islam, the jurists are unanimous that it is unlawful for a Muslim woman to marry a non-Muslim man, even if he is of the People of the Book. The reasoning is that it is expected that the father will be the head of the household and that his influence will prevail in the rearing of children. It is unacceptable that the children of a Muslim man or woman should be raised other than as Muslims.

If a Muslim man apostatizes, irrespective of the penalties for apostasy, his Muslim wife will be entitled to have the marriage dissolved. If she does not seek dissolution of the marriage and the situation comes to the attention of the legal authorities then the marriage may be dissolved without the agreement of either party.

The previous marital status of the woman is stated in the contract. She will be referred to either as *bikr* (virgin) or *thayyib* (not a virgin, being either divorced or widowed). This is considered relevant to the marriage in certain respects. First, if it is stated that she is *thayyib*, this establishes that the husband accepts that he is marrying a woman who has previously been married and is not a virgin and precludes any subsequent objection. Likewise, if it is stated that she is a virgin, then if this turns out not to be the case, he will have grounds to reject the marriage. The status of the bride may also affect the value of her dower.

Dower or bride-price

The *mahr* (dower or bride-price) is an essential element of the contract without which it is not valid. Dower is a gift of a sum of money or other commodity or service of monetary value given by the husband to the wife in consideration of the marriage. This is prescribed in the Qur'an: 'And give the women [upon marriage] their gifts graciously' (Qur'an 4.4).

Later in the same verse we find: 'So for whatever you enjoy

from them, give them their due compensation as an obligation' (Qur'an 4.24). The dower becomes the property of the bride to dispose of as she pleases, and neither her husband nor her family have the right to take possession of it. In reality, however, in some cultures and circumstances this may not be adhered to.

Normally the dower is specified in the contract. It should be in the form of money or property or anything with a monetary value, and this may include a service for which payment might otherwise be required.

> Narrated Sahl bin Sad As-Sa'idi: A woman came to Allah's Apostle and said, 'O Allah's Apostle! I have come to give you myself in marriage (without *mahr*).' Allah's Apostle looked at her and then lowered his head. When the lady saw that he did not say anything, she sat down. A man from his companions got up and said, 'O Allah's Apostle! If you are not in need of her, then marry her to me.' The Prophet said, 'Have you anything to offer?' The man said, 'No, by Allah, O Allah's Apostle!' The Prophet said (to him), 'Go to your family and see if you have something.' The man went and returned, saying, 'No, by Allah, I have not found anything.' Allah's Apostle said, '(Go again) and look for something, even if it is an iron ring.' He went again and returned, saying, 'No, by Allah, O Allah's Apostle! I could not find even an iron ring, but this is my Izar (waist sheet).' He added, 'I give half of it to her.' Allah's Apostle said, 'What will she do with your Izar? If you wear it, she will be naked, and if she wears it, you will be naked.' So that man sat down for a long while and then got up (to depart). When Allah's Apostle saw him going, he ordered that he be called back. When he came, the Prophet said, 'How much of the Quran do you know?' He said, 'I know such Sura and such Sura,' counting them. The Prophet said, 'Do you know them by heart?' He replied, 'Yes.' The Prophet said, 'Go, I marry her to you for that much of the Quran which you have.'

This *hadith* emphasizes that the *mahr* is essential for a marriage, that it may be in the form of a service of monetary value, and that lack of wealth need not be an obstacle to marriage.

The Shari'a does not specify a minimum or maximum amount; this is left to the agreement of the two parties according to their financial circumstances and to prevailing custom. The dower for a virgin will often be significantly higher than that for a woman who has previously been married. The contract will normally state the amount of dower payable immediately upon the conclusion of the contract and a deferred amount that becomes payable upon divorce or the death of the husband. The bride's family may insist on a substantial dower as recognition of the value that they place on their daughter. In many cases the immediately payable amount may be relatively small, with a large deferred amount as a deterrent to divorce. Upon irrevocable divorce it is the right of the wife to receive the deferred dower, and if she dies before it is paid then her heirs may claim it as part of her estate. If the husband dies then the widow is entitled to receive the dower from his estate as a priority debt prior to the distribution of his property. In many cases this helps to ensure that she is adequately provided for as a widow's share of her husband's estate is limited and depending on the existence of other heirs may be very small indeed.

In some cases the amount of the dower is not specified in the contract, although this is unusual. This may simply be because the parties have omitted to mention it or have made a contract on the basis that there should be no dower. Such a contract is not binding as the dower is a legal requirement of the contract, but if it occurs and is consummated then the *mahr al-mithl*, or 'appropriate dower', becomes payable. Another circumstance in which this may occur is where the dower specified is invalid, for example in an unlawful commodity such as wine. In such cases the dower payable will be that appropriate to the status of the wife according to custom in her family and community.

One of the most important considerations is that the marriage should be recognized by the community as a legitimate union. Certain rights and duties arise as a consequence of the marriage contract but these cannot be enforced where the marriage is not acknowledged. As mentioned previously, the contract is essentially verbal and does not strictly need to be written down. It does, however, have to be witnessed as this ensures that it cannot be denied nor its obligations avoided. This protects the woman in particular from accusation of adultery. As with any other contract, witnesses must be of age and of sound mind. Two male witnesses are required but if this is not possible then a man and two women will be acceptable. Both witnesses must be present at the same time to hear the words of the contract and must understand the words fully. Where both parties to the marriage are Muslim, the scholars are agreed that the witnesses should be Muslim, but some consider that where the husband is Muslim and the bride of one of the Abrahamic faiths, one of the witnesses may be Christian or Jewish. There is a *hadith* of the Prophet that 'there can be no marriage without a guardian and two upright witnesses'. Most of the scholars confirm that the witnesses should be known to be of good character and naturally most families would choose such witnesses, but if it is subsequently revealed that a witness is of immoral character this will have no effect on the validity of the contract.

In most Muslim communities and cultures it is normal for a marriage to be celebrated, and this will take a variety of forms according to local or ethnic custom. At the centre of any celebration is usually a feast. The celebrations again form part of the public acknowledgement of the marriage; they establish the new couple as a recognized and honourable part of the community, they demonstrate family pride and the mutual esteem in which the bride and groom and their respective families are held and they show approval of and happiness in the union. Celebrations may take place at the time of the contract but it is not unusual for the actual wedding party and consummation of the marriage to take place weeks, months or even years after the contract is concluded, sometimes dependent on other factors such as completion of the education of one or both of the parties or being in a position to set up home together.

It is normal for the bride to be represented in the conclusion of the contract by her marriage guardian, particularly if she is a virgin. In the Shari'a marriage guardianship is compulsory for girls who are minors on the basis that as such they do not have full capacity to act for themselves, and conventionally this is also the case for a virgin even if she is not a minor. In effect, responsibility for a woman passes from her family to her husband. In the case of mature women or those who have been previously married, guardianship is primarily a matter of etiquette and decorum. There is, however, no obstacle in law to a previously married woman contracting marriage on her own behalf. The guardian is usually the father or grandfather in the marriage of a virgin, although it may be another male relative or, in the case of an orphan, a judge. A woman may not be married without her consent but a minor girl may be given in marriage by her father or grandfather. In this case, in theory she will have *khiyar al-bulugh* or the 'option of maturity', which is the right when she reaches legal majority to apply to a judge for the marriage be dissolved on the basis that she did not give her consent. The guardian is supposed to exercise his guardianship in the interests of his ward and should seek her consent in concluding her marriage. In reality this is not always the case in some traditional societies.

If a woman who is not a minor wishes to marry a man of her own choice, her guardian has no right of *'adl*, that is, to prevent her marriage. Marriage is the preferred status for any adult and offers chastity and protection, and it is therefore improper to attempt to prevent it. The guardian may, however, prevent a proposed marriage on the grounds of lack of *kafa'a* or equivalence, meaning that the husband is not of acceptable status for the woman. If the suitor is of lower social or professional status, less affluent or of a less pious background than the woman, then the guardian may challenge this, and if it is pursued then the matter may be referred to a judge, who may overrule the guardian's objection.

Polygyny

Islam allows a man to have up to four wives.

> And if you fear that you will not deal justly with the orphan girls, then marry those that please you of [other] women, two or three or four. But if you fear that you will not be just, then [marry only] one or those your right hand possesses. (Qur'an 4.3)

Polygyny without limit is believed to have been common practice in pre-Islamic Arabia. Islam restricted this to four and some of the early converts were required to reduce the numbers of their wives to four. There are reports in the *hadith*, such as:

> Narrated Abdullah ibn Umar: 'Ghaylan ibn Salamah ath-Thaqafi accepted Islam and that he had ten wives in the pre-Islamic period who accepted Islam along with him; so the Prophet (peace be upon him) told him to keep four and separate from the rest of them.'
> Ahmad, Tirmidhi and Ibn Majah transmitted it. (*Al-Tirmidhi*, Number 945 taken from the Alim CD-ROM version)

> Narrated Al-Harith ibn Qays al-Asadi: 'I embraced Islam while I had eight wives. So I mentioned it to the Prophet (peace be upon him). The Prophet (peace be upon him) said: "Select four of them".' (*Sunan Abu Dawud*, book 12, number 2233)

A man with more than one wife is obliged to treat them with absolute equality in terms of housing, maintenance and time spent with them, but the Qur'an recognizes that it is not possible to feel equal affection towards them.

> And you will never be able to be equal [in feeling] between wives, even if you should strive [to do so]. So do not incline completely [toward one] and leave another hanging. And if you amend [your affairs] and fear Allah then indeed Allah is ever Forgiving and Merciful. (Qur'an 4.129)

The great majority of Muslim families are monogamous unions, and this is generally considered to be a licence to be used in certain exceptional circumstances rather than a normal practice.

Polygyny has always been more common in times of war, when numbers of marriageable women in a society have been greater than eligible husbands. It has also been used in the case where a woman is infertile and her husband wishes to have children but does not want to divorce her. A man should establish that he has the financial means to support more than one wife and ideally should obtain the agreement of his existing wife or wives.

There are more than 50 Muslim countries or countries with large Muslim populations that recognize polygyny. Many of these have placed certain restrictions, such as Egypt, which requires that existing wives should be formally notified of their husband's intention to take another wife and allows them to seek divorce if they object. Only a few Muslim-majority countries, including Turkey and Tunisia, have formally prohibited polygyny.

Other forms of marriage

Besides conventional marriage, which is contracted on a basis of permanency with the intention of founding a family as a unit within a society, there are certain forms of non-permanent marriage that do not entail the same consequences as a normal marriage. They are, however, concluded by contract in the same manner.

Mut'a marriage or marriage of pleasure is permitted by the Shi'a but not by Sunni Islam. It is a personal contract between a man and a woman to cohabit for a limited period of time, which may be hours or years, in return for certain remuneration payable by the man. It requires no witnesses and does not entail most of the rights involved in a conventional marriage, such as maintenance and the mutual right of inheritance. Sunni scholars agree that this was permitted in the early years of Islam but was subsequently forbidden. Most scholars agree that the temporary nature of the contract conflicts with the essential requirement that the intention in marriage should be to create a permanent union. They argue that anything in the contract indicating a temporary agreement renders the contract immediately invalid. *Mut'a* marriage is effectively a vehicle to legitimize sexual gratification on a temporary basis.

Another form of unconventional marriage is *misyar*, the traveller's marriage. This form of marriage arose during the time of the Islamic conquests, when men away from their homes were permitted to take wives on the basis of visitation but without the requirement to set up home. This type of marriage is recognized by the Sunni scholars; it is contracted as a proper marriage but the husband visits the wife by arrangement at her family's home or her own residence. Many of the contract terms are subject to agreement between the two parties. It is not contracted as a temporary marriage, but in the same way as a conventional marriage it may be terminated by divorce. In the modern world it is not uncommon for such marriages to be contracted by men away from home, whether or not they are already married. The reasoning behind this type of marriage is to legitimize a sexual relationship while avoiding adultery or fornication.

The marriage contract establishes a range of rights and obligations for husband and wife both during the marriage and after its termination by death and divorce. These will be examined in the following chapters on family life and on divorce.

3

Family Life

Judaism

Childhood

As we have seen, the bond between husband and wife is viewed as fundamental to Jewish existence. In Scripture the first commandment was given to Adam and Eve, the first human beings: it was to be fruitful and multiply (Gen. 1.28). Having children is thus a crucial element in the Jewish faith. Religious life revolves around the home as well as the synagogue, and there is a determination that the Jewish heritage must be handed down from generation to generation. Today there is a tendency to delay marriage or choose an alternative lifestyle. Many individuals are remaining single until their late 20s or early 30s, and consequently the birth rate is low. In past centuries, however, a large family was viewed as a blessing and life centred around the rearing of children.

According to Jewish law a woman is ritually unclean for seven days after giving birth to a boy and 14 days after the birth of a girl. In ancient times she was not allowed to enter the Temple precincts for 33 days (for a boy) and 66 days (for a girl). In strictly Orthodox communities the laws of purity are still observed, and a woman is forbidden to her husband for these periods. Non-Orthodox Jews, however, have abandoned these practices, regarding them as discriminatory to women. Nonetheless Jewish law is unequivocal that the life of the mother takes precedence over the life of an unborn child, whether boy or girl. Only when the baby is more than halfway emerged from the birth canal is it considered to be a full human being with rights. Thus even though abortion is regarded as an offence within Judaism, it is not perceived as infanticide.

In the past the birth of a child was accompanied by an array of superstitions. Amulets were hung near the sleeping baby to ward off evil spirits, and family and friends would gather together regularly to pray for the protection of the new arrival. Among German Jews it was the custom to swaddle infants. The strip of linen that was used to bind a little boy was kept; later it was embroidered and presented to the synagogue as a Torah binder when the lad reached *bar mitzvah* age. It was also the custom for new mothers to visit the synagogue soon after the birth to recite a blessing expressing gratitude to God. The child was named either at the circumcision ceremony (for boys) or at a baby blessing (for girls) in the synagogue. Every Jew is given a Hebrew name coupled with the name of his or her father. This is used on all formal religious documents or when an individual is called to read from the Torah scroll in the synagogue. The first time the Torah is read in the synagogue after the birth of a girl, the father is called up in honour of the new baby. The Orthodox justify such distinctions between the treatment of boys and girls by appealing to Jewish law. Feminist critics, however, insist that traditional Judaism is a patriarchal religion, appealing to the obvious sexism of the liturgy – every day in the synagogue, men recite the prayer: 'Blessed art Thou, O Lord our God, who has not made me a woman.'

According to Jewish law all male children are to be circumcised (removing the foreskin of the penis). This practice is based on God's command to Abraham in Genesis: 'This is my covenant, which you shall keep, between me and you and your descendants after you: Every male among you shall be circumcised ... and it shall be a sign of the covenant between me and you. He that is eight days old among you shall be circumcised; every male throughout your generations' (Gen. 17.10–12). The operation is performed on the eighth day after birth and can take place on the Sabbath, on festivals and even on the Day of Atonement. It should be noted that circumcision does not make the child a Jew; he is a Jew by virtue of having been born of a Jewish mother. In Hebrew the operation is described as *berit milah*, literally the covenant of circumcision.

The procedure for circumcision is as follows: the baby is handed by a godmother to a godfather and on to the *sandak*, who is responsible for holding him on his knee while the operation takes place. The operation itself is performed by a *mohel*, a professional circumciser. Once a baby is securely on the knee of the *sandak*, the father makes a blessing. After the operation is completed the *mohel* recites a prayer for the baby over a cup of wine and gives him his Hebrew name. The child is then given a few drops of wine and afterwards there is a celebratory meal.

Later, when a first-born male infant is 31 days old, the ceremony of redemption of the firstborn takes place. This practice is based on Scripture: 'The Lord said to Moses: "Consecrate to me all the first-born; whatever is the first to open the womb among the people of Israel, both of man and of beast, is mine"' (Exod. 13.1–2). During the ceremony the baby is brought into a room – sometimes on a silver platter – and the father gives him to a priest and makes a declaration: 'This is my firstborn, the firstborn of his mother, and the Holy One, Blessed be He, has given the commandment to redeem him.' The father then puts down the sum of five silver shekels in front of the priest (or a modern equivalent of a valuable object). The priest then gives the father the opportunity to redeem his son. The child is then returned to his father and a benediction is recited. Although this ceremony still takes place in Orthodox communities it has been abandoned by various branches of non-Orthodox Judaism.

Maturity

At the age of 13 a Jewish boy attains Jewish adulthood. From then on he is expected to keep the commandments, and his presence in the synagogue counts towards the quorum (*minyan*) required for prayer. From the Middle Ages, attaining this status was a cause of celebration. This was commemorated by the *bar mitzvah* (son of the commandment) ceremony, which involves reading from the Torah scroll in the synagogue. Different communities have developed varied practices. In Eastern Europe it was usual for the boy to be called up to read from the Torah on the first Monday or Thursday after his birthday. In Western Europe the tradition was that the service should take place on the Sabbath, and the boy read from the set prophetic reading as well as from the Torah.

Often he gives a short speech in which he demonstrates his knowledge of rabbinic sources.

According to tradition, girls are regarded as having reached religious maturity at the age of 12, but there is no legal obligation that this *rite de passage* should be marked in any special way. However, in modern times the non-Orthodox have instituted a *bat mitzvah* (daughter of the commandment) ceremony paralleling the *bar mitzvah*. In most cases it is identical to what is expected of a boy. Among the modern Orthodox there are still reservations about a girl reading from the Torah scroll in public, although it is accepted that she may conduct prayers and chant the prophetic reading. Alternatively some Orthodox communities conduct a collective service for all 12-year-old girls.

As we noted, for the strictly Orthodox, religious education does not end with the *bar mitzvah*. In general four years of Jewish high school follow, combining secular and Jewish studies. Then the young men will go off to a *yeshivah* (Jewish higher educational establishment) dedicated to the study of the Talmud and other sacred texts. In ancient times academies of higher learning were established in both the Holy Land and Babylonia as early as the first century CE. These establishments kept in contact with one another and attracted students from throughout the Jewish world. In the modern period, *yeshivot* were organized in Eastern Europe but were destroyed in the Nazi Holocaust. After the war new *yeshivot* were set up in the United States, Israel and Europe. Today most *yeshivot* are organized along the traditional Lithuanian lines: male students work generally in pairs, in a large hall, and together they argue out the meaning of the Talmud. The *yeshivah* world, as it is called, has become immensely influential, particularly in Israel – members are staunch upholders of Orthodoxy. Outside Orthodox circles religious education takes place in synagogues on weekdays after school or on the weekends. Rather than gaining an intensive knowledge of Jewish law, boys and girls are exposed to the riches of the Jewish heritage.

As in previous centuries, early marriage is the norm for the strictly Orthodox. Boys and girls are educated separately and are largely kept apart through adolescence. Then, during a young man's final years at a *yeshivah*, he is expected to get married, and families, friends and teachers are all co-opted to find a suitable bride. Previously in villages of Eastern Europe there was a recognized matchmaker who organized the brokering between families and made introductions. Today it is more informal. Nonetheless it is common for parents to keep a close eye on the proceedings.

> In *The American Jew: Voices from an American Jewish Community*, a strictly Orthodox Jewish mother described the process of a modern arranged marriage:
>
> With my eldest daughter, she was in seminary (an Orthodox school for young women). A friend of mine said, 'I know a real nice boy for you.' This girl had lived in this boy's parents' house, and she thought they would be a real good match ... We try to check out the boy to see if things match each other. You always know somebody who knows somebody who knows somebody. So basically we called up and checked up on the school and the synagogue and the rabbi and so on. Sometimes you check up and it's a wonderful person, but it's not for your child. You want somebody suitable for them. There were times that I called, and I didn't like what I heard. There's no point for her to go out with somebody if you know it's not going to work out. Usually a girl will go out of her parents' home. The boy will pick her up from the home. The parents will be there ... they will go out to a hotel to sit and talk.[1]

Things are not so straightforward elsewhere in the community. Most Jewish children go to secular, co-educational schools. They attend secular universities and often travel far from home to complete their studies. Parents have far less control. According to Jewish law certain marriages have no validity – in particular those that are incestuous, those that are adulterous and those between a Jew and a Gentile. It is this last that is the greatest threat today. In the past, when Jews were isolated in their own communities or

---

1 Dan and Lavinia Cohn-Sherbok, *The American Jew: Voices from an American Jewish Community*, London: HarperCollins, 1994, pp. 107–8.

when there was serious anti-Semitism, the danger of intermarriage was small. In contemporary society, however, intermarriage is a frequent occurrence. Further, in general the process of dating, premarital sex and living together has become the norm despite traditional Jewish sanctions against such practices.

Family values

In the modern world the Jewish people are frequently admired for their family values. It is commonly believed that the community has few broken families, low levels of delinquency, high standards of education and strong bonds between generations. It is true that on average Jewish children do better in school and are more likely to go on to colleges and universities than their Gentile counterparts. Nonetheless, among the non-Orthodox divorce rates increasingly parallel those of other communities and the demands of modern employment often force parents and adult children to live apart. In the diaspora (outside of Israel) most Jews are indistinguishable from their neighbours.

However, the family circle remains important. Among the Orthodox the roles of men and women remain very different. Because of her domestic duties a woman is not expected to perform all the positive time-bound commandments. She does not have to wear fringes on her clothes or lay phylacteries. She has no obligation to attend daily services, and if she does go her presence does not count towards the necessary quorum (*minyan*). Her obligations are essentially to care for the material needs of her family, to ensure her children are educated and to encourage her husband to continue with his studies. Men are commanded to love and respect their wives, and there is no doubt that within the family itself the woman is influential. In the popular sphere this is reflected in sentimental reminiscence and in regular diatribes against Jewish mothers (as in Philip Roth's novel, *Portnoy's Complaint*).

In contemporary society many women are unhappy with this traditional pattern. They believe that the maternal role has been imposed on them by men and they wish to make their mark beyond the home. It is no accident that leading feminists have been born of Jewish origin. The non-Orthodox have moved with the times. In the Reform, Conservative Reconstructionist and Humanistic movements, women can be ordained as rabbis and act as cantors. In the secular sphere most parents are anxious that their daughters as well as their sons should achieve the highest educational standards. Both in Israel and the diaspora, young people are marrying later; there are many more single people, and this lifestyle does not reflect traditional Jewish values.

At the same time the Jewish community is wistful of the old ways. Secular Jews frequently look to the family lives of the strictly Orthodox, with their clearly demarcated areas of responsibility and their large numbers of children, with a mixture of approval, dismay and envy. As the modern secular husband looks at his high-powered working wife and his one or two difficult adolescent children, traditional patterns of Jewish existence can appear attractive. Nevertheless, for most they are unobtainable. It would be pleasant to be honoured by one's offspring, to have a son who – as the Talmud puts it – does not contradict his father's words or go against his opinions. Regrettably, however, such a relationship runs counter to all modern ideas of child-rearing.

Other Jewish values are also admired by outsiders. Jewish law insists on integrity in business as the mark of a righteous person. The relationship between employer and employee should be one of mutual co-operation, fairness and trust. All Jews have a duty to support the poor and the needy and to give regularly and generously to charity. Such attitudes are still taken seriously, and Jewish welfare organizations are in general efficiently run and well supported. Hospitality to the stranger is another obligation, and most traditional Jewish households entertain guests regularly, especially on the festivals and for Sabbath dinner on Friday night. Judaism teaches that the upright person will speak the truth at all times. Gossip and slander are to be deplored. Animals must be treated with kindness and compassion and honest labour is to be commended. It is obvious that not all is right in the world. The duty of the pious Jew is to begin the work of healing the world (*tikkun olam*) and to restore the peace created by God. At its best the Jewish family is a microcosm of that ideal harmony, and as such it is seen as the beginning of the healing process. As the liturgical grace after the meal puts it: 'I have been young and now I am grown old, yet never have I seen a righteous man utterly forsaken. The Eternal will give strength unto his people, the Eternal will bless his people with his peace.'

Home life

An Orthodox bride will visit the ritual bath (*mikveh*) before her wedding. According to the Talmud a *mikveh* must be supplied partially by a spring or a tank of rain water. This is because Leviticus declares that 'a spring or a cistern holding water shall be clean' (Lev. 11.36). The rabbis interpreted this to mean that ritual contamination can be cleansed, but the water must not be poured from another container. It must come directly from nature. This natural water can subsequently be mixed with other waters to make the whole into an agent of cleanliness.

According to Jewish law, husbands and wives may not have sexual relations during the days of the wife's monthly period nor for seven clear days afterwards. This means that among the Orthodox the wedding date is calculated to fit in with the bride's menstrual flow so that she is married during her 'clean period'. During the time that she is forbidden to her husband, the couple sleep in separate beds and avoid touching each other in any way at all. This is why Orthodox men avoid having any physical contact with women. Then, after the flow has stopped and seven full days have elapsed, the wife visits the ritual bath.

Before immersion in the *mikveh* the woman must have a thorough wash. For the immersion to be valid every inch of the surface of her body must come into contact with the ritual waters – all traces of dirt must be removed. Fingernails and toenails are trimmed and the hair is thoroughly combed out. Among the strictly Orthodox it is the practice for a married woman to cut off her hair and wear a wig. This has the double benefit of fulfilling the commandment that a married woman must cover her hair, and it makes the monthly visit to the ritual bath easier to manage. When the *mikveh* supervisor – a pious respected woman of the community – is satisfied that the woman is completely clean and her hair free from tangles, she is directed to the ritual bath itself. There she immerses herself completely, so that the waters cover her head, and she recites the traditional blessings. Then she can resume marital relations with her husband. It should be noted that although the laws concerning the *mikveh* are followed rigorously by the strictly Orthodox, such regulations have been largely abandoned by Jewry as a whole. Both Reform and secular Jews have rejected these complex laws of ritual purity, regarding them as primitive and discriminatory to women.

Turning to practices within the home, strictly Orthodox Jews say the *Shema* prayer both when they rise and when they go to bed at night. This prayer contains the reminder that God's words, his Torah, should be bound 'as a sign upon your hand, and they shall be as frontlets between your eyes. And you shall write them on the doorposts of your house and on your gates' (Deut. 6.8–9). For generations the Jewish community has understood these words as referring to the duties of putting on phylacteries and nailing a *mezuzah* to the doorpost.

Phylacteries are boxes containing biblical verses written by hand on parchment. The verses are Exodus 13.1–10 (on the laws relating to the dedication of the firstborn to God's service), Exodus 13.11–16 (repeating the laws of the firstborn and the commandment to teach children about the miraculous deliverance from slavery in Egypt), Deuteronomy 6.4–6 (the first paragraph of the *Shema* prayer stressing the oneness of God) and Deuteronomy 11.13–21 (the second paragraph of the *Shema* prayer on reward and punishment). These boxes are attached to straps. One is placed over the head so that the box sits squarely upon the forehead between the eyes. The other is wound round the left arm so that the box faces the heart. The strap is placed in a special way so that it forms the Hebrew letter *shin*, the first letter of God's name *El Shaddai*. Putting on phylacteries should be observed by all male Jews of *bar mitzvah* age and above, and is performed every weekday at home or in the synagogue.

A *mezuzah* is another small box containing parchment. The verses are Deuteronomy 6.4–9 and 11.13–21, the first two paragraphs of the *Shema* prayer. The word *Shaddai* (Almighty) is written on the back. The parchment is then inserted into a small opening in the box and it is nailed on the right-hand doorpost. It is placed about two-thirds of the way up in a slanting position.

Almost all Jews, if they are in any way observant, put *mezuzahs* on their front doors. The strictly Orthodox put one on the doorpost of every room in the house except the bathroom and lavatory.

Both the *mezuzah* and phylacteries are visible signs that remind the Jew of his obligation towards God. Every day he dedicates himself anew, when he puts on his *tephillin*. Every time he enters or leaves his house he is recalled to his awesome obligations as a member of God's chosen people. The sages taught that the purpose of the *mezuzah* is to remind the Jew that all material possessions are a gift from God. Today among secular Jews, the *mezuzah* is perceived as a badge of identity, a sign that the house is a Jewish home. Among the pious the *mezuzah* is a constant affirmation of the all-embracing nature of God's Torah, and it is not uncommon to see the Orthodox reverently touch their *mezuzahs* as they enter and leave their house.

One of the most recognizable signs of masculine Orthodox dress is the skullcap. Today all Orthodox men keep their heads covered at all times – to the extent that it is not uncommon to see a pious man take off his large outdoor hat and find that he is wearing a skullcap underneath. Hence in traditional Jewish households, men wear a skullcap at all times. Members of non-Orthodox congregations, however, wear a head covering in the synagogue but go about bareheaded on secular occasions. Among the Hasidim and the strictly Orthodox it is common for men to allow their side-locks to grow in accordance with the biblical prescription not to cut the corners of the beard (Lev. 19.27). Another element of Orthodox appearance is fringes (*tziztzit*). In accordance with Leviticus 15.37–8, Orthodox men wear an undergarment with fringes on four corners; known as a *tallit katan*, the garment is largely hidden although the fringes are brought out above the trouser waistband and are directly tucked into a pocket. Women's dress is characterized by modesty. As previously noted, married women traditionally cover their heads, and the Orthodox continue this practice either by wearing a wig or by swathing the head in a large scarf. Skirts cover the knee and sleeves the elbow. The non-Orthodox, however, ignore these customs.

Turning to home observance, the laws of *kashrut* govern what may be eaten. The eating of meat is hedged about with numerous restrictions. The slaughter of prescribed animals must be performed in accordance with biblical and rabbinic law. Because of the prohibition against eating blood, ritual slaughter involves getting rid of as much blood as possible from the carcass. There are no rules for the slaughter of fish, but not all sea creatures may be eaten. According to Deuteronomy, 'Of all that are in the waters you may eat these: whatever has fins and scales you may eat. And whatever does not have fins and scales you shall not eat; it is unclean for you (Deut. 14.9–10). This means that all shellfish are forbidden. It is also not permitted to eat both meat foods and dairy products at the same meal.

In a traditional Jewish home the housewife will set up her own kosher kitchen to ensure that food is properly prepared. The first necessity is to keep milk and meat products completely separate. It is not enough to avoid serving them together: minute particles of food can permeate crockery, cutlery and cooking utensils and thereby mingle during the process of preparation. To avoid this the housewife has two completely different sets of plates and saucepans. There must even be separate washing-up bowls, draining boards and preparation areas. Once kosher meat is brought into the kitchen it must undergo further treatment. In order to avoid the eating of blood the meat must be soaked in clean water for 30 minutes; it is then thoroughly salted and put on a grooved board for an hour. Keeping a kosher home is a serious commitment for a Jewish family. Among the strictly Orthodox it is of vital concern. Yet within the non-Orthodox world the complex laws of *kashrut* generally no longer remain in force, although Conservative, Reform and Reconstructionist Jews attempt to put into practice a modified version of kosher ritual. In addition it is not uncommon for even the most assimilated Jews to refrain from eating pork and shellfish.

Jewish festivals and home ceremonies

Although Jewish festivals are celebrated in the synagogue, home ritual is also of central importance. The Sabbath, for example, begins on Friday evening before sunset. Just before it begins, candles are lit by the mother of the household, who recites the benediction: 'Blessed art Thou, O Lord our God, King of the Universe, who has sanctified us by Thy commandments and hast commanded us to kindle the Sabbath lights.' After returning from the synagogue the father blesses his children, praying to God to make the boys like Ephraim and Menasseh and the girls like the matriarchs Sarah, Rebecca, Leah and Rachel. Then he says the *kiddush*, the sanctifying prayer, over a cup of wine. This is followed by a ritual washing of the hands and the blessing and sharing of bread. The Friday-night meal is the central family occasion of the week. After the food has been eaten, special songs are sung and the proceedings conclude with the grace after meals. Sabbath observance concludes with the *Havdalah* ceremony, which generally takes place at home. The ritual consists of blessings over wine, spices and lights. Not all Jews follow these elaborate home rituals, yet even among the non-Orthodox it is common for certain aspects of Sabbath observance to be followed.

Passover is also a major home festival. Traditionally it is kept for seven days, and its main focus is the Passover *seder*, which takes place on the first night. Even the most secular Jews often attend a Passover *seder* and most have vivid childhood memories of the occasion. It is an opportunity for the extended family to get together – grandparents, aunts and uncles, miscellaneous cousins, parents and children. The meal fulfils the commandment in the book of Exodus (13.8): 'And you shall tell your son on that day, "It is because of what the LORD did for me when I came out of Egypt."' On the table is placed an array of symbolic food. There are three pieces of *matzot* (unleavened bread). The top and bottom represent the double portion of manna that was provided for the Israelites on their wanderings in the wilderness. The middle piece is divided into two; one part is described as the 'bread of affliction', reminding the participants of the miseries of slavery, while the other is hidden.

Also laid out are bitter herbs representing the bitterness of slavery, the green herb associated with the spring, salt water representing the tears of the Israelite slaves, *haroset* (a mixture of apples, nuts, cinnamon and wine) reminiscent of the mortar the Jews were compelled to mix in Egypt, a roasted bone symbolizing the Passover sacrifice and an egg commemorating the festival sacrifice in the Temple. Also on the table is the cup of Elijah. According to tradition the Messiah will reveal himself at Passover time and the prophet Malachi promises that he will be heralded by the prophet Elijah. During the course of the evening the front door is opened in the hope that this year Elijah will be waiting. Each participant drinks four cups of wine. These are linked with the four expressions of redemption in the book of Exodus. During the course of the evening, blessings are said, the symbolic food is eaten and the Passover story is told. Then the full meal is eaten. This is followed by grace after the meal, the reciting of the *Hallel* (Psalms 113–118), a concluding liturgy and the singing of various songs and hymns.

The festival of Hanukkah is celebrated for eight days – it commemorates an episode in Jewish history in which the devout Maccabee family overcame the Greek ruling Seleucid dynasty in the second century BCE. After a three-year struggle, in 165 BCE Judah Maccabee captured the city and rebuilt the altar in the Temple. According to legend, one day's worth of sacred oil miraculously kept the candelabrum burning for eight days. The festival celebrates this miracle. Commemoration centres on the lighting of the Hanukkah lights. On the first evening one candle or lamp is ignited, on the second night two and so on for eight days. The best-known Hanukkah game involves a spinning top that is inscribed with four Hebrew letters forming an acrostic for the Hebrew phrase: 'a great miracle occurred here'. It is customary to eat potato pancakes and sugar doughnuts during the festival, and the hymn *Maoz Tsur* ('Rock of Ages') is sung. Even fairly secular households have Hanukkah candlesticks, and some attempt is made to provide children with presents during this period.

The home is also the setting for rituals of sadness. Once an Orthodox family returns from the funeral of a loved one, a period of seven days' mourning takes place, known as *shiva*. During this period visitors from the community come to the house to offer their condolences. The first meal after the funeral is prepared by friends or neighbours. Visitors are not expected to greet the bereaved – instead they sit down quietly with the family, sympathizing with their loss. It is the custom for visitors to bring food with them. The *Kaddish* prayer for the dead can only be recited when a quorum (*minyan*) of ten adult men is present. *Shiva* ends on the morning of the seventh day. Often the rabbi or other leading members of the community will come to the house to escort the mourners on their first walk outside. During this period the family should still avoid shaving, having their hair cut, attending parties or wearing new clothes. But they go back to work and life begins to return to normality. The practice of sitting *shiva* is unique to the Jewish tradition. It gives the family a clear space to adjust to their new situation, to be surrounded by family members and to be sustained by the love and concern of the community as a whole. In non-Orthodox homes *shiva* is not normally observed; instead a funeral, with a graveside ceremony or a cremation, takes its place.

Christianity

Families and the Bible

> The sexual characteristics of man and the human faculty of reproduction wonderfully exceed the dispositions of lower forms of life. Hence the acts themselves which are proper to conjugal love and which are exercised in accord with genuine human dignity must be honored with great reverence. Hence when there is question of harmonizing conjugal love with the responsible transmission of life, the moral aspect of any procedure does not depend solely on sincere intentions or on an evaluation of motives, but must be determined by objective standards. These, based on the nature of the human person and his acts, preserve the full sense of mutual self-giving and human procreation in the context of true love. Such a goal cannot be achieved unless the virtue of conjugal chastity is sincerely practiced. Relying on these principles, sons of the Church may not undertake methods of birth control which are found blameworthy by the teaching authority of the Church in its unfolding of the divine law. (*Gaudium et spes*)

Since the most obvious function of sex and marriage is procreation, family life is the next stage. God's first commandment to

Adam and Eve is 'Be fruitful and increase in number' (Gen. 1.28). Humankind's first family is scarcely a role model for the Christian family, however. Adam and Eve disobey God, causing sin to enter the world, and Cain murders his younger brother Abel. However, religion is about striving for perfection rather than having already attained it, and when we reach the story of Abraham in the Bible we find God telling Abraham that in his progeny will all the earth's families be blessed. Many Christians see God's covenant with Abraham as fulfilled in Jesus Christ, whose lineage the Bible purports to trace back to Abraham and indeed beyond. Christ's coming did not bring about a perfect world either, or even perfect families, and sin, being endemic in human nature, needs to be addressed in the context of family life. Dealing with improper conduct and maintaining discipline must be features of Christian families.

The majority of Christians become married, and most married couples have children. Marriage and raising children is not an obligation, however, and most Christians respect the decision of individuals who choose to remain single and couples who elect not to have children. Some couples are unable to have families, and childlessness is a theme that is addressed by a number of denominations. Increasingly in the West, single-parent families and same-sex partners find their way into Christian congregations.

The Bible teaches that conventional earthly families reflect Christ's relationship with the Church, which is sometimes referred to as 'the bride of Christ', and there is much use of family metaphors to describe the Christian's relationship with God. We are described as God's children or God's family, God being referring to as 'Father', and the expression 'mother Church' is not uncommon. Just as entry to the human world is by physical birth, Christians often talk about being 'born again'. Jesus says to Nicodemus, 'No one can see the kingdom of God unless they are born again' (John 3.3), and when Nicodemus fails to understand Jesus' meaning, Jesus explains:

> Very truly I tell you, no one can enter the kingdom of God unless they are born of water and the Spirit. Flesh gives birth to flesh, but the Spirit gives birth to spirit. You should not be surprised at my saying, 'You must be born again.' (John 3.5–7)

A number of points are worth noting about this passage. First, Jesus mentions the kingdom of God in this context. There has been much discussion among biblical scholars as to the precise meaning of the expressions 'kingdom of God' and 'kingdom of heaven', but most Christians look to its completion in an after-death state. This entails that God's family is not merely the community of believers on earth but includes the living, the dead and those who are yet unborn. Second, children have a place in the Church's congregational life, and their entry into the Christian family is normally marked by baptism. The baptismal ceremony, significantly, is one that involves the parents, and typically the event will be a celebration involving the parents' wider family. Because children are usually baptized in the first year of their lives, they cannot understand the meaning of baptism or even remember the event. Some Christians therefore see baptism more as an expression of commitment on the part of the parents, who vow that they will bring up their child in the Christian faith.

Some denominations, particularly the Baptist churches, prefer to wait until children have grown to an age at which they can make a profession of the Christian faith for themselves and belong to the Church voluntarily. Denominations that practise infant baptism enable the baptismal candidates to profess their faith with understanding at another ceremony later in life, known as confirmation in the Anglican and Roman Catholic traditions or simply as 'admission to membership' in other Protestant denominations. After this ceremony they are entitled to receive the sacrament of Holy Communion – the common symbolic meal that is shared by the Christian community. Just as secular families eat together, so Christians symbolize their oneness by sharing the bread and wine, which are distributed during the sacrament. In the Orthodox tradition, all baptized children are immediately eligible to receive the sacrament, and it is not uncommon to see babies being brought to the altar in an Orthodox church to receive the bread and wine from the priest.

Family planning

> Unless the L ORD builds the house,
>   the builders labour in vain.
> Unless the L ORD watches over the city,
>   the guards stand watch in vain.
> In vain you rise early
>   and stay up late,
> toiling for food to eat –
>   for he grants sleep to those he loves.
> Children are a heritage from the L ORD,
>   offspring a reward from him.
> Like arrows in the hands of a warrior
>   are children born in one's youth.
> Blessed is the man
>   whose quiver is full of them.
> They will not be put to shame
>   when they contend with their opponents in court.
>
> (Psalm 127)

For most Christians family life is the norm. On marriage, in common with most members of western society, couples choose to set up a new home, independent of their parents, and the nuclear family consisting of two generations – parents and children – is favoured. This is not a religious requirement, however; although Christianity favours family life, it concedes that there are other non-familiar lifestyles that enable a Christian to practise his or her faith.

There is no agreed view throughout Christendom about the optimum size of a family, although there are theological doctrines that underpin decisions about family planning. Central to Christian ideas on family life is the notion that a child is a gift from God and is therefore to be valued as such. Jesus himself valued children: he is recorded in the Bible as taking children into his arms and blessing them (Mark 10.13–16), and when his disciples start arguing about who will be the greatest in God's kingdom, he makes a child stand beside him and says: 'Whoever welcomes this little child in my name welcomes me; and whoever welcomes me welcomes the one who sent me. For it is the one who is least among you all who is the greatest' (Luke 9.48).

The valuing of new life entails opposition to abortion, on which the vast majority of Christians are agreed. The prophet Jeremiah is frequently cited in this connection: 'Before I formed you in the womb I knew you, before you were born I set you apart' (Jer. 1.5), and Augustine asserted that the soul entered the body at the moment of conception. Hence prenatal life is also to be valued.

The metaphor of the child being the 'gift of God' has led different Christians to different conclusions. There is no certainty that any copulative act will give rise to birth, hence there is an element of 'grace' that is involved in the creation of a new life; hence, as the *Catechism of the Catholic Church* puts it, 'A child is not something *owed* to one, but is a *gift*' (2378; italics original). In contrast with the Roman Catholic view that any sexual act should leave open the possibility of procreation, the majority of Protestants hold that viewing a child as a gift means that he or she should be wanted and cherished, being freely chosen.

At the more extreme end of the US Protestant tradition there are Christians who believe in maximizing the size of one's family, viewing God's command to Adam and Eve as requiring fecundity even today. One organization promoting large families has adopted the name 'Quiverfull', being an allusion to Psalm 127 quoted above. While the image of arrows contained in a quiver may connote several children being neatly contained in a Christian home, some supporters of Quiverfull note the fact that in the days of the psalmist, the arrows and quiver were part of a warrior's arsenal, and thus the large family is conceived in militaristic terms. Some might regard the imagery as signifying that a large number of sons can aid preparation for war, while other slightly more moderate supporters see the metaphor as alluding to spiritual warfare, viewing large families as adding strength to the opponents of evil. At a more pragmatic level, supporters of large families argue that such families help to promote virtues such as sharing, co-operation, willingness to negotiate and compromise and helping their siblings.

Families require extra resources, both from one's domestic budget and from the world's dwindling natural resources. A key concept in the Christian tradition is 'stewardship' and most Christians, in common with their non-religious counterparts, support the concept of family planning. Population is also an important issue: in 1960 the world had three billion inhabitants, but since then the population has increased by around a billion every 13 years, passing the seven billion mark in 2012. The instruction to 'be fruitful and increase in number' may have made sense in a world where the population was small, but most twenty-first-century Christians would view God's words to Adam and Eve as a permission rather than a command and view fertility as a blessing to be used responsibly.

Parenting

A few Christian organizations have engaged in communal living, bringing up children collectively. Notable examples are the Amish, the Bruderhof and the Twelve Tribes. The Family International (formerly the Children of God) used to live in communal homes, providing their own home education, but have now largely abandoned the practice. The practice of communal living is based on an early Church practice: the Bible records that 'All the believers were together and had everything in common' (Acts 2.44). The majority of later Christians often claim that although there was an attempt by Christians to share everything in common, this was an early experiment that proved unsuccessful.

The Church of Scotland, in which I was brought up, asks parents to make the following vow when presenting a child for baptism:

> Do you promise, in dependence on Divine grace, to teach *him* the truths and duties of the Christian faith; and by prayer, precept and example, to bring *him* up in the nurture and admonition of the Lord, and in the ways of the Church of God? (*Book of Common Order* 91)

These words effectively sum up Christians' duty to their children. Christian parents recognize the obligation to provide a loving environment for their children, to enable them to have a good education and to spend time with them. In this regard they are no different from their secular counterparts but additionally they have the task of passing on their faith to their offspring by teaching, example and discipline. As the *Catechism of the Catholic Church* puts it, the 'home is the first school of Christian life' (*Catechism* 1657). Some households have family worship, say grace before meals and teach children to pray, typically when retiring for the night. Such practices still prevail among evangelical Protestant Christians but in Britain they are not so commonplace. The Church, of course, plays its role in spiritual nurturing. The setting up of Sunday Schools, although much in decline in Britain, serves the obvious purpose of helping children to understand the faith. Some churches now prefer the name 'Sunday Club' since 'school' has connotations of hard work.

A further source of guidance comes from godparents. The precise role of godparents has varied over the centuries and with different traditions. The institution of godparents goes back at least as far as Augustine, although it is not altogether clear how or why the practice originated. In the book of Acts we read that new converts to the Christian faith were baptized as households (Acts 16.15), parents assuming responsibility for their children's spiritual nurture. The role of the godparent may have grown out of the desirability of having witnesses to a baptism, or other adults may have taken on a quasi-parental role where no parents existed. The Protestant Reformers tended to disapprove of the practice and hence it is not normally found in Protestant circles. However, in Roman Catholicism, Orthodoxy and Anglicanism it is common for two adults, one of each gender, to be present at a baptism and to take vows. Certain rules surround the appointment of godparents, with slight differences according to tradition. The two godparents need not be husband and wife or related to each other but should be practising adult Christians who have been baptized, confirmed and eligible to receive the sacraments. Particularly in the Orthodox tradition it is common practice to choose the best man and a bridesmaid from the parents' wedding to perform the role. The godparents are expected to take an interest in the child's personal development and religious education.

Traditionally it was expected that godparents would be responsible for the child's care if he or she were orphaned. In practice the presence of godparents amounts to little more than the keeping up of a tradition, and the relationship between godparent and godchild is left to develop organically or even to fade away. When a baptized Christian becomes confirmed, it is customary to have sponsors who – at least in theory – have a similar role.

Childlessness

> In the time of Herod king of Judea there was a priest named Zechariah, who belonged to the priestly division of Abijah; his wife Elizabeth was also a descendant of Aaron. Both of them were righteous in the sight of God, observing all the Lord's commands and decrees blamelessly. But they were childless because Elizabeth was not able to conceive, and they were both very old. Once when Zechariah's division was on duty and he was serving as priest before God, he was chosen by lot, according to the custom of the priesthood, to go into the temple of the Lord and burn incense. And when the time for the burning of incense came, all the assembled worshippers were praying outside. Then an angel of the Lord appeared to him, standing at the right side of the altar of incense. When Zechariah saw him, he was startled and was gripped with fear. But the angel said to him: 'Do not be afraid, Zechariah; your prayer has been heard. Your wife Elizabeth will bear you a son, and you are to call him John.' (Luke 1.5–13)

Traditionally the Christian faith has entailed a commitment to protecting those who are socially marginalized or disadvantaged. Caring for orphans and widows is specifically mentioned in Scripture as a Christian obligation (James 1.27). Theologically the obligation is associated with every Christian's relationship to God. Jesus said to his disciples, 'I will not leave you as orphans; I will come to you' (John 14.18). Not only is God described as 'Father' but Jesus taught that his followers should address him as *abba*, which is a Hebrew term connoting intimacy and the word a child would use to speak to his or her own father. Paul uses the word 'adoption' in connection with his people: the Jews are originally his chosen or 'adopted' people (Rom. 9.4) – a relationship that still stands (Rom. 11.1) but now, as a result of Christ's redeeming work and the power of God's Spirit, also applies to all who have faith in him (Gal. 3.26).

One contributor to the online journal *Christianity Today* has written, 'What our heavenly Father does spiritually, he expects us to do physically.' Some Christians have therefore offered practical support for homeless children. Perhaps the best-known British organization that specializes in this work is Barnardo's. In Britain, children's homes declined following a number of scandals relating to child abuse, and the government tended to favour foster care rather than institutions dedicated to the care of children. However, worldwide, Christians continue to offer care homes for children, with a particular concern for those who are orphaned as a result of the AIDS epidemic. In the United States, the Christian Alliance for Orphans is an interdenominational coalition uniting around 75 institutions dedicated to the care of orphans, of which there are some 18.3 million worldwide. In order to raise consciousness about their plight, the Alliance has attempted to institute an annual Sunday – 'Orphan Sunday' – on which congregational worship focuses specifically on the theme.

Most Christians are likely to agree that a child thrives better in a loving home rather than in an institution, however well-run and caring it seeks to be. Adoption is therefore a course of action that numerous Christians have considered, and Christian organizations exist to promote it, such as Christian Adoption Services in the United States. Adoption may therefore appear to serve a dual purpose: it helps a mother who is unable or unwilling to support her offspring and it gives a childless couple the opportunity of raising a family. However, for some women the problem is not so much the desire to have a child but the strong urge to go through the normal biological process of conception, pregnancy and childbirth itself. The Bible portrays the state of infertility (or 'barrenness') as regrettable, and numerous key women in biblical history are portrayed as having their infertility miraculously cured. Sarah, Rebecca, Rachel, the (unnamed) mother of Samson and Hannah (the mother of the prophet Samuel) all bear their children when God effects a cure (Gen. 11.30; 25.21; 29.31; Judg. 13.3; 1 Sam. 1.1–20). Such situations are not confined to Hebrew Scripture: Paul reminds his readers about Sarah (Gal. 4.27); and Elizabeth, the mother of John the Baptist, is infertile until her husband Zechariah receives an angelic visitation (Luke 1.5–17, above).

Some conservative Christians believe that the ancient biblical solution of prayer still works, and I have come across couples who have maintained that they were childless until they prayed about their condition, as a result of which the wife became pregnant. Other Christians regard such solutions as oversimplistic, pointing out that many have prayed but not experienced any such miraculous remedy. Moreover those who appear to have experienced miraculous answers to prayer can appear smug and spiritually superior, causing unsuccessful couples to feel that they not only continue to have a physical or psycho-sexual problem but that their spiritual life is inadequate too. Whether or not infertile Christian couples seek spiritual help, there are few who would not make use of conventional medical treatment. The Church positively welcomes scientific research into fertility and has no objection to couples seeking medical help for such conditions, which may be due to impotence, low sperm count or psycho-sexual problems. Recent scientific advances have given rise to a number of important ethical issues that Christians continue to debate, for example artificial insemination by donor (AID), sperm and ovum donation, *in vitro* fertilization (IVF) and surrogate mothering.

The Roman Catholic Church has tended to be conservative about these ways of attaining parenthood, and bases its teachings on three fundamental principles. First, a child is a 'gift' from God: there is no innate 'right to a child' and hence infertility may simply need to be accepted. Life comes from God and technology should not be allowed to dominate the potential for child-bearing. Second, life should come from the procreative act between the husband and wife, with no third party intervening. Third, the child should have the right to know who his or her natural parents are and to be born of parents who are united in marriage.

These principles entail that 'artificial' methods of inducing pregnancy are unacceptable. Sperm and ovum donation involve a third party, the resulting embryo being genetically unrelated to one of the parents. The same holds for artificial insemination by donor (AID). It is frequently the case that such techniques cause the child to be ignorant of one parent's real identity, and the child's genetic parents are not 'bound to each other by marriage'. Surrogate mothering involves a third party and is described as 'gravely immoral' (*Catechism* 2376–7). Artificial insemination by husband (AIH) is regarded as not as bad since the resulting child is born of his or her natural parents, but the technique involves a separation of the sexual act and the procreative act and is therefore unacceptable.

Protestant attitudes to artificial insemination are not unanimous. I know of no Protestant denomination that has expressed official opposition; they prefer to leave such matters to their members' individual conscience with the support of pastoral counselling. There is certainly a great deal of debate on the subject, and Christians identify similar issues to those of their non-religious counterparts. For example, medics typically grade embryos for IVF according to their likelihood of fertility. Should an embryo, which is a living being, be 'graded' in this way? IVF involves the availability of surplus embryos: what should become of them? They can be stored for the potential future use by the couple; they could be donated to another infertile couple; or they could simply be destroyed – which many Christians regard as morally no different from abortion. IVF treatment has given rise to multiple births, when most couples simply want a single child: an unexpectedly large family can cause financial hardship and multiply the amount of care that is needed.

Separating the biological from the relational in such ways raises the prospect of a 'slippery slope'. How far down the route of artificial means of human reproduction should one legitimately go? What about a single woman who wants to be a mother, or a lesbian couple? What about the possibility – now a reality – of preselecting the sex of one's child? Should one terminate a pregnancy when an embryo is seriously deformed? Is a 'designer baby' more of a commodity than a person to be respected? And more generally, should children be born simply to meet the desires of parents rather than to be valued for themselves? I do not profess to have answers to these questions, but merely to highlight the current state of the debate.

Alternatives to family: holy orders and Christian singles

In contrast with Judaism and Islam, where founder-leaders like Abraham, Moses and Muhammad were married and had families, Jesus was probably unmarried, and Paul was certainly single. Paul seems singularly unenthusiastic about the institution of marriage when he makes statements like:

> Now to the unmarried and the widows, I say: It is good for them to stay unmarried, as I do. But if they cannot control themselves, they should marry, for it is better to marry than to burn with passion. (1 Cor. 7.8–9)

When the Bible refers to the 'marriage of the Lamb' (that is, Jesus the Lamb of God: see John 1.29; Rev. 19.7), John the Divine paints a somewhat surreal picture of the bride as the Holy City of Jerusalem, which comes down from God in heavenly splendour (Rev. 21.9–11). The mystical union between Christ and the Church finds expression in the traditional convention of referring to the Church as 'she', and there is therefore a sense in which all Christians, being part of the Church, are Christ's marriage partners. A number of Christian mystics, such as Bernard of Clairvaux (1090–1153) and John of the Cross (1542–91), have used imagery that verges on the erotic to express this relationship and finds expression in a few Christian hymns. For example, in John Newton's hymn 'How sweet the name of Jesus sounds', the line 'Jesus my shepherd, husband, friend' was sung by both men and women, although – perhaps because some men found it embarrassing to call Christ their husband – the words have been modified in some hymnals.

For the majority of Christians the Church as the Bride of Christ is perfectly compatible with conventional marriage. There are some, however, who have viewed this relationship with Christ as a special relationship that excludes any human matrimonial relationship and have entered holy orders as a full-time commitment, involving celibacy. In the Roman Catholic and Orthodox traditions, admission to holy orders is a sacrament, equivalent and alternative to marriage. There are two types of holy orders: priesthood and monasticism. Only men are eligible for the former in these two traditions, although the Anglican and Protestant traditions, with some exceptions, have progressively permitted women's ordination. The monastic life, by contrast, is open to both sexes, monks and nuns being segregated into single-sex communities. The difference between a priest and a monk or nun is that a priest normally has responsibility for a congregation, officiates at public worship and has the authority to celebrate the sacraments of baptism and Eucharist. Monks or nuns traditionally commit themselves to a disciplined rule of life involving prayer and meditation.

The celibate life in these holy orders serves to foster self-control. Mastery over the senses is something that few of us achieve, and abstinence from sexual relationships is regarded as good self-discipline, demonstrating that desires can be brought under control. Allied to this is the quest to become God-like. As the Church of England's *Thirty-Nine Articles* puts it, God is 'without body, parts, or passions' (Article I). Although achieving a disembodied state is not possible on this side of death, at least Christians can attempt to control their bodies, and monasticism presents a way of controlling or even eliminating one's passions. The celibacy of the clergy was one of the controversial issues at the time of the Protestant Reformation. One of the ways in which the Protestant churches, as well as the Anglican tradition, attempted to distance itself from Roman Catholicism was by allowing its clergy to marry. Most Protestant and Anglican clergy tend to be married, usually with a family. Although making time for one's wife – or husband these days – and family takes time and attention away from one's work as a Christian minister, many in their congregations believe that married clergy are likely to have a better understanding of marriage and raising families and can therefore offer better guidance to those seeking advice on such matters. Spouses and families can offer help with congregational activities:

a pastor's wife can be involved in women's organizations, and children in youth ministries.

Although most Christian laypeople become married, marriage is by no means a requirement and there are many single Christians. They fall into a variety of categories: some are widowed, some are separated or divorced and some have never married, either because they have not found marriage a particularly appealing lifestyle or because they have not found a suitable partner. To a considerable degree marrying is tying: one has to organize one's life around another person's schedule, being home for meals, synchronizing diaries and spending time with children if one has a family. To a large extent, therefore, the single Christian has greater freedom and independence and more independently free time to spend doing work for their church. Some single Christians have therefore seen their state as a vocation or an opportunity, enabling them to devote more time to their faith, perhaps taking on additional responsibilities in one's church. Unmarried Christians may be more inclined to appreciate the role of friendship rather than a relationship with a sexual dimension.

Christian churches often uphold the nuclear family as the ideal unit to target for evangelism. It is not uncommon to see congregations advertise 'family worship' on their notice boards or websites and to offer 'family services', which frequently mean services aimed largely at children. Single adult Christians sometimes find this alienating since they do not fit into the role of parents or young people. They can feel left out of church activities geared to couples, such as a church dance or a Valentine's Day party. The biblical idea of Adam and Eve being created as 'one flesh' can convey the notion that the single person is incomplete: colloquially we refer to partners as our 'other half' or 'better half', reinforcing the belief that someone who is unmarried is only half a person.

Some attempts have been made to address the situations that Christian singles encounter. In 1986 Network Christians was set up with a view to bringing single Christian people together for holidays and other events. The aim was not merely social: the organization seeks to help singles make sense of their situation and God's purpose for them. It is non-denominational and brings together Christians from different backgrounds. Some participants meet their ideal partner but Network Christians is not a dating agency. Other organizations exist to facilitate Christian dating among those who want to emerge from the lifestyle of being single.

Islam

The model for family life

Muslims take the life of the Prophet Muhammad as their model for family life. Muhammad married his first wife Khadija when he was around 25 years of age, and it is thought that she was about 40. Khadija was a wealthy woman who had inherited her father's trading business. She employed trustworthy agents known for their honesty and respectability to accompany her caravans and act for her in doing business in Syria and on other trading journeys. Muhammad worked for her as her trusted business agent, and it was she who proposed marriage to him, having turned down the proposal of more prominent and prosperous men who sought her hand due to her wealth. Khadija was already twice widowed and had two sons and a daughter from her earlier marriages. She bore Muhammad six children but their two sons died in infancy. During her lifetime Muhammad took no other wives, and the accounts of their life together indicate that their marriage was a relationship of genuine love and affection and a true partnership of mutual support. When the Angel Jibril appeared to Muhammad bringing the first Revelation, it was Khadija to whom he turned in his emotional turmoil. It is reported that he came to her shaking with fear and emotion, pleading with her 'Cover me, cover me', upon which she wrapped him in a blanket and held him until his terror subsided and he was able to speak and explain to her what had happened. Khadija believed in him and supported him immediately and unconditionally and sought guidance from a cousin of hers, Waraqa ibn Nawfal, an Ebionite Christian priest, who confirmed to her the authenticity of Muhammad's prophethood.

Muhammad's father died before his birth and his mother died when he was around six years of age, so in Khadija he found not only the fulfilment of a loving marriage but perhaps also the kind-

FAMILY LIFE

ness and support of a maternal figure. The reports in the *hadith* indicate that Muhammad had great respect for women and deep reverence for wives and mothers. He treated his wives as partners and companions.

The Prophet said: 'Among the Muslims the most perfect, as regards his faith, is the one whose character is excellent, and the best among you are those who treat their wives well.'

> When asked by one of his followers, 'To whom do I owe the greatest respect?', he answered 'Your mother', and when asked 'And after that?' he replied again 'Your mother', and again to the same question 'Your mother'. Only after giving the same answer three times did he then say 'Your father'.
>
> He is also reported to have said that '[p]aradise lies at the feet of mothers'.

Muhammad and Khadija were married for some 24 years until her death, by which he was deeply affected. The year of her death is often referred to as the Year of Sorrow, as Muhammad's uncle who had raised him died in the same year. Khadija is sometimes referred to as the Mother of Islam, and both she and the later wives of Muhammad are usually referred to as the Mothers of the Faithful as a term of respect and reverence.

Only after Khadija's death did Muhammad marry again. The first woman he married was Sawda bint Zam'a, who was older than him, and their marriage brought both companionship to him in his loneliness following his great loss, and shelter to her as she was the widow of one of the early Muslims. Muhammad's marriage to Aisha sometime later was his only other true love match after Khadija. The marriage was proposed initially to support his alliance to her father, Abu Bakr, one of his closest companions and the first Caliph following his death. Aisha is reported to have been six or seven years of age when the marriage was contracted and nine or ten when it was consummated. This has been a subject of debate over centuries, but most scholars will say that it has to be viewed in the context of the times, when child marriage was common and life expectancy relatively short. Some have suggested that because of her importance as a figure in early Islam, Aisha's age was highlighted in the early histories to emphasize her purity prior to marriage, which was of great importance in Arab culture.

Muhammad made a number of further marriages, all of them to widows and divorcees, some of whom were significantly older than him. Some of these were political alliances and some intended to provide shelter to vulnerable women. None of them is given the same prominence as Aisha. In exception to the injunction limiting the number of wives a man may have to four, Muhammad at certain points had more wives than this at the same time. The scholars have long agreed that this was a specific exemption given to Muhammad due to his status as Prophet.

The mutual rights of husband and wife as a consequence of the marriage contract

> O People, it is true that you have certain rights with regard to your women, but they also have rights over you. Remember that you have taken them as your wives only under Allah's trust and with His permission. If they abide by your right then to them belongs the right to be fed and clothed in kindness. Do treat your women well and be kind to them for they are your partners and committed helpers. And it is your right that they do not make friends with any one of whom you do not approve, as well as never to be unchaste.
>
> (From the Prophet's farewell sermon shortly before his death in 632 CE)

The rights established on the basis of a valid marriage contract are divided into three main categories: mutual rights, rights of the husband and rights of the wife.

> And due to the wives is similar to what is expected of them, according to what is reasonable. But the men have a degree over them [in responsibility and authority]. (Qur'an 2.228)

Although in reality sexual relations within marriage are not normally governed by law but form a natural part of a marriage, among the mutual rights created by the marriage contract is the legitimizing of *mu'ashara jinsiyya* or conjugal relations, entitling both parties to sexual gratification and the possibility of procreation on a lawful basis.

There is some debate among the jurists, however, as to whether conjugal relations are a right or a duty with regard to each of the parties. On the whole they agree that intercourse is a right of the husband at any time, providing the wife has no justification to refuse, such as menstruation, recent childbirth or illness, on the basis of the verse already mentioned: 'Your wives are a place of sowing of seed for you, so come to your place of cultivation however you wish and put forth [righteousness] for yourselves' (Qur'an 2.223). By definition, then, there is no notion of rape within marriage in Islam.

Most of the jurists hold that intercourse is also a right of the wife but they disagree as to what is demanded of the husband in fulfilment of this right. They base these opinions on a range of factors. One opinion is that the husband should have intercourse with his wife at least once every four months by analogy with *iyla*, the oath of abstinence for four months, which results in dissolution of the marriage. An alternative view is that the minimum is once every four nights, as he is permitted four wives and a wife is entitled to his attention one night in four (whether or not he has other wives). Other views include that it should be one night in two on the basis of the *hadith* 'the male is entitled to the lot of two females' (which usually refers to shares in inheritance), or that it should be once a month on the basis of a ruling by Umar ibn al-Khattab (the second of the rightly guided Caliphs), as this is all that may be required for conception to occur. The Hanafis, however, hold that intercourse is an absolute right for the husband and a duty for the wife, and the husband is only ever obliged to fulfil this once in consummation of the marriage.

There is a principle in Shari'a of causing no harm, and it is therefore considered by some to be improper for a man to deprive his wife of sexual gratification. In some cases a judge may grant a woman a divorce if she claims that this is harming her to the extent that she is unable to continue married life in this way or that she is in danger of falling into immorality. It is also forbidden for him to have intercourse with her in such a way as to hurt or harm her, such as if she is too weak or sick to bear the act or if he is affected by a sexually transmitted disease or engages in or proposes any 'unnatural' practice that she finds unacceptable, such as oral or anal sex. If intercourse causes the death of the wife, then the husband will be deemed responsible and may be liable to pay the *diya'* or bloodwit to her family, depending on the circumstances.

The second of the main mutual rights is the right of mutual inheritance according to the shares prescribed in the Qur'an.

The rights of the husband

> Men are in charge of women by [right of] what Allah has given one over the other and what they spend [for maintenance] from their wealth. So righteous women are devoutly obedient, guarding in [the husband's] absence what Allah would have them guard. But those [wives] from whom you fear arrogance – [first] advise them; [then if they persist], forsake them in bed; and [finally], strike them. But if they obey you [once more], seek no means against them. Indeed, Allah is ever Exalted and Grand.
>
> (Qur'an 4.34)

Among the rights of the husband is the right of obedience (*ta'a*). Although this means a general right in the sense that a wife should normally follow the lead of her husband, in practical terms it usually means that she should not leave the marital home except with his agreement or for some lawful purpose. The husband is not permitted to ask her to do anything that contradicts with the Shari'a, and if he does so she is entitled to refuse and should suffer no detriment from doing so.

If she refuses obedience and leaves the marital home without justification she will be deemed disobedient (*nashiz*) and will lose her right to maintenance. The husband will then be entitled to ask for a judge's ruling requiring her to return to the marital home, which is referred to in this context as *bayt al-ta'a*, the 'house of obedience'. In many Islamic jurisdictions, this is enforceable by the courts and the wife may only refuse with justification such as fear of harm or if the marital home does not fulfil the legal requirements. What will be deemed disobedience will vary according to culture and custom, but in many Islamic jurisdictions it will not be considered disobedience if the wife goes out of the home for lawful employment or education.

An aspect of the right of obedience is the right of discipline. Sura 4, verse 34 gives men permission in the case of disobedience to admonish their wives and if this does not correct their behaviour to desert the marital bed and even to beat them. However unacceptable this may appear to most people, including many Muslims, the Qur'an is infallible and therefore the verse above has to be accepted as it stands. Over the centuries, however, the scholars and jurists have attempted to soften the interpretation of this verse. Many of the scholars indicate that discipline should only be used where there is no alternative to resolve a situation that endangers the stability of the family, and the majority insist that in no way should any form of chastisement cause real harm to the wife. In the case where a husband abuses his right of discipline, the Maliki school gives the wife the right to request divorce on the grounds of harm. According to the Shafi'i school, if the husband is so ill-tempered or violent that admonition by a judge is of no avail, the judge may separate them without divorce until such time as the husband amends his behaviour, and the husband will continue to be liable for maintenance during this period.

The Qur'an gives the husband the right to choose his wife's domicile: 'Lodge them [in a section] of where you dwell out of your means and do not harm them in order to oppress them' (Qur'an 65.6).

The scholars are agreed upon this but indicate that there are two main restrictions. The first is that the husband should not force his wife to relocate simply to hurt or dominate her. Any move should be for a legitimate purpose such as work in another town. He should not ask her to move to a place where she will be in danger of harm such as a war or famine zone.

The rights of the wife

The rights of the wife are based on the principle of *al-mu'ashara bi'l-ma'ruf* or 'fair cohabitation'.

The wife has three main rights with regard to the husband. The first of these is to receive the dower (*mahr*) or at least the first portion thereof (as discussed earlier) on the conclusion of the contract. This becomes her property and no one else has any claim on it. The wife has complete financial independence from her husband. Her own money, property and business interests are hers alone and her husband has no right of possession or control of them.

She is also entitled to maintenance (*nafaqa*) immediately upon consummation of the marriage, provided she is not *nashiz* (disobedient) or *murtadda* (apostate), in which case maintenance is immediately forfeit. Maintenance should comprise all that the wife requires in the way of food, clothing, housing and running a household. This is irrespective of her own means and she is not required to contribute to the household budget, although in reality in the modern world many women do work to support their families. There is a *hadith* indicating that when the Prophet was asked, 'What rights do our wives have?' he replied, 'That you feed them as you eat, that you provide them with clothing as you clothe yourselves, that you do not strike their faces, that you do nothing disgraceful and that you do not desert them except within the house [i.e. desert the marital bed].'

He is also reported to have said in his farewell sermon on his final pilgrimage: 'If they abide by your right, then to them belongs the right to be fed and clothed in kindness.'

If the husband fails to provide maintenance, the wife may apply to a judge to require him to do so. If he has assets the judge may order their sale and pass on what is owed to the wife out of the proceeds, as maintenance is a debt like any other. If he has no assets that may be liquidated, the wife may request that he be imprisoned. This may be counterproductive if he is suffering hardship, and it means that he is unable to work, but it may be used at the discretion of the judge if the husband is affluent but simply recalcitrant. Where there is no resolution of the situation, many jurists are of the opinion that the judge may dissolve the marriage.

If he goes away leaving no maintenance and no means of contacting him then the judge may order the sale of a sufficient part of his assets to provide maintenance if this is possible, or he may authorize the wife to incur debt in the name of the husband, who will be legally responsible for this as and when he returns or is contacted.

> And if you fear that you will not deal justly with the orphan girls, then marry those that please you of [other] women, two or three or four. But if you fear that you will not be just, then [marry only] one or those your right hand possesses. That is more suitable that you may not incline [to injustice].
>
> (Qur'an 4.3)
>
> And you will never be able to be equal [in feeling] between wives, even if you should strive [to do so]. So do not incline completely [towards one] and leave another hanging. And if you amend [your affairs] and fear Allah – then indeed, Allah is ever Forgiving and Merciful.
>
> (Qur'an 4.129)

Monogamy is the norm for the majority of Muslims, who will find the financial and emotional demands of one family quite enough to cope with. Most will, however, acknowledge the legitimacy of polygyny as to deny this would be to contradict their faith. Many will even support the wisdom behind its permissibility, even if they would not consider it for themselves.

If a man is married to more than one woman then they are both or all entitled to be treated fairly and equally. This is the right of *qasm* or equity of treatment between wives.

The Qur'an recognizes, however, that human nature means it is not possible for a man to have the same feelings for more than one woman, but it is his duty to treat them fairly in material terms. They should be provided with equivalent accommodation of an acceptable standard, each private and independent of the other or others, and they should receive equal provision for themselves and for their children in terms of food and clothing. If a husband is unable or unwilling to meet these conditions then he should only take one wife. There is a *hadith* that the Prophet said: 'If a man has two wives and is inclined towards one of them, then on the Day of Judgement he will be punished for his injustice.' If a man does not treat his wives equitably then they may appeal to a judge to compel him to do so. A husband is also required to share his time equally between his wives and to treat them with equal respect and consideration. Aisha, the second wife of the Prophet, is reported to have said:

> The Prophet used to share and be fair [among his wives], but he said 'O God, this is my *qasm* in that over which I have the power, so do not blame me for that which is your power and over which I have no control.'

Aisha was Muhammad's favourite wife after the death of Khadija; she was his beloved and his confidante. Towards the end of his life, when he was gravely ill, his other wives voluntarily gave up their rights to his time, allowing him to spend his last days in the house of Aisha, where he was cared for and comforted by her, and it is reported that he died peacefully in her arms.

Parents, children and family life

Children are the natural consequence of marriage and it is extremely unusual in all Muslim communities for married couples to remain childless by choice. In many Islamic cultures, large families are normal, indeed desirable, although in urban society and among Muslims in non-Muslim countries numbers of children may be smaller. The Qur'an is silent on the matter of contraception but there are *hadith* referring to it, such as a report by Jabir: 'We used to practise '*azl* (coitus interruptus) during the Prophet's lifetime. News of this reached him and he did not forbid us.' But according to 'Umar Ibn Khattab: 'The Prophet forbade the practice of '*azl* with a free woman except with her permission.' The scholars are generally agreed that temporary forms of contraception are undesirable but not forbidden, provided both parties consent to this. In reality, temporary contraception is widely used in many Muslim communities either to help with the spacing of pregnancies or to limit family size, particularly among professional families. On the other hand, sterilization or procedures that result in sterility, such as hysterectomy, are prohibited unless there is a pressing medical need for them. There is no sense in this that sex is not to be enjoyed for itself but only that it is not the right of human beings to attempt to control something that is in God's hands.

Opinions on abortion vary among the scholars. In general it is considered to be wrong. There is strong Qur'anic support for the concept of the sanctity of life:

> Whosoever has spared the life of a soul, it is as though he has spared the life of all people. Whosoever has killed a soul, it is as though he has murdered all of mankind. (Qur'an 5.32)

> And do not kill your children for fear of poverty. We provide for them and for you. Indeed, their killing is ever a great sin. (Qur'an 17.31)

Some scholars allow abortion up to 120 days on the basis of a *hadith* that is interpreted to mean that life as such only begins at this point with the ensoulment of the foetus.

> Allah's Apostle, the true and truly inspired said, '(as regards your creation), every one of you is collected as a seed in the womb of his mother for the first forty days, and then he becomes a clot for another forty days, and then a piece of flesh for another forty days. Then Allah sends an angel to write four words: He writes his deeds, time of his death, means of his livelihood, and whether he will be wretched or blessed (in religion). Then the soul is breathed into his body ...'
>
> (*Sahih Bukhari*, Volume 4, Book 55, Number 549 – narrated by Abdullah)

Even in the case of rape the life of the foetus is considered sacred. The only case in which some of the modern jurists consider abortion permissible is where the life of the mother is in danger or where the child is expected to suffer from a severe mental or physical handicap.

There is no ruling concerning the attendance of the father at the birth of his child, but in traditional societies birth has normally been an all-female event. In some Muslim cultures it is not acceptable for a woman to be attended by a male doctor, and births are assisted by trained or traditional midwives, female family members or female doctors. This is generally the preference, but in many Muslim countries births are attended by male obstetricians. Birth customs vary according to culture, but a newborn child should be washed and clothed and then have the *adhan* or call to prayer whispered into his or her ear, usually by the father.

Many Muslims celebrate the seventh day following the birth. This will usually involve the slaughter of one or more sheep and the distribution of part of the meat to the poor. Children are usually named by the seventh day, and it is the duty of the parents to give a child a good name to live up to. There is a report that the Prophet said: 'On the Day of Resurrection, you will be called by your names and by your fathers' names, so give yourselves good names' (*Hadith* Abu Dawud). Naming customs vary and children are often given the names of their grandparents as a gesture of respect. Many Muslims name their children after the Prophet, his family and his companions. The name Muhammad and its variant Ahmad are probably the most commonly given. Children have a given name, followed by the name of their father and grandfather, which indicate their lineage. The family name in the western form is a recent adaptation in some Muslim countries, but it has always been the case that following the patrilineal name a person would be further identified by his tribe or clan ('of the house of ...'), his town, region or country of origin or his profession.

Traditionally, if a son is born it is customary for his parents to be called after him, for example Umm Ahmad and Abu Ahmad (mother and father of Ahmad respectively). This is a mark of pride for parents and the most polite form of address. Occasionally, if there are no sons, they may be named after the eldest daughter.

Circumcision of male children is expected although there are no sanctions as such if it is not performed. This may take place at any time between birth and puberty according to the custom of the community. Traditionally this was done by community circumcisers or 'barber surgeons', and this remains the case in many poor or rural communities, but today it is more commonly performed by a qualified medical professional. Muslims consider it essential for purposes of hygiene and the requirements of the ablution for prayer.

Female circumcision is not prescribed in Islam but pre-dates it. In the countries where it is most prevalent, such as Egypt and some African countries, it is also practised by Christians. There are differences of opinion among religious scholars. Some have condemned it as having nothing to do with Islam while others consider it permissible on the basis of the *hadith*: 'Circumcision is obligatory for men, and it is an honour for women, but it is not obligatory for them' (al-Mughni 1/70). There is also a report by Umm 'Atiyah according to which a woman used to perform circumcisions in Madina. The Prophet told her: 'Do not abuse [that is, do not go to extremes in circumcising]; that is better for the woman and more liked by her husband' (reported by Abu Dawud in *al-Sunan, Kitab al-Adab*). The latter *hadith* is, however, considered to be weak.

Mothers are encouraged but not obliged to suckle their offspring, and the duration of suckling is given as two years. If the mother cannot or will not suckle her child, the child may be given to a wet nurse and the father will be responsible for paying for this service.

Mothers may breastfeed their children two complete years for whoever wishes to complete the nursing. Upon the father is the mothers' provision and their clothing according to what is acceptable. No person is charged with more than his capacity. No mother should be harmed through her child, and no father through his child. And upon the [father's] heir is [a duty] like that [of the father]. And if they both desire weaning through mutual consent from both of them and consultation, there is no blame upon either of them. And if you wish to have your children nursed by a substitute, there is no blame upon you as long as you give payment according to what is acceptable ...

(Qur'an 2.223)

Both parents have a duty to care for their children and to raise them as Muslims. Although many women work at all levels of employment from the most basic to the highest professional levels, gender roles are still predominantly traditional. Mothers are the nurturers of children and the centre of the family, and it is the duty of fathers to provide for them.

Parents teach their children to pray and are responsible for their religious education. It is the aspiration of all Muslims to learn the Qur'an by heart, and many achieve this in childhood. Fathers will take their sons to the mosque for the Friday prayer from an early age and introduce them to the Muslim community. Children are introduced from infancy to stories from the Sunna, or biography of the Prophet, as guidance and as a model for their lives.

> And We have enjoined upon man, to his parents, good treatment. His mother carried him with hardship and gave birth to him with hardship, and his gestation and weaning [period] is thirty months. [He grows] until, when he reaches maturity and reaches [the age of] forty years, he says, 'My Lord, enable me to be grateful for Your favor which You have bestowed upon me and upon my parents and to work righteousness of which You will approve and make righteous for me my offspring. Indeed, I have repented to You, and indeed, I am of the Muslims.'
>
> (Qur'an 46.15)
>
> And your Lord has decreed that you not worship except Him, and to parents, good treatment. Whether one or both of them reach old age [while] with you, say not to them [so much as], 'uff,' and do not repel them but speak to them a noble word. And lower to them the wing of humility out of mercy and say, 'My Lord, have mercy upon them as they brought me up [when I was] small.'
>
> (Qur'an 17.23–4)

Although the model of the nuclear family has become more common in recent decades, particularly in urban contexts,

FAMILY LIFE

the multi-generational family is still an accepted norm in most Muslim communities. In many Islamic cultures it is the norm for newly married couples to live with the parents of the husband. This obviously has many advantages for all concerned in terms of mutual support, childcare, care for the elderly and sharing of duties and resources. Naturally there are potential disadvantages, such as lack of privacy and autonomy. It is, however, very much an expectation that older generations are to be respected and not discarded; that their care is an honour and not a burden.

Families pray together, they observe the fast of Ramadan together and come together in their families and communities to break the fast at the end of the day. They celebrate together *Eid ul-Fitr*, the festival that marks the end of the month of fasting, and *Eid ul-Adha*, the Feast of the Sacrifice, which commemorates Ibrahim's willingness to sacrifice his son Ismail in devotion to God and God's substitution of an animal sacrifice in his place. The family is at the centre of a Muslim's world and is considered to be the essential building block of a stable and prosperous society.

4

Divorce

Judaism

Divorce in the tradition

Biblical law specifies the procedure for divorce. According to the book of Deuteronomy, 'When a man takes a wife and marries her, if then she finds no favour in his eyes because he has found some indecency in her, he writes her a bill of divorce, and puts it in her hand and sends her out of his house' (Deut. 24.1). This verse stipulates that the power of divorce rests with the husband and the act of divorce must be in the form of a legal document. Among early rabbinic scholars there was disagreement as to the meaning of the term 'indecency'. The School of Shammai interpreted it as referring to unchastity whereas the School of Hillel understood the term more widely. Nonetheless, in two instances it was not permitted for divorce to take place: first, if a man claimed that his wife was not a virgin at the time of marriage, and his charge was disproved (Deut. 22.13–19); or second, if he raped a virgin whom he later married (Deut. 22.28–9). Conversely, a man was not allowed to remarry his divorced wife if she had married another person and had not been divorced or widowed (Deut. 24.2–4). Nor could a priest marry a divorced woman (Lev. 21.7).

The role of the husband in divorce

> According to this biblical verse (Deut. 24.1), the husband writes the bill of divorce (a *get*), gives it to his wife, and banishes her

> from his house. Professor Zev Falk described biblical divorce as the 'arbitrary, unilateral, private, act of the husband.' The husband initiated and executed the divorce at his will and in accordance with his subjective evaluation of the nature and quality of his marriage. His wife had no capacity, voice or power to protest. It did not matter whether she was at fault for the breakdown of the marriage, having refused conjugal relations with her husband, committed adultery or merely burnt his dinner (in accordance with the opinion of Bet Hillel). Judith Romney Wegner maintains that even in the time of the Mishnah, a woman could be discarded like an 'old shoe.' It is from this verse in Deuteronomy that Jewish Law establishes that a Jewish divorce occurs only when a man issues a bill of divorce to his wife (a *get*). A Jewish woman cannot give a bill of divorce to her husband.
>
> (From Jewish Women's Archive, article by Susan Weiss: www.jwa.org/encyclopedia/article/divorce-halakhic-perspective)

In the Talmudic period the law of divorce underwent considerable development, including the elaboration of various situations under which the court could compel a husband to divorce his wife if she remained barren over a period of ten years, if the husband contracted a loathsome disease, if he refused to support his wife or was not in a position to do so, if he denied his wife her conjugal rights or if he beat her despite the court's warnings. In such cases the Talmud states that the husband is coerced by the court only to the extent that he would in fact want to divorce his wife.

The bill of divorce (*get*) is to be drawn up by a scribe following a formula based on Mishnaic law. This document is written almost entirely in Aramaic on parchment. Once it has been given to the wife it is retained by the rabbi, who cuts it in a criss-cross fashion so that it cannot be used a second time. The husband then gives the wife a document that affirms that she has been divorced and may remarry. The wife is permitted to remarry only after 90 days, so as to ascertain whether she was pregnant at the stage of divorce. This document must be witnessed by two males over the age of 13 who are not related to each other or to the divorcing husband and wife.

The traditional understanding of marriage and divorce

> According to the Orthodox Jewish scholar David Bleich, Jewish marriage is comparable to a purchase arrangement: 'The legalistic essence of [Jewish] marriage is in effect an exclusive conjugal servitude conveyed by the bride to the groom. All other rights, responsibilities, duties and perquisites are secondary and flow therefrom. The three methods of solemnizing a marriage, i.e. *kesef, shetar* and *bi'ah* (money, deed and sexual intercourse) parallel the conveyances prescribed for the transfer of real property (in Jewish law). Title to real estate is transferred by payment of the purchase price; marriage is effected by *kesef* (delivery of an object of value, usually specified in the form of a ring, by the groom (the "purchaser") to the bride). Transfer of real property can be effected by a delivery of deed: a man can acquire a wife by delivery to her of a *shetar kiddushin* ... Real property can be transferred by *hazakah*, i.e. the recipient performing an overt act demonstrating proprietorship, e.g. plowing a furrow ... *Bi'ah*, or cohabitation for purposes of marriage, is the counterpart of *hazakah*; it is an overt demonstration of the exercise of the servitude that is being acquired. Understanding that the essence of marriage lies in a conveyance of a "property" interest by the bride to the groom serves to explain why it is that only the husband can dissolve the marriage. As the beneficiary of the servitude, divesture requires the husband's voluntary surrender of the right that he has acquired.'
>
> (Quoted in Jewish Women's Archive, article by Susan Weiss: www.jwa.org/encyclopedia/article/divorce-halakhic)

Get

The legal requirements for giving a *get* consist of several conditions:

- A divorce document must be written. This is usually done by a professional religious scribe (*sofer*). It must be written on the explicit instruction and free-willed approval of the husband, with the intention that it is to be used by the man for the specific woman (it cannot be initially written with blanks to be filled in later).
- It must be delivered to the wife, whose physical acceptance of the *get* is required to complete and validate the process.
- There are detailed requirements relating to the legal and religious nature of the *get*. For example: it must be written on a fresh document; there must be no possibility of erasing the text; it may not be written on anything that is attached to the ground; it may not be pre-dated.

A *get* must be given of the free will of the husband – consent of the wife is not biblically mandated. However, the Ashkenazi tradition is that a husband may not divorce his wife without her consent. A *get* should not be given out of the fear of any obligation either party undertakes to fulfil in a separation agreement. Such an agreement may provide for matters such as custody of the children and their maintenance, as well as a property settlement. Yet either party may withdraw from such an agreement if they can satisfy the court of a genuine desire to restore marital harmony.

The laws relating to a *get* only provide for a divorce initiated by the husband. However, the wife has the right to sue for divorce in a rabbinical court. If the court finds just cause it can require the husband to divorce his wife. According to tradition a husband who refuses the court's demand that he divorce his wife is subject to various penalties in order to pressure him into granting a divorce. These include excommunication, monetary punishment, corporal punishment (including forcing the husband to spend the night at an unmarked grave with the implication that it could become his grave). In Israel rabbinic courts have the power to sentence a husband to prison and impose additional penalties within prison, such as solitary confinement, to compel the husband to grant his wife a *get*. Rabbinical courts in the diaspora do not have sufficient power to enforce such penalties; this sometimes leads to a situation in which the husband makes demands of the court and his wife, insisting on a monetary settlement or other benefits including child custody.

Occasionally a man will refuse to grant a divorce despite such pressure. This leaves the wife with no possibility to remarry according to Jewish law. Such a woman is called a *mesorevet get* (refused a divorce). If the court determined that she is entitled to a divorce, the husband is frequently spurned by the Orthodox community and excluded from religious activities. It is hoped that such pressure will persuade him to agree to the court's demands. Although it is widely assumed that the problem lies primarily in the man refusing to grant a divorce to his wife, in Israel figures released from the chief rabbinate illustrate that men are equally victimized. Nonetheless, such a husband has the option of seeking a *heter meah rabbanim*, while no similar option is available to women.

A *heter meah rabbanim* (permission by 100 rabbis) is a term in Jewish law that means that 100 rabbis agree with a rabbinical court that a particular situation warrants an exemption to permit a man to remarry, even though his wife refuses or is unable to accept a *get*. In certain cases – such as the case of a man whose wife refuses to accept a *get* for an extended period – the Bet Din will permit him to remarry after 100 rabbis agree with them to issue an exemption. After receiving a *heter meah rabbanim*, the Bet Din will require the husband to write a *get* for his wife and deposit it with them. She will remain married until she receives the *get*.

Situations where the Bet Din might embark on this process include:

- Where the law requires a man to divorce his wife, and she refuses to accept it (such as in the case of adultery).
- Where the wife has abandoned her husband and refuses to accept a *get*.
- Where the wife disappeared and her whereabouts are unknown.

- Where the wife is mentally unable to give her consent to receiving a *get*.
- Where the wife is in a coma.

Ashkenazi Jews have followed Rabbenu Gershom's ruling banning polygamy since the beginning of the eleventh century. However, some Sephardi and Mizrahi Jews discontinued polygamy much more recently as they emigrated to countries where it was forbidden. Israel has forbidden polygamous marriages but instituted provisions for existing polygamous families immigrating from countries such as Yemen and Iran where the practice was legal.

> **The *get***
>
> On the _____ day of the week, the _____ day of the month of _____ in the year _____ after creation of the world, according to the calendaric calculations that we count here in the city, _____ which is situated on the _____ river, and situated near springs of water. I, _____, the son of _____, who today am present in the city _____, which is situated on the _____ river, and situated near springs of water, willingly consent, being under no duress, to release, discharge, and divorce you [to be] on your own, you, my wife, _____, daughter of _____, who are today in the city of _____, which is situated on the _____ river, and situated near springs of water, who has hitherto been my wife. And now I do release, discharge, and divorce you [to be] on our own, so that you are permitted and have authority over yourself to go and marry any man you desire. No person may object against you from this day onward, and you are permitted to every man. This shall be for you from me a bill of dismissal, a letter of release, and a document of absolution, in accordance with the law of Moses and Israel.
>
> _____, the son of _____ – witness
>
> _____, the son of _____ – witness

The divorce procedure

The traditional procedure for divorce is based on the *Code of Jewish Law*. The officiating rabbi initially asks the husband if he gives the bill of divorce (*get*) of his own free will without duress and compulsion. After receiving the writing materials from a scribe, he instructs the scribe to write a *get*. The *get* is written, and the witnesses must be present during the writing of the first line; the witnesses as well as the scribe then make a distinguishing mark on the *get*. When the *get* is completed and the ink is dry, the witnesses read the *get*. The rabbi then questions the scribe to ensure that the document was written by him on the instruction of the husband. Turning to the witnesses, the rabbi asks if they heard the husband instruct the scribe to write the *get*, as well as observed him writing it. In addition the rabbi questions the witnesses about their signatures on the bill of divorce. Finally the rabbi asks the husband if the *get* was given freely. The wife is then asked if she freely accepts the *get*:

> Rabbi: 'Are you accepting this *get* of your own free will?
> Wife: 'Yes.'
> Rabbi: 'Did you bind yourself by any statement or vow that would compel you to accept this *get* against your will?'
> Wife: 'No.'
> Rabbi: 'Perhaps you have unwittingly made such a statement that would nullify the *get*. In order to prevent that, will you kindly retract all such declarations?'
> Wife: 'I revoke all such statements that may nullify the *get*, in the presence of the witnesses.'

The rabbi tells the wife to remove all jewellery from her hands and hold her hands together with open palms upward to receive the bill of divorce. The scribe holds the *get* and gives it to the rabbi. The rabbi then gives the *get* to her husband; he holds it in both hands and drops it into the palms of the wife and states: 'This be your *get* and with it be you divorced from this time forth so that you may become the wife of any man.' When the wife receives the bill of divorce, she walks with it a short distance and returns. She gives the *get* to the rabbi, who reads it again in the presence of the witnesses; the rabbi then asks the scribe and the witnesses to identify the *get* as well as the signatures. Following this the rabbi states: 'Hear all you present that Rabbenu Tam has issued a ban against all those who try to invalidate a *get* after it has been delivered.' The four corners of the *get* are cut and it is placed in the rabbi's files. The husband and the wife receive written statements certifying that their marriage has been dissolved in accordance with Jewish law.

It is customary for the husband and wife to be present during the divorce proceedings, but if this is not possible, Jewish law stipulates that an agent can take the place of either party. The husband may appoint an agent to deliver the *get* to his wife; if this agent is unable to complete this task he has the right to appoint another one, and the second agent another. The wife can also appoint an agent to receive the *get*. Thus it is possible for the entire procedure to take place without the husband or wife seeing one another; this is sometimes done to avoid the emotional strain of the husband and wife meeting each other if a bitter divorce has occurred.

In certain instances a *get* of benefit (*get zikkui*) may be arranged. Jewish law stipulates that a woman's consent to a divorce is not necessary. However, the ordinance of Rabbenu Gershom prohibits divorcing a woman without her consent. According to Talmudic scholars, a benefit can be conferred upon an individual even when that person is not present. That is, if the procedure can bring about a benefit for an individual, it is logical to assume that this person would give his or her consent if he or she knew about it. In the case of civil divorce it can be assumed that if the husband and wife have already obtained a divorce from the secular authorities, she has given consent to the divorce. In such a case the rabbinical court (Bet Din) can appoint an agent to receive the *get* for her even without her consent. Here the wife would be receiving a benefit because she would be able to remarry according to the *halakah* without risking being considered an adulteress. In such instances the procedure of divorce is the same, except that instead of giving the bill of divorce to the wife, the husband gives the *get* to an agent who is appointed by the court.

Throughout history a number of modifications have been made to divorce legislation. In the Middle Ages, Rabbenu Gershom brought about a fundamental change in the law of divorce among Ashkenazim as well as some Sephardic communities. In an enactment he decreed that a husband may not divorce his wife without her consent. This decree in essence made the rights of the wife nearly equivalent to those of the husband; from this time forth divorce could only be by mutual consent. Later scholars strengthened this enactment by stating that any writ of divorce issued in violation of this ruling was null and void. Some time later Jacob Tam declared that in certain emergencies the stipulation requiring mutual consent could be set aside, such as in the case of a woman who apostatized and left the Jewish community.

Yet despite such modifications certain difficulties still remain about the granting of a *get*. Since it is the husband who must give the bill of divorce to his wife, if he cannot be located this presents an insuperable problem. Similarly, in the diaspora rabbinic scholars have no authority to compel a husband to comply with their instructions. In both cases the wife has the status of being an *agunah* (a 'tied' woman) who is not able to remarry according to traditional Jewish law.

The agunah

The term *agunah* denotes a Jewish woman who is 'chained' to her marriage. As we have seen, Jewish law requires that a man grant his wife a *get* of his own free will. Without such a document no new marriage can be recognized according to Jewish law. Any child she has with another man is deemed a *mamzer* (bastard). The circumstances leading to a woman being regarded an *agunah* are:

- The husband disappears without any witnesses declaring that he is dead.
- The husband succumbs to a physical or mental disease that leaves him in a coma or insane and thereby unable to grant a divorce.

- The husband refuses to grant his wife a *get* even though she is entitled to a divorce according to Jewish law. In such a case she is referred to as a *mesorevet get*, although the term *agunah* is more frequently used.

Because of the nature of adultery in Jewish law, an *agunah* is forbidden to marry another man regardless of the circumstances whereby she has become an *agunah*. The amount of time that has passed since she first became an *agunah* is irrelevant. As noted, any child born from another man to an *agunah* is a *mamzer* and may only marry another *mamzer* or a convert.

Due to the serious nature of this situation, every effort is made to release a wife from her marriage. This can be done in several ways:

- locating the husband and persuading him to give his wife a *get*;
- providing evidence that her husband is dead;
- finding a flaw in the original marriage ceremony – this annuls the marriage.

In the view of most rabbis, reasonable circumstantial evidence is sufficient to prove the death of the husband. This is based on the Talmudic assertion (Yevamot 121a): 'The rabbis taught, "if he fell into a lion's den [being witnesses to] testify [that he is dead], if he fell into a ditch of snakes and scorpions – [there is] no [need] to testify [that he is dead]".' In other words, if it is known that the man fell into a ditch of snakes and scorpions and did not come out, it can be assumed that he is dead and there is no need for further evidence (unlike falling into a lion's den, where there is a chance of survival). If, however, it is later discovered that the husband is not dead, the woman will find herself in particularly difficult circumstances. The children of her second marriage will be regarded as *mamzerim* and she will be forced to divorce both husbands subject to the halakhic ruling that an adulterous woman is forbidden to her husband and the man with whom she fornicated.

Discovering a flaw in the marriage ceremony is regarded as a last resort in releasing an *agunah*. In Jewish law a marriage must be performed in front of two witnesses. In order to release the *agunah*, efforts must be made to identify why one of the witnesses is ineligible. If this were the case then the marriage would be null and void. Another possibility is to prove that the woman did not consent to the marriage clearly and of her own free will, so that the ceremony is regarded as invalid. Annulling a marriage has no impact on the status of the children. However, since it is not a generally accepted mechanism, it could have the adverse effect of leaving the wife susceptible to the halakhic ruling that she was still married, and any subsequent relations with another man would be adulterous.

Only a woman can be declared to be an *agunah*. None of the prohibitions listed above goes into effect for a man whose wife has disappeared. This is because there is no legal prohibition in the Torah for a man to have two wives. In such cases any child born is not considered a *mamzer*. In the eleventh century, however, Rabbenu Gershom issued a decree prohibiting Jewish men from practising bigamy (although this ruling was not accepted by certain Jewish communities). Further, Rabbenu Gershom also decreed that a woman may not be divorced against her will. In certain extreme cases – as for example when a wife is missing or when she refuses to accept a *get* – a *heter meah rabbanim* (exemption by 100 rabbis) may permit him to take a second wife after depositing a *get*. This exemption is only rarely used in contemporary society.

In modern times, warfare has become a major cause of a woman being declared an *agunah*, since a soldier can be killed in battle without anyone knowing. As a result, efforts have been made to resolve this problem. During the Second World War, some American Jewish and other chaplains provided combat soldiers with a 'provisional *get*', which would only go into effect if the husband were missing in action. This is based on the Talmudic explanation of the union of King David and Bathsheba. According to tradition, David did not sin by lying with a married woman since all of his soldiers gave a 'provisional *get*' to their wives before going into battle (Shabbat 56a).

As we noted, if a husband refuses to give his wife a *get*, various measures can be taken by a rabbinical court (such as shunning and denying him communal benefits and honours). In Israel, rabbinical courts can decide to revoke a driver's licence, revoke bank accounts, invalidate professional licences and cancel a passport. Imprisonment is also an option. In the diaspora, however, rabbinical courts do not have such powers. In recent times rabbinical groups and women's organizations have decried the increasing number of cases where the husband refuses to give a *get* despite such pressure; as a result various task forces have been created to deal with the issue of the *agunah* and to help individual victims.

The problem of the agunah

In the view of Jewish women's groups, rabbinical courts have failed to use adequate measures to force men to give their wives a *get*. This situation has permitted husbands to blackmail their wives. In response to this situation a number of solutions have been proposed:

- Increasing the means available to rabbinic courts to force husbands to grant their wives a *get*. In Israel, rabbinic courts can imprison men until they acquiesce and grant *gets* to their wives. In the diaspora this is not an option.
- Couples can sign a prenuptial agreement that requires the husband to pay support to his wife if he denies her a *get*. This would provide an incentive for a couple not to delay a divorce. Halakhic authorities in the United States have validated such prenuptial agreements to deal with this problem.
- Couples can prepare a provisional *get*, which will go into effect under certain agreed circumstances.
- Couples can agree to a conditional marriage, which includes a stipulation in the marriage ceremony citing that under certain circumstances – such as living apart – the marriage itself would be nullified with no need for a *get*.

In 2004 Justice Menahem HaCohen of the Jerusalem Family Court offered hope to *agunahs* when he ruled that a man refusing his wife a *get* must pay her 425,000 shekels in punitive damages because refusal to grant a *get* constitutes a severe infringement on her ability to lead a reasonable, normal life. This would constitute emotional abuse lasting for several years. He noted that this is not another sanction against someone refusing to give a *get*, intended to speed up the process of granting a *get*. Further, he went on to explain that the court was not involving itself in any future arrangements for the granting of a *get* – rather this solution is a direct response to the consequences that stem from not granting a *get*: the right of the woman is to receive punitive damages. This ruling resulted from the Public Litigation Project initiated by the Centre for Women's Justice, as one of a number of successful lawsuits filed in Israeli civil courts claiming financial damages against recalcitrant husbands.

Adopting a more liberal approach, the Conservative movement has sought to find remedies to the problem of the *agunah*. At the 1998 Jerusalem Agunot Conference, Rabbi Mayer Rabinowitz, the Chairman of the Joint Bet Din of the Conservative movement, explained the four approaches taken by leaders of Conservative Judaism.

The first, beginning in the 1950s, was the inclusion of the Liberman clause (named for a Talmudic scholar at the Jewish Theological Seminary, and discussed in Chapter 2) in the *ketubah* requiring that a *get* be granted if a civil divorce is issued. Most Orthodox rabbis have rejected this clause, although leaders of the Conservative movement claim that the original intent was to find a solution that could be used by both Orthodox and Conservative Jews. Later, because some civil courts viewed the enforcement of a religious document as a violation of the constitutional principle of separation of church and state, Conservative rabbis began to require couples to sign a separate letter stating that the clause had been explained to them as part of premarital counselling and that both parties had agreed to its conditions. Some Conservative rabbis, however, have expressed reservations about the use of the Liberman clause.

The second approach is based in part on past approaches used by both the French and Turkish rabbinates. The *ketubah* was not changed but a separate premarital agreement was signed, and in the presence of a rabbinical court the prospective groom read it and the prospective bride stated that she agreed to it. The agreement is that the parties understood that if a civil divorce were ever granted, then a *get* must be delivered within six months. A refusal to abide by the agreement would give the court no choice but to consider the original marriage, and the original declaration of the groom, so flawed that it would be as if the marriage never took place.

A third approach, using contacts both within Judaism and external to it, was to coerce the recalcitrant husband to grant a *get*. One example was a case where the civilly divorced husband planned to remarry a Catholic woman in a Catholic ceremony. The Conservative Bet Din contacted the Catholic Church, which agreed to refuse to have the marriage performed until the previous marriage was religiously dissolved.

The fourth approach – agreed by a vote of the law committee – is that the Joint Bet Din of the Conservative movement could annul marriages as a last resort, based on the Talmudic principle of *halka'at kiddushin*.

Within the Orthodox community there has been a long history of concern for the *agunah*, and a number of proposals have been put forward for consideration. So far no solution has been found that satisfies most Orthodox religious leaders. Yet as discussions of this issue continue, a number of modern studies and conferences have cited the work of past Orthodox rabbis, including Yaakov Moshe Toledo, who recommended in the 1930s that every Jewish marriage should be made contingent on the continuing agreement of the local rabbinic court, so that the court could retroactively annul the marriage as a remedy for the *agunah*. During the same period Menachem Risikoff recommended that such consideration be given to the Jerusalem rabbinic court. He also proposed discussing the reinstatement of the biblical status of the *pilgesh*, a relationship status between a man and a woman that does not require a *get* upon dissolution. Other approaches include the possibility of prenuptial agreements not incorporated in the *ketubah* or mentioned by the groom during the ceremony.

Christianity

A realistic view of marriage

> Divorce is a grave offence against the natural law. It claims to break the contract, to which the spouses freely consented, to live with each other until death. Sacramental marriage is the sign of the covenant of salvation, to which divorce does incredible injury. Contracting a new union, even if it is recognized by civil law, adds to the gravity of the rupture: the remarried spouse is then in a situation of public and permanent adultery. If a husband, separated from his wife, becomes involved with another woman, he is an adulterer because he makes that woman commit adultery; and the woman who lives with him is an adulteress, because she has drawn another's husband to herself.
>
> (*Catechism of the Catholic Church*, 2384)
>
> The divorce that God approves of is one of His major surgical procedures to save the people of the marriage (but not necessarily the marriage itself). But it has been turned into something detestable and abhorred. And because of this, many husbands and wives will live life with no joy, dead hearts, and guilt from not divorcing just to save the marriage, but themselves being lost because they were kept from a surgical operation they so desperately needed.
>
> (Divorce Hope: www.divorcehope.com/motivebehinddivorce.htm)

The words 'till death us do part' in the marriage ceremony indicate the Christian ideal of marriage as a lifelong relationship, which is not dependent on one's spouse's condition. One cannot be sure what fortune or misfortune life will bring, but one's marriage vows entail that marriage transcends any condition in which husbands and wives might find themselves. A beautiful bride or a handsome husband may become disfigured by a calamitous accident or, perhaps more likely as medical science prolongs people's lives, old age may bring ill health, disability or dementia. The commitments one makes on marriage are intended to ensure that one's spouse is not abandoned if he or she becomes a burden.

Most couples will affirm that the experience of 'being in love', which occurs early in one's relationship, changes as the years progress. For many the relationship develops into more mature companionship while for others love fades or a partner might even come to acknowledge that his or her choice of partner was a mistake. While emphasizing the seriousness of the marriage vows and the lifelong commitment they entail, the Christian faith seeks to be realistic and compassionate where things go wrong.

The Church does not teach that sequential monogamy is acceptable. A Unitarian minister whom I once knew wanted to dispense with the clause 'till death us do part' and substitute 'as long as our love shall last'. While this proposed change was in the interests of greater realism, it is unacceptable as part of the ceremony, and is not legal in most western countries.

The Gospels do not provide a wholly consistent view of Jesus' teaching on divorce. Jesus appears to have agreed with Moses that divorce is permissible but it is not clear whether or not he gave permission to remarry after divorce. According to Mark and Luke, Jesus teaches that remarrying after divorce is tantamount to placing one's wife in the position of an adulteress. Matthew portrays Jesus as slightly more liberal: if the divorce was occasioned through the adultery of one's first spouse then remarriage is acceptable (Mark 10.12; Luke 16.18; Matt. 19.9). According to Jewish teaching it was permissible for a husband to write out a certificate of divorce if his wife had been sexually promiscuous and to send her away (Deut. 24.1–4).

Divorce militates against the idea that marriage is an unbreakable and permanent bond between a man and a woman, and therefore the dissolution of a marriage is not to be entered into lightly. From a Christian standpoint it is not a sufficient reason that one's partner does not espouse the Christian faith (1 Cor. 7.11–13), that one's love has diminished or that a couple repeatedly quarrel. Adultery, however, presents a special exception. Marriage is viewed as a bonding between one man and one woman, and a breach of marital fidelity is a breaking of the marriage covenant that unites the husband and wife. Jesus' words, 'what God has joined together, let no one separate' (Matt. 19.6), are typically reiterated at Christian marriages, and the words 'forsaking all others' form part of a Declaration of Consent that is normally used in Church of England ceremonies and at most religious weddings in the United States. The Roman Catholic Church teaches that the marriage ceremony enacts a covenant between a man and woman that is a reflection of God's covenant with his people, and that breaking one's marriage vows is a breaking of God's covenant. Divorce disrupts family life, causing instability and trauma to the couple and to their children. Further, it is contagious, 'a plague on society' (*Catechism* 2385): once divorce becomes widespread and socially acceptable, greater numbers of couples are more likely to seek divorce as a solution to matrimonial difficulties.

Roman Catholicism takes the notion of sacramental marriage a stage further: such a union is irrevocable. Just as God's covenant cannot be broken, so the marriage bond is unbreakable. The Catholic view is therefore that there is no such thing as divorce, only annulment of a marriage. What this means is that in order to dissolve a marriage one must demonstrate that the marriage did not legitimately take place. Grounds for annulment would be that a marriage had never been consummated or that it was in breach of civil or ecclesiastical law – for example if one of the partners was already married. Another possible ground would be that the marriage was not freely entered into – for example if one partner had been coerced by parents or instilled with fear at possible repercussions of not agreeing to the union. If it is believed that such grounds exist, one can apply for an ecclesiastical tribunal to examine the circumstances. If it is agreed that the marriage is void, then both partners are free to marry (not 'remarry') but each must ensure that any obligations to their partner are fulfilled.

If an annulment cannot be obtained, two options remain: reconciliation or separation. If a couple decide to separate they still remain married in the eyes of the Church and are not free to remarry or to have sexual relationships with other partners. If a couple decides to have a civil divorce this does not affect the sacramental bond that has been forged by the Church's ceremony, although Roman Catholic teaching states that such a state can be 'tolerated'. It is not inherently immoral and can be an appropriate way to guarantee legal rights – for example to property or to having access to one's children. However, unless there is a formal annulment or dissolution of one's marriage, any new union is not regarded as valid. Having sexual relationships with anyone other than one's first spouse constitutes adultery and bars one from receiving the sacraments or from holding any office in the church. Divorcees are nonetheless encouraged to attend the Mass, to hear God's word there and to endeavour to live a Christian life. If they are penitent, do penance for their sin and undertake to accept a life of continence within any new civil marriage, they can be reinstated and receive the holy bread and wine once more.

In the Protestant tradition divorce is viewed somewhat more leniently. Although splitting up is a matter of regret, there are no sanctions attached to it. If a partner is guilty of an offence such as adultery, then of course this would attract severe disapproval, although Christianity preaches forgiveness and reconciliation. Divorced couples may continue to receive the sacrament and divorce normally presents no bar to holding office in a congregation or from seeking ordination as a member of the clergy.

Are Christian marriages more stable?

> Researchers frequently postulate a strong relationship between religiosity and marital stability ... While no single dimension of religiosity adequately describes the effect of religious experience on marital stability, the frequency of religious attendance has the greatest positive impact on marital stability. When both spouses attend church regularly, the couple has the lowest risk of divorce. Spouse differences in church attendance increase the risk of dissolution. All significant religious affiliation influences disappear once demographic characteristics are controlled. The wife's religious beliefs concerning marital commitment and nonmarital sex are more important to the stability of the marriage than the husband's beliefs.
>
> (Vaughn R. A. Call and Tim B. Heaton (1997), 'Religious Influence on Marital Stability', *Journal for the Scientific Study of Religion* 3(2), pp. 382–92)

One would like to be able to say that the Christian faith made marriage more stable and that substantially fewer Christian marriages failed. Unfortunately statistics prove otherwise. In a survey carried out in 2008 by George Barna Research – an organization that carries out surveys on a wide variety of religious issues – some 33 per cent of the US population (Christian and non-Christian) who have been married at least once have become divorced. The statistics for Christians are little different: 34 per cent of married Protestants have undergone a divorce, although Roman Catholics fare somewhat better, with 28 per cent of married Catholics divorcing. This compares with 30 per cent of married atheists and agnostics who become divorced. 'Born again' Christians (those who have personally committed themselves to Jesus Christ and expect to enter heaven after death) are no different: again 33 per cent. There appears to be less correlation between Christianity and divorce rates than other social factors, such as social status and ethnicity. Only 22 per cent of married 'upscale' Americans (those with a college education, earning over $20,000 annually) are divorced, compared with 39 per cent 'downscale'. Only 20 per cent of married Asians were divorced, and 38 per cent of those 'associated with other faiths'.[1] Bradley Wright, a sociologist at the University of Connecticut, paints a slightly brighter overall picture of the US scene, claiming that the average divorce rate in the United States is 50 per cent, compared with 42 per cent among Christians. Wright questions Barna's approach, which uses broad categories such as 'evangelical' and 'born again'. Wright's contention is that these broad affiliations have less to do with marital stability and divorce than more specific forms of religious behaviour such as church attendance. He claims that of evangelical Christians who rarely attend church, some 60 per cent of those who have been married have also been divorced, compared with 38 per cent who attend regularly. Brad Wilcox of the National Marriage Project at the University of Virginia claims that those who attend Christian worship regularly – several times a month – are 35 per cent less likely to divorce compared with those without

---

1 www.barna.org/barna-update/article/15-familykids/42-new-marriage-and-divorce-statistics-released. Accessed 27 April 2012.

a religious affiliation, but that 'nominal Christians' are 20 per cent more likely to divorce than the religiously unaffiliated.[2]

Whatever the statistics suggest, Christians recognize that lasting marriages and stable loving families are the ideal, and the Church has therefore made attempts to reduce divorce and to strengthen the marriage bond. One initiative is to ensure that couples receive appropriate preparation for marriage. The Roman Catholic Church insists that couples undergo a preparatory course reminding them of the sacramental nature of marriage, the seriousness of the vows they are making and the commitment into which they are entering. Other denominations organize seminars for couples, encouraging them to reflect on their motives for getting married, how they might prepare for their weddings (practically, emotionally and spiritually) and how they ought to respect each other and deal with disharmonies that are bound to arise at least occasionally. In most churches a wedding couple can at least expect an informal interview with the priest or minister who will conduct the ceremony, or a pastoral visit in which guidance is offered to promote a successful marriage. At a later stage if things are going wrong with a marriage, a priest or minister will provide counselling in an attempt to rescue precarious matrimonial relationships.

A rather different attempt, initiated from the Protestant tradition, is the idea of 'covenant marriage'. This was piloted in three US states, beginning in 1997 when the state of Louisiana passed a law enabling couples to choose between two types of marriage. Instead of the conventional marriage contract, which allows divorce on the grounds of 'irreconcilable differences', a couple entering into a covenant marriage agree to be legally bound only to seek a divorce where there is 'fault'. Examples of fault would be adultery, committing a serious felony, deserting one's spouse or sexual or physical abuse of a family member. Following Louisiana's initiative, Arizona passed similar legislation in 1998, Arkansas following suit in 2001. Supporters of the new law no doubt hoped that couples would make serious and binding commitments to each other and that the increased difficulty of divorce that resulted from a more stringent contract would cause them to

---

2 www.usatoday.com/news/religion/2011-03-14-divorce-christians_N.htm.

reflect carefully on the commitment each was making, and make dissolution of marriage less likely. Such supporters may have had high hopes about cementing the marriage bond but unfortunately they were disappointed – covenant marriage proved tremendously unpopular. On its inception only around 2 per cent of couples in Louisiana elected to enter into a covenant marriage; in Arizona it proved even less popular, only 0.25 per cent of couples taking up the option; and by the first half of 2003 in Arkansas only 0.04 per cent of marriages were covenant marriages.

Roman Catholicism and divorce

> Today there are numerous Catholics in many countries who have recourse to civil divorce and contract new civil unions. In fidelity to the words of Jesus Christ – 'Whoever divorces his wife and marries another, commits adultery against her; and if she divorces her husband and marries another, she commits adultery' – the Church maintains that a new union cannot be recognized as valid, if the first marriage was. If the divorced are remarried civilly, they find themselves in a situation that objectively contravenes God's law. Consequently, they cannot receive Eucharistic communion as long as this situation persists. For the same reason, they cannot exercise certain ecclesial responsibilities. Reconciliation through the sacrament of Penance can be granted only to those who have repented for having violated the sign of the covenant and of fidelity to Christ, and who are committed to living in complete continence …
>
> The remarriage of persons divorced from a living, lawful spouse contravenes the plan and law of God as taught by Christ. They are not separated from the Church, but they cannot receive Eucharistic communion. They will lead Christian lives especially by educating their children in the faith …
>
> The Church teaches that the separation of spouses while maintaining the marriage bond can be legitimate in certain cases. The Catechism states: 'If civil divorce remains the only possible way of ensuring certain legal rights, the care of the children, or the

> protection of inheritance, it can be tolerated and does not constitute a moral offence.
>
> (*Catechism of the Catholic Church*, 1650, 1665, 2383)

Superficially the Roman Catholic Church's position on divorce seems straightforward: marriage is for life and there is no such thing as divorce. As with most matters in religion, the situation is much more complex. This seemingly straightforward position applies exclusively to 'sacramental marriage', that is, the joining of a baptized man and woman within the Roman Church's marriage ceremony. Theologically the man and woman have 'become one flesh' and the marriage is a three-way relationship between God, the husband and the wife. As Jesus said, 'So they are no longer two but one flesh. What therefore God has joined together, let not man put asunder' (Matt. 19.6). Although human actions can make a couple unable to live together, they cannot dissolve this bond that God has created through the Church's sacrament. The only way a couple can extricate themselves from such a union is to seek an annulment, by means of which the Church certifies that no sacramental marriage ever took place. This is not a divorce but an acknowledgement that there never was a marriage: it is null and void. A sacramental marriage is null and void if one or more of the following conditions hold: at least one partner was not baptized, had entered holy orders, was already married, was under age (defined as 14 years for a woman, 16 for a man), is a blood relation up to the fourth degree, has a spiritual relationship such as being a godparent, or if the marriage has not been consummated.

These conditions apply to 'sacramental marriage' but there is a different type of marriage: 'natural marriage'. A natural marriage is considered a 'valid' marriage and may or may not take place within a Catholic church. Although it is not particularly favoured, the permission for a 'mixed marriage' to take place in church is often regarded as the lesser of two evils since it prevents the couple from marrying outside the Church. The Roman Catholic Church does acknowledge the validity of civil marriages and marriages of another denomination. These are not sacramental marriages but they are nonetheless regarded as serious commitments: if one partner had an affair with a third party, this would be regarded as adulterous and hence gravely sinful. However, being non-sacramental, such marriages can be 'dissolved' under certain conditions, known as the Pauline and the Petrine privileges.

The Pauline privilege is so-called because it is based on Paul's teaching on marriage:

> To the rest I say, not the Lord, that if any brother has a wife who is an unbeliever, and she consents to live with him, he should not divorce her. If any woman has a husband who is an unbeliever, and he consents to live with her, she should not divorce him ... But if the unbelieving partner desires to separate, let it be so; in such a case the brother or sister is not bound. For God has called us to peace. (1 Cor. 7.12–15)

However, only the unbelieving partner may initiate the marriage's breakup. If the unbeliever instigates civil divorce proceedings then the believer has grounds for exercising the Pauline privilege and applying for dissolution. He or she is then free to remarry and to have a subsequent marriage consecrated in church as a sacramental marriage. The original partner's grievance, however, must relate to the spouse's Catholic faith; the Pauline convention cannot be exercised on the grounds that the partner has committed adultery or been physically or mentally abusive. To obtain a dissolution under the Pauline privilege, an application must be filed with the diocese. The case is then investigated by a tribunal, who receive statements from the partners and may call witnesses. At the time of writing, the number of dissolutions granted in the United States is in excess of 60,000 a year.

The exercise of the Petrine privilege is much rarer. This applies to a marriage where one partner is unbaptized and has remained so throughout the marriage, but the marriage has broken down and the baptized partner is not at fault. If the believing partner then wishes to marry a Catholic, he or she can apply for a dissolution. An application of this kind cannot be dealt with locally but can only be granted by the Pope himself. The name 'Petrine privilege' is given since the Pope is regarded as the successor of Saint Peter, to whom Jesus gave the authority to be the custodian of his Church (Matt. 16.18).

Celebrating divorce?

In the past divorce has often been regarded as a stigma, a mark of marital failure and even something to be ashamed of. It is often surrounded by animosity, at least one partner feeling that he or she has been wronged by the other. Disputes over ownership of possessions, custody battles and alimony payments are commonplace. Increasingly, however, there are those who take a more positive view of divorce, regarding it as ground for celebration. It marks the end of an unfortunate relationship and is the beginning of a new life, either on one's own or with a new partner. At a secular level, card shops have already attempted to market divorce cards, and divorce parties are gaining in popularity. Although these attempts at celebrating divorce emphasize its positive aspects, they frequently underscore the old grudges and resentments that existed in the former marriage. Card messages like, 'Congratulations – you've got rid of the creep!' do little to promote the more Christian values of love and forgiveness. A quick browse on the internet revealed photographs of 'divorce cakes' displaying an effigy of the husband, stabbed to death by his former partner and with red icing flowing down the tiers of cake to simulate blood.

Might it be possible for Christians to celebrate divorce in a way that is dignified, forgiving and non-spiteful? A small but growing number of Christians have sought to place their divorce within a religious framework and participate in a religious 'divorce ceremony'. Since divorce is now such a widespread phenomenon, it could be argued that for many it is a life-cycle event that is appropriately marked by a religious rite of passage. Where a couple has entered into marriage by means of a religious ceremony, their marriage is a religious as well as a civil phenomenon, yet usually a divorce is a purely civil matter. Ought not divorcing couples therefore seek to end their marriage in a religious as well as a civil way?

Already the United Methodist Church and the United Church of Christ have pioneered liturgies for the dissolution of a marriage, and for many years – outside the mainstream – Unitarian churches have offered ceremonies for divorcing couples. Since there is no historical tradition of such services, a religious divorce ritual can be tailored to meet the needs of the participants. Essentially such ceremonies serve a variety of purposes. First, they make divorce a matter of open acknowledgement rather than embarrassment, eliciting the support of friends, family and congregation. Second, since divorces can frequently be acrimonious, the emphasis of such services is on love, forgiveness and peace. The presence of one's children can underline the fact that they are still cared for despite the marital breakup. The ceremony acknowledges the good times in the marriage – of which there were usually many – as well as the bad ones. The service can involve one partner or both. Where both partners are present, ritual elements relating to the marriage ceremony can be incorporated, such as the giving back of wedding rings or declarations in which the 'I do' of the marriage ceremony is replaced by 'I'm sorry'. Another ritual suggested by the United Methodist Church is the presence of three candles on the altar: one is already burning before the commencement of the ceremony and is extinguished during the service, whereupon the two remaining separate candles are lit. Prayers are said and readings from the Bible might include passages relating to marriage or stories emphasizing forgiveness and reconciliation. Celebrating communion is a recommended component. The commensality involved in sharing this symbolic meal underscores the wish that, despite the dissolution of one's marriage, all parties involved nonetheless remain part of Christ's family who can share fellowship together. Concerning his own divorce in 1986, the controversial Bishop of New Hampshire, Gene Robinson, recounts:

> We tried to do the dissolution in a very holy way. We took a priest with us to the judge's chambers for the decree and went back to his church. In the context of the holy Eucharist we released each other from the vows we had taken, asked each other's forgiveness for ways in which we might have hurt one another, pledged ourselves to the joint raising of our children

and gave our rings back as a symbol of the vows we no longer held each other to. It was one of the most healing moments of my whole life.[3]

As one might expect, such liturgical innovations are controversial. Critics see it as the Church's sanctioning of divorce and a degradation of marriage. Can a bride and groom really take a vow at their wedding ceremony that commits them to a lifelong bond, when another ceremony is available to sever it? The availability of such a rite may cause spouses to take their wedding vows less seriously and to regard marriage as a disposable rather than an enduring relationship.

Divorce and polygamy

> This Conference upholds monogamy as God's plan, and as the ideal relationship of love between husband and wife; nevertheless recommends that a polygamist who responds to the Gospel and wishes to join the Anglican Church may be baptized and confirmed with his believing wives and children on the following conditions: (1) that the polygamist shall promise not to marry again as long as any of his wives at the time of his conversion are alive; (2) that the receiving of such a polygamist has the consent of the local Anglican community; (3) that such a polygamist shall not be compelled to put away any of his wives, on account of the social deprivation they would suffer; (4) and recommends that provinces where the Churches face problems of polygamy are encouraged to share information of their pastoral approach to Christians who become polygamists so that the most appropriate way of disciplining and pastoring them can be found, and that the ACC be requested to facilitate the sharing of that information.
>
> (Lambeth Conference, 1988)

---

[3] www.scotsman.com/news/millions-believe-this-man-is-the-antichrist-1-910905.

Christianity is a constantly changing religion and has continually faced challenges as it has moved to different cultures. One thorny issue it has faced on entering Africa is the question of polygamy. Throughout its history Christianity has presupposed that marriage will be between one man and one woman. However, in several African countries, polygamy – or perhaps more accurately, polygyny – has been practised for many generations. While any religion can set its own rules for its hearers to accept or reject, a catechumen with several wives presented the Christian missionaries with a fait accompli. The missionaries during the colonial period took a firm stance: polygamy is sinful, and the Christian faith involves abandoning sin and following Christ. Hence to be eligible for baptism and receiving the Eucharist, the would-be convert must give up all but one of his wives, sending away the others and divorcing them. Some African churches took the view that polygamous converts could attend worship but could not have any leadership role or even a more modest position such as singing in the church choir. In many cases they were barred from receiving the sacrament.

Unsurprisingly the question of whether the new convert should divorce his 'surplus wives' is contentious. Wives and families who had been sent away in such circumstances faced obvious economic problems. Some returned to their parental homes, having lost face and status. Some entered a new polygamous marriage while others were reduced to prostitution. As has been mentioned throughout my discussion of Christian marriage and family life, it is a fundamental obligation for a Christian to provide for his or her family, and hence forcing a new convert to abandon such obligations runs counter to the key principles of love and compassion. In some cases polygamous converts continued to provide for additional wives and families by merely pretending to have given them up. They might give them new accommodation at a distance from their former home, perhaps housing them on the edge of the village. The price of compassion was deception and often caused other unconverted villagers to scorn the missionaries.

As African Christians grew in their understanding of the faith, many came to question whether monogamy is in fact a prerequisite of accepting Christianity. The practice is nowhere explicitly condemned in the Bible, and many of the key figures in the Old Testament had polygamous marriages. King Solomon is recorded as having 700 wives and 300 concubines (1 Kings 11.3) and is never taken to task for this. The practice is never mentioned in the New Testament. The one and only apparent requirement of monogamy is found in the instructions to Timothy about the qualities of a congregation's overseer: 'Now the overseer must be above reproach, the husband of but one wife' (1 Tim. 3.2). This instruction raises an array of questions. If the overseer may only have one wife, does this mean his congregation might be allowed more? Does the instruction imply that a polygamous convert could be admitted to the Christian faith but would be ineligible for any office within the congregation? Or does it simply mean that overseers should be married rather than unmarried?

Christians who oppose polygamy have pointed out that although the practice is not explicitly proscribed (except for the congregation's leader), the fact that it is mentioned in the Bible does not mean that it is acceptable. The Genesis story of Adam and Eve presupposes a one-to-one relationship between a husband and wife. God says that Adam needs 'a helper', not several, and that a man will be 'united to his wife', not 'wives' (Gen. 2.18, 24). In response to a question on divorce, Jesus recounts the story of Adam and Eve and uses the expression, 'the two will become one flesh' (Matt. 19.5), not 'the three' or 'the four'. As we noted in a previous chapter, Christian theology regards human marriage as analogous to God's relationship to his people – the Church – which again is a one-to-one relationship.

African Christians have found no easy solution to the problem. The mission-founded churches have tended to take an unsympathetic stance towards polygamy, while the African-Instituted Churches (AICs) do not want their polygamous members to be treated as second-class citizens. Many of the latter ask why the remedy for polygamy, which the Bible does not explicitly condemn, should be divorce, which Jesus did condemn. One would not expect partners in other 'irregular marriages' to divorce: for example, if a same-sex couple had undergone a ceremony to seal their relationship, a church would not require them to dissolve it although, as previously mentioned, conservative Christians would demand that they be celibate.

The preference for monogamy, many argue, is a cultural rather than a religious one and reflects western imperialism from which Africa has emerged. Conventions change: Christianity's stance on slavery and on usury have altered, so why not monogamy? Is polygamy really so bad? At the Lambeth Conference in 1988, it was stated that: 'It has long been recognized in the Anglican Communion that polygamy in parts of Africa, and traditional marriage, do genuinely have features of both faithfulness and righteousness.' The World Council of Churches, however, continues to exclude churches with polygamous leaders. In 1998 the Celestial Church of Christ, an AIC that allows polygamy among its clergy, applied for membership but was advised that it could not gain admission unless it changed this policy. In 2008 the Lambeth Conference passed a further resolution affirming that polygamy was sinful, excluding polygamists from holy orders and leadership roles and prohibiting new converts from marrying additional wives. Across the churches the issue remains highly contentious, with no sign of any agreed policy.

Islam

> A *hadith* of the Prophet Muhammad says:
>
> Of all the things that are permitted, divorce is the most hated by God.
>
> (Abu Dawud)

Talaq *or unilateral divorce*

As already noted, although marriage is encouraged in Islam it is very much a worldly agreement rather than a sacrament; it is not a holy and indissoluble union. The partners in a marriage should enter matrimony with the intention of it being a permanent bond, but Islam recognizes that discord and irreconcilable differences may arise. Divorce is permitted where the spouses cannot find a way to continue their married life together. Where marital problems occur it is considered to be the responsibility of the family and the community to support the couple and to attempt to solve the problems.

> And if you fear dissension between the two, send an arbitrator from his people and an arbitrator from her people. If they both desire reconciliation, Allah will cause it between them. Indeed, Allah is ever Knowing and Acquainted with all things.
>
> (Qur'an 4.35)

If a breakdown of the marriage is feared, an arbitrator should be nominated from each of the two families to try to bring about reconciliation, but if this fails then divorce may be the practical way to minimize the harm to both parties. In many Islamic jurisdictions, including the Personal Status laws of most of the Arab countries, there is provision for arbitration and conciliation.

Although divorce is undesirable, Islamic law gives the husband the right to pronounce divorce unilaterally. Some of the jurists consider that this is a licence rather than a right, to be used only where absolutely necessary, but in fact there are no legal restrictions to a man's power to divorce his wife at any time and for any or for no reason. It is, however, required that he should be of sound mind at the time of the pronouncement. He should not be intoxicated, confused, enraged or under duress, nor may the divorce be pronounced as conditional or suspended either upon the performance or avoidance of some other action either by the wife or by a third party. At one end of the scale this means that a husband may not use this as a form of control, for example, 'if you speak to your sister, you are divorced', and at the other it means that grand rhetoric, such as an oath pronounced before a guest, 'may I be three times divorced, if you do not stay for dinner with us tonight', does not actually have the legal effect of bringing about a divorce where there was never any real intention for this.

The term for unilateral divorce is *talaq*, which means releasing or letting go. It is often translated as repudiation. Sura 65, entitled Al-Talaq, gives considerable detail on the legal requirements for the pronouncement of unilateral divorce and the behaviour expected in the exercise of this. Injunctions and guidance exist in other Suras, notably Sura 2, Al-Baqara. The process of unilateral divorce takes different forms: *talaq hasan* (approved divorce), *talaq ahsan* (most approved divorce) and *talaq al-bid'a* (innovative divorce – in that it is believed to employ a deviant understanding of the threefold divorce).

Unilateral divorce should be pronounced during a period of *tuhr* or purity, while the wife is not menstruating and where no intercourse has taken place since the last menstruation. Following this the wife is required to observe the *'idda* or waiting period, during which the divorce is considered revocable and the husband has the right to take his wife back with or without her consent and without any kind of formal procedure, either verbally by expressing his decision or simply by resuming normal marital relations. Until the waiting period is completed, the wife is still under his marital authority and may not refuse the resumption of married life. The Qur'an is clear, however, that this should not be used to harm or manipulate the wife.

> And when you divorce women and they have [nearly] fulfilled their term, either retain them according to acceptable terms or release them according to acceptable terms, and do not keep them, intending harm, to transgress [against them]. And whoever does that has certainly wronged himself. (Qur'an 2.231)

She is not considered divorced until the waiting period is completed and is, therefore, not permitted to marry another man during this time. If the husband does not take the wife back during this time, the divorce will be *talaq ba'in baynuna sughra* or the lesser irrevocable divorce. This terminates the marriage, and the divorced wife is then entitled to receive her deferred dower and is free to remarry. Thereafter the partners may remarry each other, but this will have to be by a new contract, and a new dower will be required. The husband may only divorce his wife this way twice and still be permitted to marry her again: 'Divorce is twice. Then, either keep [her] in an acceptable manner or release [her] with good treatment' (Qur'an 2.229).

If this is repeated a third time it will be considered to be *talaq ba'in baynuna kubra* or greater irrevocable divorce. This form of divorce is known as *talaq ahsan*, being a divorce conducted according to proper procedure. In this case the partners will be prohibited permanently from marrying each other unless the wife subsequently marries another man in a legitimate consummated marriage and is widowed or divorced.

> And if he has divorced her [for the third time], then she is not lawful to him afterward until [after] she marries a husband other than him. And if the latter husband divorces her [or dies], there is no blame upon the woman and her former husband for returning to each other if they think that they can keep [within] the limits of Allah. (Qur'an 2.230)

Talaq hasan is also completed by three consecutive pronouncements of divorce, but these must be in three consecutive periods of *tuhr* between menstrual periods, during which overall time frame intercourse has not taken place. Upon completion of these three pronouncements and the observation of the *'idda* following the final pronouncement, the marriage is dissolved irrevocably and the couple will be forbidden to remarry unless the wife has subsequently married another man as described above.

A form of divorce that is strongly disapproved of but nevertheless recognized as legal in some Islamic countries is the triple divorce whereby the husband pronounces the divorce formula three times in succession on a single occasion, thereby effecting an immediate irrevocable divorce. This is referred to as *talaq al-bid'a* and is generally frowned upon as being contrary to the intention of the Shari'a. In the legislation of several countries where registration of a divorce is required, it is stipulated that the court will only record it as a single divorce.

If a husband divorces his wife before consummation of the marriage the divorce is immediately irrevocable. Divorce may be pronounced verbally by the husband himself or by a person whom he authorizes to do this (for instance if the spouses are not in the same country), or it may be conducted in writing. Most Muslim countries today require divorce to be conducted formally before a *qadi* or notary or registered with the courts. In the last decade or so there has been controversy in several Muslim countries with regard to the validity of divorce effected by email or SMS. Judges in Saudi Arabia, Dubai and Malaysia have accepted divorces by text message whereas other countries such as Singapore have expressly forbidden it.

It would be a mistake to think, however, that all cases of *talaq* or unilateral divorce are simply the action of the husband against the will of the wife. In many cases it may simply be that the marriage has broken down irretrievably and the couple have agreed to divorce, in which case the pronouncement of the divorce formula by the husband is simply a matter of procedure. There are also certain other circumstances in which divorce takes place where it is effected by means of the *talaq*, including cases where the husband is required to do so by a judge or in compliance with law. This will be discussed below.

There are other provisions by which a divorce may be sought or effected by either or both parties.

Women's access to divorce

The methods by which a wife may seek divorce are more limited. Both parties have the right to stipulate additional conditions to the marriage contract, provided these do not contradict or conflict with the Shari'a in overall terms or as it applies to marriage, and the bride may stipulate that she should have the right to terminate the marriage, although this is obviously subject to the husband's agreement at the time of the contract. She may also set other conditions, such as that she should be entitled to a divorce without prejudice to her marital financial rights if the husband takes another wife or if he asks her to emigrate or move away from her hometown with him. In reality, however, these scenarios are uncommon.

A wife may seek dissolution of the marriage by a *qadi* on grounds of injury if her husband mistreats or abuses her, whether physically or psychologically. In some jurisdictions the wife may be able to prove to a judge that she has suffered significant emotional and psychological harm by her husband taking a further wife and thereby obtain a judicial divorce. Wilful and persistent failure to pay maintenance or imprisonment of the husband for an extended period are further possible grounds, as is significant mental or physical defect in the husband that the wife was unaware of at the time of the contract, including impotence.

A further form of access to divorce for women that is supported by the Qur'an is *khul'*, sometimes referred to as *mubara'a*.

> And it is not lawful for you to take anything of what you have given them unless both fear that they will not be able to keep [within] the limits of Allah. But if you fear that they will not keep [within] the limits of Allah, then there is no blame upon either of them concerning that by which she ransoms herself. (Qur'an 2.29)

There are reports in the *hadith* that support this:

> A woman came to the Prophet Muhammad seeking the dissolution of her marriage, she told the Prophet that she did not have any complaints against her husband's character or manners. Her only problem was that she honestly did not like him to the extent of not being able to live with him any longer. The Prophet asked her: 'Would you give him his garden (the marriage gift he had given her) back?' she said: 'Yes'. The Prophet then instructed the man to take back his garden and accept the dissolution of the marriage.

Believed to originate in a pre-Islamic system of divorce, *khul'*, meaning detaching, uprooting or taking off, is a process by which a wife may free herself from an unhappy marriage, without having to give grounds or prove any fault or injury, by waiving all of her financial rights and compensating her husband, usually by repaying any dower she has received. This is, however, subject to the agreement of the husband. Reformers in several countries have attempted to develop this into a formal workable system to enable women to free themselves from intolerable marriages where their husbands are unwilling to divorce them, particularly where this is because of the financial implications. The Egyptian legislature introduced a law permitting and regulating *khul'* in 2000, in an attempt to provide relief to the thousands of women whose petitions to the courts for divorce are delayed sometimes by years in an overworked judicial system. On the surface it appears to offer the possibility of speeding up the process and avoiding the distress and expense involved in lengthy court proceedings, but in reality it is an option available only to the privileged few who are able to afford it. It involves sacrificing financial rights to which a woman otherwise may be legitimately entitled, and there is always the possibility that a man who wishes to divorce his wife but does not want to pay the deferred dower or maintenance may make life so unbearable for her that she requests *khul'* in desperation. This is specifically forbidden:

> And do not make difficulties for them in order to take [back] part of what you gave them unless they commit a clear immorality. And how could you take it while you have gone in unto each other and they have taken from you a solemn covenant? (Qur'an 4.20–1)

Some archaic and obscure forms of divorce

There are other procedures recognized by the Shari'a by which a marriage may be terminated, although these are virtually obsolete. In the process of *li'an*, mutual imprecation (referred to in Chapter 1), a husband who believes that his wife has been unfaithful but cannot meet the standard of proof required by the Shari'a could accuse her of adultery and, where relevant, deny paternity of a child whether newborn or unborn. He is required to take four oaths in the name of God that he is telling the truth and then invoke God's wrath upon himself if he is not. The wife then takes four oaths that her husband is lying and that she is truthful, and then invokes God's wrath upon herself if he is telling the truth. In this way husband and wife avert the penalties for slander and adultery respectively. The jurists differ as to whether the marriage is automatically dissolved in this way, but intercourse between the husband and wife is prohibited with immediate effect. Certain schools require the *qadi* (judge) to call upon the husband to divorce his wife, and if he refuses the *qadi* himself will dissolve the marriage. If the husband then withdraws his accusation the marriage will continue, but the husband will be liable for the Shari'a penalty of 80 lashes for slander of a virtuous woman. According to other schools, the marriage is automatically dissolved as soon as both spouses have sworn the oaths. In either case the divorce that results from *li'an* is irrevocable.

In the process of *ila* a husband swears an oath not to have intercourse with his wife for a period of four months or more. 'For those who swear not to have sexual relations with their wives is a waiting time of four months, but if they return [to normal relations] – then indeed, Allah is Forgiving and Merciful' (Qur'an 2.226). If he then resumes marital relations with her before this period has expired, he is required to make expiation (*kaffara*) for breaking an oath. If he fulfils the oath and does not resume marital relations, some jurists are of the opinion that the marriage is dissolved automatically. Others consider that the wife is entitled to apply to a *qadi*, who will order the husband to resume marital relations or divorce her, and if the husband does not comply then the *qadi* will pronounce the divorce on his behalf.

Zihar is a process in which the husband compares his wife to his mother, sister or any of his female relatives who are forbidden to him in marriage. This is a pre-Islamic custom, and while the Qur'an expresses clear disapproval of it, it is nevertheless recognized. 'Those who pronounce *zihar* among you [to separate] from their wives – they are not [consequently] their mothers. Their mothers are none but those who gave birth to them. And indeed, they are saying an objectionable statement and a falsehood. But indeed, Allah is Pardoning and Forgiving' (Qur'an 58.2).

In *zihar*, the man will use an expression such as, 'You are to me like my mother's back (*zahr*)'. The effect of *zihar* is that the husband is forbidden to have sexual relations with his wife until he has made expiation for this by fasting for two months or by feeding 60 poor people (or, archaically, by freeing a slave). If the husband does not make expiation, the wife may refuse marital relations and this will not be considered to be marital disobedience. She will not be entitled to dissolution of the marriage in these circumstances. If the husband continues to refrain from sexual relations, according to some of the jurists when four months have elapsed this will effectively be *ila,* and the marriage will therefore be dissolved.

Consequences of divorce including custody and guardianship

Divorce entails a range of material and moral consequences, many of which are specified clearly in the Qur'an. The first of these is the *'idda* or waiting period during which the wife is technically still under the marital authority of the husband. She is not permitted to marry another man until this is completed. This is considered to be the right of the husband which, apart from being a form of cooling-off period during which reconciliation is possible after the first two divorces, ensures that if the woman is pregnant there is no doubt regarding paternity. The rights of the woman and the child are also protected in this way as paternity, and the rights and protections that it entails, cannot be denied. The duration of the waiting period is the completion of three menstrual cycles or, for women who do not menstruate, three months of the Islamic calendar. If the wife is pregnant at the time of the divorce, the waiting period is until she gives birth (or miscarries).

> Divorced women remain in waiting for three periods, and it is not lawful for them to conceal what Allah has created in their wombs if they believe in Allah and the Last Day. And their husbands have more right to take them back in this [period] if they want reconciliation. (Qur'an 2.228)

> And those who no longer expect menstruation among your women – if you doubt, then their period is three months, and [also for] those who have not menstruated. And for those who are pregnant, their term is until they give birth. (Qur'an 65.4)

DIVORCE

The husband is required to house and maintain the woman during the waiting period, provided they remain chaste during this time.

> O Prophet, when you [Muslims] divorce women, divorce them for [the commencement of] their waiting period and keep count of the waiting period, and fear Allah, your Lord. Do not turn them out of their [husbands'] houses, nor should they [themselves] leave [during that period] unless they are committing a clear immorality. (Qur'an 65.1)

The wife is under no obligation to suckle her infant child, but if she does so then the husband is required to provide her with maintenance during the period of suckling, which is deemed to be up to two years. The emphasis in the Qur'anic verse in which this is set out appears to be on ensuring an amicable agreement in which the child is cared for and does not become a pawn in any dispute between the parents.

> Mothers may suckle their children two complete years for whoever wishes to complete the nursing [period]. Upon the father is the mothers' provision and their clothing according to what is acceptable. No person is charged with more than his capacity. No mother should be harmed through her child, and no father through his child. And upon the [father's] heir is [a duty] like that [of the father]. And if they both desire weaning through mutual consent from both of them and consultation, there is no blame upon either of them. And if you wish to have your children nursed by a substitute, there is no blame upon you as long as you give payment according to what is acceptable. And fear Allah and know that Allah is Seeing of what you do. (Qur'an 2.233)

The completion of the waiting period following either of the forms of irrevocable divorce makes the husband liable to pay the deferred portion of the dower immediately.

In the case of divorce before consummation, if the dower has been agreed upon he must give her half of it as compensation. If it has not been agreed upon he must give her a gift of appropriate value.

There is no blame on you if you divorce women before consummation or the fixing of their dower, but bestow on them a suitable gift, the wealthy according to his means and the poor according to his means. A gift of a reasonable amount is due from those who wish to do the right thing also.

And if you divorce them before you have touched them and you have already specified for them an obligation, then [give] half of what you specified – unless they forego the right or the one in whose hand is the marriage contract foregoes it. And to forego it is nearer to righteousness. And do not forget graciousness between you. (Qur'an 2.236–7)

In this case no waiting period is required as it is as if the marriage had never existed and there is no chance of pregnancy.

O you who believe, when you marry believing women and then divorce them before you have touched them, no period of 'idda shall you have with regard to them, so give them a gift and release them in a handsome manner. (Qur'an 33.49)

In addition to this, however, many of the jurists are agreed that in the case where a husband uses his right of divorce arbitrarily due to no cause on the part of his wife and without her consent, she should be given compensation, referred to as *mut'at at-talaq*: 'And for divorced women is a provision according to what is acceptable – a duty upon the righteous' (Qur'an 2.241). Some scholars are of the opinion that this verse refers to the specified or appropriate dower and that the husband is under no further financial duty towards her, whereas others consider it to be an additional obligation. It has been incorporated into the divorce law of a number of Muslim countries and the amount, if not agreed upon, is assessed by a court.

Moreover if the husband divorces his wife simply because he wishes to marry someone else, he is forbidden to take back any gifts he has given to her: 'But if you want to replace one wife with another and you have given one of them a great amount [in gifts], do not take [back] from it anything. Would you take it in injustice and manifest sin?' (Qur'an 2.20).

In the Shari'a there are two categories of responsibility for the welfare of a child. The first is guardianship (*wilaya*), which entails overall authority and responsibility for decision-making in the upbringing and education of the child, oversight of his or her physical, religious, moral and educational well-being and development and management of his or her money and property. This is normally vested in the father or his authorized trustee or the paternal grandfather or his authorized trustee. The second category is custody (*hadana*), which entails residence, day-to-day care of the child and responsibility for his or her physical, religious, moral and educational well-being and development. This is normally vested in the mother during early childhood, or if she is deceased, unfit, unable or unwilling to care for the child, the order of entitlement to custody is then the maternal grandmother, followed by the paternal grandmother with the father being fourth in line. There are no specific references to custody in the Qur'an but there are several references in the *hadith*:

> A woman came to the Messenger of God and said: 'O messenger of God, verily my son here was in my womb, my breasts gave him milk, and from my lap he gets affection. His father divorced me and he wants to take him away from me'. He [the Messenger] said: 'You are most entitled to him if you do not remarry'. (Reported by Abu Dawud)
>
> In a separate report a woman came to the Prophet saying 'my husband wants to take away my son, who has helped me and provided me with drinking water from Abu Inaba's well'. Then her husband came and the Prophet said: 'Boy, this is your father and this is your mother, so take whoever of them you wish by the hand.' He took his mother's hand and she went away with him. (Abu Dawud)

In the second *hadith* the child is old enough to perform tasks such as fetching water and therefore old enough to be asked his opinion in the matter. On the basis of these *hadith*, the mother's right of custody is traditionally considered to continue to the age of seven years or until seven for a boy and until puberty for a girl, although the legislatures of several Muslim countries have set higher age limits to this. Thereafter some scholars consider that the child is entitled to choose whom he wishes to live with, while others insist that custody reverts to the father.

Both of these roles are dependent on the guardian or custodian being deemed competent and morally fit to fulfil them, and with regard to custody certain other provisions apply concerning the composition of the household of the female custodian – for example, in the case of a daughter where there is a male cousin or other relative who is not within the degrees of relationship that prohibit marriage. If the mother remarries, the father will be entitled to remove the children from her custody. It is considered generally unacceptable for children to live in a home with a man who is not their father, although this may be tolerated where the father is deceased. In any case, both guardianship and custody are intended to be primarily in the interests of the child, and any judicial decisions in relation to custody must take this into account.

Overview and contemporary legislation

Overall, divorce rates among Muslims are relatively low. For most Muslims marriage represents a commitment to the founding of a family, which is considered to be a sounder basis for living than romantic love alone. On this basis the majority of Muslims will consider the impact on family and the wider social implications before seeking divorce.

For a woman, being a divorcee carries a degree of stigma and many women will tolerate extreme marital difficulties rather than be divorced, and their families may encourage them in this. This may even extend to preferring that their husbands take a second wife rather than divorce them. In addition to the shame involved they risk losing custody of their children once they reach a certain age and at any age if they remarry. In some close-knit traditional communities marriages often consolidate alliances, and their dissolution may bring shame upon the families.

It is a normal expectation that a woman who is divorced will return to her family, whatever her age and professional status. It is not generally acceptable for a divorced woman, like any other single woman, to live alone. In many cases, however, particularly in modern urban society, a divorced woman who has custody of children may remain in the family home. This may depend on local legislation and the ruling of a judge.

There is no restriction or disapproval of remarriage once a woman has completed her *'idda*, but the prospects of marriage for a divorcee (or widow) are very much more limited than those of a previously unmarried woman.

It is notable that in all the texts referring to divorce, the spouses are encouraged, with the support of their families and communities, to try to find a way to live together in harmony. Where this is impossible, however, the emphasis is on fair treatment and amicable settlement to minimize the harm to both parties and in particular to the children.

Over the course of the last century or so, reformers in many Muslim countries have tried to make the application of the Shari'a in the area of divorce more equitable. While there is no scope to alter the essential elements of the law there have been attempts to select more favourable juristic opinions. Throughout much of the Middle East the prevailing Hanafi school of jurisprudence is particularly conservative concerning divorce, considering **talaq** the absolute right of the husband, irrespective of his state of mind, and judicial divorce restricted for women to the case where the husband is unable to consummate the marriage. Legislators in a number of countries have therefore made provision for the opinions of other schools to be substituted, in an effort to restrict arbitrary divorce for men and to expand the range of grounds on which a woman might seek divorce on grounds of harm. This has not been without objection from religious conservatives who reject any attempt to restrict the Shari'a.

Part 2

Trialogue

5

Sex before Marriage

George

I think our various contributions to this book have highlighted a number of similarities in our ways of thinking on sex and marriage, as well as a number of important differences, and I hope we can have a frank yet friendly discussion about these. We seem to agree that our respective religions recognize marriage as the most common lifestyle, providing a relatively stable environment for bringing up children. Do we all agree that there are risks and problems attached to promiscuity: sexually transmitted diseases, unwanted pregnancies, unstable relationships and children not knowing the identity of their biological father? And do we all agree in rejecting the idea that 'anything goes' in sexual matters?

Assuming we are agreed that there are at least some definite obligations, I think that one of the key issues is the question of whether our ethical systems are God-given absolutes or whether we need to move with the times, adapting to our twenty-first-century world and recognizing new insights. A generation ago we denounced 'fornication', cohabiting was called 'living in sin' and children born out of wedlock were referred to as 'bastards'. Times have indeed changed. In the United States the number of cohabiting couples multiplied by 15 between 1960 and 2010, and in Britain 44 per cent of children are born out of wedlock, 25 per cent to cohabiting couples. The Church of England recently decided to accept reality, and in 2009 made itself controversial by offering a 'two in one' wedding ceremony in which the marriage rite was immediately followed by the baptism of the children. I have seen many church weddings at which the couple's children were present, including my own godson who was married recently.

Two things changed society. One was the availability of contraceptive measures, the 'pill' becoming available on prescription from 1960. The other change was an increasing prevalence of theological liberalism. In his highly controversial *Honest to God*, published in 1963, John A. T. Robinson, then Bishop of Woolwich, included a chapter on 'The New Morality' in which he rejected the absolutism that was inherent in the Christian tradition. Love is the essence of the law, he pointed out, not rules, and hence, for example, prohibitions on extramarital sex are not rules to be slavishly followed. If one is in a loving relationship then what is the harm in expressing it sexually? In fact the vast majority of Christians have had sex before marriage – probably somewhere upward of 80 per cent if statistical evidence is to be believed.

It's interesting, Dan, that you have disabused readers of the idea that Jews obsessively have to obey lots of seemingly pointless rules. This is a stereotype that unfortunately continues to be held by Christians and still proclaimed from some pulpits. An important question I'd want to put to you – and it's one that applies to me too – is this. How does one distinguish between new legitimate insights on one's tradition and what is simply a rationalization of imperfect practice? Most people enjoy sex and most couples don't seem to want to save it up for the traditional wedding night. So are we giving in to secular societal pressure or might the secular world be causing us to reappraise what is and isn't important within our tradition?

Dawoud, your exposition of Islamic law on such matters seems to suggest a more absolutist stance. I don't detect any desire to move with the times and, in fact, I'm rather surprised at the emphasis on flogging and stoning as punishments for fornication and adultery. My own impression, before reading your discussion, was that few Muslim states continued to carry out such severe penalties, and when they do – for example in Iran – there is considerable public outcry in the West, with campaigning groups trying to persuade politicians to intervene. I was under the impression that Islam has seen a different sort of change from Judaism and Christianity, with the way the political situation has changed over the centuries. My understanding is that Muhammad presided over a single unified state, and hence the Qur'an makes little if any distinction between religious and political obligations. With the Muslim world having fragmented into several different nation states, does not each have its own laws, some states being more liberal than others? So does your discussion mean that you favour the conservative, traditional view of Islamic law you describe, or is there scope for new interpretations in the light of political change?

Dan

George is right that our three traditions extol marriage as the ideal relationship between a man and a woman. This has been so since ancient times. But there has been a major change in attitudes regarding sex before marriage. In the first chapter I outlined some of the highly restrictive laws laid down in rabbinic sources. The numerous prohibitions illustrate Judaism's intolerance of sex outside of marriage. Moral sensitivity to illicit sex as well as the fear of unwanted pregnancy have been central to Jewish attitudes to human sexuality. No doubt, among the strictly Orthodox, the *Code of Jewish Law* is still rigorously followed, yet in modern society most Jews simply ignore this legislation. Even among those who identify with Orthodox Judaism there is little if any awareness of the manifold regulations regarding sexual behaviour.

Recently my wife and I went to two Jewish weddings that in different ways illustrate the changes in attitude that have taken place within the Jewish community. The first was an Orthodox wedding held in Leeds. The bride (from an Orthodox home) and the groom (whose parents are Reform) had been living together – and obviously having sexual relations – for several years. The service was conducted by a bearded Orthodox rabbi who chanted the blessings and read out the *ketubah* under the *huppah* (wedding canopy). This was followed by a lavish reception that began with cheering as the bride and groom were lifted up on chairs; men danced together and there was raucous singing. Later, however, as the band played slower music, men wearing skullcaps danced with women (some of whom were not their wives). The second wedding took place in the United States. The groom – a newly ordained Reform rabbi – was the son of one of my close rabbinical friends. He and I were students together in the late 1960s at the Hebrew Union College–Jewish Institute of Religion in Cincinnati, Ohio, the American rabbinical seminary of Reform Judaism. His son David and his bride-to-be had been living together for over four years, and it appears that no one in his congregation ever complained.

These two examples clearly demonstrate that rabbinic legislation regarding sexual behaviour has largely lost its hold on Jewish consciousness. Except among the Haredim (strictly Orthodox Jews), unmarried Jewish young men and women engage in premarital sexual activity without official censure. This includes dating, sexual foreplay and sexual intercourse, and it is not uncommon for couples to live together before any engagement is announced. In some cases they even have children prior to marriage. In this respect there is no difference between premarital sexual encounter in the Jewish community and society at large. The only God-given absolute appears to be the conviction that marriage itself is a sacred bond. In this respect contemporary Judaism is like Christianity: there is a widespread acceptance of sex before marriage as well as cohabitation. And it should be noted that the non-Orthodox branches of Judaism (including Reform, Conservative, Reconstructionist and Humanistic Judaism) also accept the viability of homosexual and lesbian relationships prior to marriage (as well as gay marriage itself).

But from what Dawoud has written it is clear that such liberalism is totally absent within Islamic circles. Like George, I am curious what Dawoud has to say about this. He gives the impression that Islam has not undergone major reforms in the contemporary world. Even if officially Islamic law vigorously condemns premarital sex and only sanctions sex within marriage, are we to assume that Muslims follow such precepts? Or is there a major rift between theory and practice? Like Christians and Jews, do Muslim young men and women ignore Shari'a law? Do they engage in premarital sex just as Jews and Christians do? Do they live together before marriage without official censure? Do they have children out of wedlock and subsequently marry in a traditional way?

George has asked how it is possible to distinguish between new legitimate insights on one's tradition and what is simply a rationalization of imperfect practice. He implies that there is a danger of giving in to secular pressure. This is a key question that we will need to pursue throughout our discussion of our three traditions. For strictly Orthodox Jews there is a bedrock of certainty: God's revelation to Moses as interpreted by the rabbis. God's revelation and rabbinical exegesis provide absolute certainty about all matters, including human sexuality. Yet as I noted in Chapter 1, the vast majority of Jews do not share this view. Instead most religious Jews regard the Hebrew Bible as divinely inspired – but not the word of God. As a result they select for themselves those aspects of the tradition that they regard as spiritually significant. What this means in practice is that moral judgments are ultimately based on subjective considerations rather than grounded on absolute principles.

Dawoud

Both of you are correct in observing that Islam is very much more absolute in its stance on sexual morality than modern mainstream Judaism and Christianity. The fact that the Qur'an is clear on these matters means that this cannot be challenged, and this is entrenched in the mind of the Muslim community. For Muslims there is no separation between religion and worldly life; they are part of the same whole. A Muslim will never say that sex outside marriage is acceptable. The word for fornication or adultery, *zina'*, is still used with the same sense of moral condemnation that you refer to George, and illegitimacy is still a great social stigma. The expression *ibn haram*, 'bastard', is a term of abuse, and if used simply to describe the fact of a person's paternity it reflects negatively on the person despite their own innocence in the matter. No respectable family will allow their son or daughter to marry someone who is 'illegitimate'.

An important element in this is perhaps that Islam still puts great emphasis on family and community and less on individual freedoms. Acts considered to be immoral are seen as a danger to the cohesion and stability of society. This is not to say that fornication and adultery do not exist, but no attempt would ever be made to justify them. There is a general precept in Islam of *Al-Amr bi'l Ma'ruf wa'l-Nahy 'an al-Munkar* – sometimes given as 'commanding good and forbidding evil' but more accurately translated as 'the enforcing of what is accepted [by the community] and the prevention of that which is rejected'. This means that all aspects of sexual morality, including fornication and adultery, are not simply private matters but issues of public concern.

Adultery is unlawful in all Islamic countries but the ways in which it is dealt with vary greatly. In Iran, for example, adultery is a capital crime. Stoning as punishment only came into force in the early 1980s under the Islamic Penal Code introduced by the revolutionary regime, but officially has been set aside since 2008 while new legislation is considered, perhaps in response to international condemnation. In Aceh the Islamic legislature was given permission to introduce Shari'a penalties, including stoning, in an agreement with the Indonesian government. However, although flogging for unmarried adulterers has been used, no incidents of stoning have yet been reported. On the other hand, in Egypt legal proceedings will normally only be instigated on the basis of a complaint by a spouse. If an accusation of adultery is proved against a married woman, she may be sentenced to up to two years in jail, but for a man, to be considered as adultery the act must take place in the marital home and the sentence will only be six months. A man who kills his wife upon finding her in flagrante delicto will face a sentence of not more than three years and may escape punishment completely, as he will be seen to be defending his honour; whereas a woman may face 15 years for murder in the same circumstances.

Cohabitation without marriage will not be tolerated by any Islamic community, but there is recognition of the reality of human needs, which is why the legal scholars permit a range of forms of marriage to accommodate these needs within a lawful framework, including the traveller's marriage or the temporary or *mut'a* marriage allowed by the Shi'a.

There is no scope for liberalization of the fundamental elements of the laws relating to sex in the Shari'a and, moreover, there is no societal pressure for liberalization. For the most part Muslims do not see this as a restriction but as a protection for their families and a clear and safe path for their children to follow. Dan, you say that the belief that the Hebrew Bible is divinely inspired but not the word of God means that Jews can make their own moral judgements. In contrast to this, it is central to Islam that the Qur'an is the word of God, which means that anything that is clearly enjoined or prohibited is an absolute and there is no scope for subjective consideration.

6

Marriage

Dan

Reading through our respective discussions of sex within marriage, I was struck by the similarities between George's and my approach. Both of us have emphasized the multiplicity of interpretations of sacred texts within the various branches of our faiths. In particular we have stressed the liberalizing developments that have taken place in the contemporary world. In Chapter 1 I stressed that the numerous restrictions regarding sexual behaviour in Scripture and rabbinic sources – particularly the *Code of Jewish Law* – have been discarded by the vast majority of Jews today. Only among the strictly Orthodox – which constitute a tiny minority within the Jewish world – do these regulations have any binding authority. Although marriage is regarded as central to Jewish life, most modern Jews are ignorant of the multifarious traditional rules regarding sexual behaviour within marriage. Instead of following these prescriptions they regard sex as a natural part of married life. Similarly, as George explained in Chapter 1, Christians in general view sex as an essential element of married life. Conjugal love is regarded as natural and a source of pleasure. The only controversy, he notes, is whether the prime purpose is enjoyment or procreation.

Dawoud has just explained to us that such liberalizing tendencies have not taken place in the Islamic world. This, I believe, is profoundly disturbing, and I want to highlight some of the concerns I have had reading through his discussion of the Islamic teaching regarding sexual morality in his section of our book. In Chapter 1 he points out that unmarried women are expected to be virgins when they are married – this is a matter of honour for families. However, when virginity cannot be proved the consequences can be catastrophic for the bride: not only can she be rejected by her husband but she may be ostracized by her family and the community. At worst she could be killed by either her husband or her own family. Recently there have been descriptions of such honour killing in the media. In my view such attitudes are monstrous. No right-minded person could condone such actions.

The same applies to Dawoud's discussion in the same chapter of the numerous restrictions placed on women in the Islamic world. Traditional Islamic culture, he states, does not permit socialization between men and women. Islamic custom requires that women are veiled as a sign of modesty; they should not wear clothes that accentuate their figures. In some cultures complete bodily covering is worn, with a mask over the face, and in some cases gloves and shoes or stockings that conceal the hands, feet and ankles are worn. As I noted, similar attitudes and modifications to clothing take place within the strictly Orthodox Jewish community. Yet such regulations make it virtually impossible for women to live normal lives. Arguably they reflect the inferior status of women. Among non-Orthodox Jews there have been enormous advances in the liberation of women. Head coverings for women – including shawls and wigs – have been discarded by the vast majority of Jewish women, and in modern society women can serve as rabbis and cantors and play an equal role in the Jewish community. Such liberalization, however, seems to be entirely absent in the Islamic world.

Equally disturbing is Dawoud's discussion in Chapter 2 of *mut'a* marriage. This, he explains, is a marriage of pleasure permitted by Shi'a Islam. Such a marriage gives permission for a man and a woman to cohabit for a limited period of time (hours or years) in return for certain remuneration payable by the man. *Misyar* marriage (traveller marriage) is equally disturbing. Here, marriage is permitted when men are away from their homes. Dawoud notes that such marriages are not uncommon, even if men are already married. Is this not a form of legalized prostitution in which women are exploited? In the western world such arrangements would rightly be morally condemned.

He tells us in his response to George and me that in Egypt,

if adultery is proved against a married woman, she may be sentenced to up to two years in jail, whereas if it is against a man the sentence will only be up to six months. Further, a man who kills his wife upon finding her in flagrante delicto will face a sentence of not more than three years and may even escape punishment completely because he is defending his honour. A woman, on the other hand, may face 15 years for murder in similar circumstances. This, I believe, is deeply disturbing. Clearly Islamic jurisprudence – and theology for that matter – has not undergone the same evolutionary process that has taken place in Judaism and Christianity. This is a tragedy.

George

I think Dan has made many of the points that I would also wish to put to Dawoud, and I hope that he does not feel that he is becoming the target of criticism. But I hope Dawoud won't mind if I pursue some points about *mut'a* marriage first of all. First, should it be called a marriage? And second, is it a desirable arrangement that takes marriage sufficiently seriously?

Mut'a and *misyar* marriage highlight a number of contrasting points that Christians would want to make about marriage. Christian marriage is an institution that is not merely entered into through a religious ceremony; a state-appointed registrar or other authorized official is also involved, so that the marriage goes on public record. The social and legal conventions make it difficult to disengage from a marriage partnership. The estimated cost of the average British wedding is slightly in excess of £20,000, which makes any subsequent wedding a daunting prospect. Although divorce is not so expensive, cost and legal formalities make it a serious undertaking. As I pointed out in Chapter 2, marriage involves the sharing of property and rights of inheritance, with due provision for one's spouse and one's children.

Most of this contrasts with *mut'a* marriage. As far as I am aware, it is not publicly recorded, there are no conditions like 'till death us do part' and there are no strings attached once the 'marriage' is over. The only proviso, as I understand it, is that the husband rather than the wife is obliged to look after any child who is born as a consequence, although I imagine this could be difficult to enforce if the woman has been in more than one similar relationship. I also gather that many *mut'a* and *misyar* marriages may be enacted secretly. If a traveller is away from home, presumably his wife need not know about any such arrangement. I would therefore agree with Dan that a *mut'a* marriage that only lasts a matter of hours sounds rather like hiring the services of a prostitute, and a more extended relationship lasting the duration of a business trip sounds a bit like having an affair. Christian businessmen – and business women – would take the view that we should exercise restraint, and that abstinence does no harm. Having sexual encounters outside marriage can erode the relationship with one's spouse, as well as bearing other obvious risks. I am not trying to take the moral high ground here: Christians have committed their share of sexual impropriety, and regrettably this goes for clergy as well as laity.

I should also like to comment on the role of relationships between men and women more widely. Dawoud notes that women are still not permitted to drive in Saudi Arabia, and recent news reports about possible relaxation of the ban stated that Majlis al-Ifta' al-A'ala, the country's highest religious authority, apparently feared that such a change would mean there would be no more virgins, and that it would 'provoke a surge in prostitution, pornography, homosexuality and divorce' (*Daily Telegraph*, 2 December 2011). I know that Dawoud would not endorse everything that happens in Saudi Arabia by any means. But it is very difficult to understand this kind of thought process, and it helps to reinforce the popular western perception that Islam represses women. Why should a lone woman driver pick up a man, any more than a lone male driver might give a lift to a woman?

And what is so wrong with being alone with someone of the opposite sex to whom one is not married? Not all relationships with the opposite sex have to be sexual. I mentioned C. S. Lewis's *The Four Loves* earlier (Chapter 1), and I think it is very limiting to see *erōs* (erotic love) as the only way of relating to someone. In common with many colleagues and many fellow Christians, I have no problem about one-to-one socializing with a woman. Recently I arrived a day early for a conference in the United States. By chance I met a female colleague: we had each gone to the tourist office to find a city map, so we decided to spend the day sightseeing together. I don't think it occurred to either of us to spend the night together! There was enough *storgē* (mutual liking to make it a pleasant day), *philia* (Platonic love, which enabled us to discuss the study of religion) and of course *agapē* (Christian love, which one is expected to show to all). And I could tell my wife, who sometimes finds herself in similar circumstances.

Dawoud

I understand the points that both Dan and George make, but the difficulty lies in the fact that Islam does not allow the believer to select the bits they like and ignore the bits that do not suit them. It is difficult to generalize about the practice of an entire religion that has as many ethnic and cultural manifestations as Islam and, of course, the same must be true for Christianity and Judaism. Naturally there will be significant differences in culture and custom between, for example, a village in rural Bangladesh, a middle-class area of Cairo and Muslim communities in Britain or the United States, but there are certain elements that are universal because they are contained in the Qur'an, which for Muslims is immutable and infallible, literally the word of God as revealed to the Prophet Muhammad. To contradict the injunctions of the Qur'an is therefore tantamount to apostasy. The law is not separate from the faith. The provisions on sex and marriage are among the clearest in the Qur'an and are familiar to all Muslims. This does not mean that all Muslims are perfect in their practice of their faith and it does not mean that there is no premarital sex or infidelity. It does mean, however, that there is no scope for this to be considered a valid alternative to lawful marriage.

The consequences of the discovery of sexual impropriety will depend very much upon the society. For the great majority, the discovery of adultery will result in divorce rather than any more serious consequences. As I mentioned, in Egypt as with several other countries, prosecution for adultery will only take place where the injured spouse raises a case before the courts, but in reality many will divorce quietly rather than publicize their shame. Honour crimes do exist but are not common, and for the most part this occurs in traditional tribal societies and again the majority of Muslims would not support it. Governments and reforming organizations such as WLUML (Women Living Under Muslim Law) and VNC (Violence is Not our Culture) have been working to end this and other abuses.

As far as *mut'a* marriage is concerned, the majority of Muslims would disapprove as strongly as Dan and George do. It is completely unacceptable to Sunni Muslims. In Shi'i jurisprudence in Iran, the religious authorities accept it as being lawful according to the Shari'a, but it cannot be legally registered due to its temporary nature. Although the intentions behind it may not always be honourable, in many cases it may be used for practical purposes, such as an interim solution for couples who wish to marry but cannot afford the dower or to set up home. In such cases it provides a legal structure for young people to have romantic and sexual relationships without fear of accusation of adultery. *Mut'a* may subsequently be converted into a registered legal marriage by agreement between the two parties or by a judge's ruling, and in the latter case, where there is dispute a judge will make a presumption of permanence. Nevertheless it is generally frowned upon socially and no respectable family will allow their daughters to marry in this way. It involves risk for a woman who enters into such a marriage in good faith, on the understanding that it will lead to a permanent marriage, if she is deceived or let down by her partner or if he dies, because her future marriage prospects will be poor.

The issue of men and women being alone together is deeply entrenched in Muslim culture. This is not seen particularly as a restriction because there is no real notion of socialization between men and women alone in the first instance. Traditionally they have occupied different spheres of life. The requirement of chaperoning is seen as being for the protection of women and their honour against both real threats and against gossip and slander. Having said that, it is also relevant to mention that very similar rules have always applied within Christian and Jewish communities in the Middle East.

On the other hand, Muslims commonly perceive that in western society families do not care enough for their children, both boys and girls, to protect them from the risks of unsupervised socialization. They question why anyone would value their teenage girls so little as to allow them to wear unnecessarily revealing clothing, exposing them to undesirable attention, or why they would let them go out with teenage boys and run the risk of becoming unmarried teenage mothers abandoned to cope on their own. Obviously this is a difference of worldview, but is it so far removed from western values of only a couple of generations ago?

7

Sex within Marriage

Dawoud

It is clear that our three faiths are in agreement about the place of marriage at the centre of a person's life and faith and about the ideal of exclusivity of the sexual relationship within marriage. From my reading of Dan's description of attitudes towards sex within marriage among Orthodox and non-Orthodox Jews, it is easy to understand why most non-Orthodox Jews have chosen to disregard the provisions that make it sinful for a couple to approach sexual intercourse with any desire other than for procreation. This seems to be in complete contrast to the Islamic view of marital sex. While procreation is important, Islam has no objection to husbands and wives enjoying a fulfilling sexual relationship in its own right, and there are *hadith* of the Prophet that encourage men not to approach their wives as animals do but to take their time, speak gentle words to them and to kiss and caress them prior to engaging in intercourse. The Qur'an says nothing explicitly about what is or is not permitted sexually between spouses, and on the basis that what is not forbidden is permitted, many scholars believe that there is no restriction to what sexual practices are permissible between husband and wife, provided that everything is consensual and causes no harm. The only sexual practice that receives almost universal disapproval even where both spouses agree to it is anal sex.

The openness with which such topics are treated depends on culture and context. Egyptian TV broadcasts a popular 'sex therapy' programme to the Arab world hosted by sex therapist Heba Kotb, a 40-something mother of three who wears *hijab* and, basing her opinions on the Qur'an and *hadith*, tells her viewers that they should have more sex, with their lawful spouses of course. The religious establishment has accused her of encouraging perversion, but the programme is tolerated so long as it is limited to guidance for married couples and those who are to be married. Among her key opinions is that a woman should not explore her sexuality in any way prior to marriage, so that she can be a 'blank canvas' to develop her sexuality with her husband, and to this end she gives advice on avoiding 'the secret habit', masturbation. She does, however, stress that fulfilment for both parties is essential to create and maintain a healthy relationship and minimize the risk of infidelity due to sexual frustration. Her interactive programme attracts a large audience, and viewers across the Middle East and beyond phone in or email or text their problems and questions, which are dealt with live on air. More recently she has established a Facebook presence, where she has over 40,000 'likes'. While what she can discuss is still relatively limited, she has had some influence in raising awareness among women that their sex lives can be more fulfilling, and among men that their wives are equally entitled to enjoy sex and that by making sure their wives are satisfied they will enhance their own enjoyment.

Even a cursory search of the internet will find a vast array of websites and forums offering advice on sex to married Muslim couples, and these range from the very conservative to some really quite explicit guidance. There is even some very practical advice to husbands suggesting that should they wish to encourage their wives to feel more amorous towards them, they might consider cleaning the house, doing the laundry or cooking dinner (and washing up) without being asked. The feature that appears most commonly, however, is the recommendation that spouses should demonstrate their love and affection towards each other as a means to a truly fulfilling relationship.

As discussed previously, views on contraception within marriage vary between absolute prohibition to general acceptance of non-permanent forms of birth control, provided both partners agree to this. Again, every shade of opinion in this can be found on advice websites and forums, and in effect it is possible for a person to choose the opinion that best suits and supports their own situation.

Views regarding internet and media resources are divided. Some Muslims consider them to be intrusive, degrading and unnecessary while others believe that by encouraging happier relationships they can help to preserve the institution of marriage.

George has referred to online resources for married Christian couples aimed at enhancing their sexual relationships. I would like to ask Dan whether there are similar resources specifically aimed at Jewish couples, and I would like to ask both Dan and George whether they consider that such resources have the potential to enhance and support marital relationships or whether they degrade the institution of marriage.

George

It's interesting that Dan's and Dawoud's accounts of Judaism and Islam lay much more emphasis on the pleasurable function of sex and have little room for the asceticism and abstinence that are often found within the Christian tradition. I pointed out earlier (Chapter 1) that Christianity has been divided on the question of whether one's personal identity consists of an immaterial soul or a resurrectable body, and this ambiguity has given rise to fundamental issues, such as whether to give up conventional living – including sexual activity – in favour of a contemplative spiritual life and whether it is pleasure or procreation that should be the prime purpose of sex.

Dawoud asks about resources that enhance sexual relationships. Personally I have no problem about people using devices like sex toys, if that's what they want to do. I don't know if any of my Christian friends use them since people don't normally talk about what goes on in their bedroom. In the Church of England and in the Protestant tradition there are no prescriptions about how one has sexual intercourse, and couples are perfectly free to adopt whatever physical positions they enjoy. There are no prohibitions on oral or anal sex, sex during a woman's menstrual period or the use of sex toys to enhance one's enjoyment. The only provisos would be that one's sexual practices should be consensual and not harmful. As western society has become more permissive and more open on sexual matters, some Christians have followed the example of the secular world and created quite an industry of Christian books on how to 'spice up your sex life', Christian sex toys and websites with names like Christian Nymphos, Hot Christian Marriage and BetterSex4Christians.com.

Many Christians are uncomfortable with all this, however. Some are inherently conservative while others are concerned that although sex toys themselves may be inherently harmless, they are part of a wider sex industry encompassing pornography, clip joints and sleazy-looking 'private shops'. The creation of specifically Christian distributors of sex products, of course, is an attempt to allow Christians to enjoy them without the sleaze.

Roman Catholicism takes a somewhat different view. One author, who simply calls himself 'Catholic Writer', suggests two important principles that are involved in the use of sex aids.[1] The first is the traditional Catholic moral principle of 'double effect'. This principle applies where an action has two sets of consequences, one good and one bad. For example, if I injure a burglar to protect my property, my act has a bad effect (injuring a person) and a good one (protecting my property). The principle of double effect allows me to produce the bad effect provided the good and not the bad effect is intended, the bad effect outweighs the good one and is the means towards producing the good effect. By this logic a sex aid that enhances pleasure – not a desirable aim from the Catholic standpoint – may legitimately be used if it helps procreative sex. If a device helps to improve, say, retarded ejaculation, then it would be permissible provided that its purpose is to assist the procreative function rather than to enhance sexual pleasure.

Catholic Writer's second consideration is that sex toys should respect human dignity – a similar point to Dawoud's. I have to confess that I have never personally tried S & M or fantasy role-plays with uniforms (two of the writer's examples): neither particularly appeals to me, but I am not convinced that dressing up as a schoolgirl or a chamber maid is necessarily demeaning, any more than acting out such roles in a church play would demean the actor. Since sexual activity is a private activity, such matters are left

---

1 'Catholic Writer', http://catholicwriter.wordpress.com/2006/09/13/question-is-the-usage-of-sex-toys-allowed-during-sexual-intercourse/.

to individual preference and conscience, and religious authorities cannot draw up lists of permitted and forbidden sexual devices.

By way of conclusion I'd like to make a small correction to Dawoud's opening statement that 'our three faiths are in agreement about the place of marriage at the centre of a person's life and faith'. Although marriage is the most common Christian lifestyle it is not an obligation, and many Christians adopt different lifestyles, including remaining single, living as a single parent, gay and lesbian partnerships (to be discussed later) and the monastic life. (The last of these tends to be absent in Judaism and Islam.) Although family life tends to be presented as the norm, increasing numbers of Christians are trying to ensure these alternatives are not neglected.

Dan

In the Talmud there is a saying that a man will be obliged to render account before his Maker in the Hereafter for every legitimate pleasure he denied himself. In this context sex within marriage should be regarded as a pleasurable obligation that every Jew should fulfil. Even though Judaism shares Christianity's view of the soul as distinct from the body (which will eventually return to God), sexual activity within marriage is viewed as essential. The first commandment recorded in Scripture is 'Be fruitful and multiply'. As I stressed throughout my discussion of the Jewish view of sex and marriage in the book, Jewish men and women are commanded to marry and have sexual intercourse with the aim of continuing the Jewish people. For this reason abstinence from sex in the pursuit of a contemplative spiritual life has never been regarded as a virtue. The great Jewish mystics of the past were invariably married men with fulfilled sexual lives.

However, as I noted in Chapter 1, sexual behaviour was traditionally highly regulated. The *Code of Jewish Law* contains a wide range of laws regarding legitimate sexual behaviour. No doubt in previous centuries Jews strictly observed these obligations. And in contemporary society the strictly Orthodox continue such practices. In their view the Torah was revealed on Mount Sinai and the rabbis' amplification of Jewish law is seen as the continuation of this process of revelation. Biblical and rabbinic law is therefore binding and unalterable. However, within the various non-Orthodox branches of Judaism both biblical and rabbinic ordinances have ceased to retain their hold on Jewish consciousness. Instead the vast majority of Jews today have completely disregarded the manifold regulations concerning sexual behaviour within marriage. Quite simply, most Jews are entirely ignorant of the wide range of prescriptions contained in rabbinic sources.

Let me turn to Dawoud's observation about our two faiths: he contrasts the Islamic and Jewish attitude to sex by stating that within Judaism it is sinful for a couple to approach sexual intercourse with any desire other than that for procreation – Islam, on the other hand, stresses enjoyment and pleasure alongside the desire for procreation. I think my discussion of sex within marriage in Chapter 1 may have given the wrong impression. It is true that procreation is central to Jewish sexual activity, yet the enjoyment of sex is an essential feature of married life. If you look at websites dealing with Judaism and sex, such as Judaism 101, My Jewish Learning or the Jewish Virtual Library, you will see that they all emphasize the importance of sexual pleasure and enjoyment within marriage. Islam and Judaism are thus much closer than Dawoud suggests. Yet if Islam is not concerned with what is or is not permitted sexually between spouses, then there is a clear distinction between our two faiths as far as Orthodox Judaism is concerned.

Like Dawoud, George notes that he is unaware of Christian prescriptions about how one has sexual intercourse: as a result couples are free to adopt whatever practices they enjoy. As a consequence there are no rules regarding oral and anal sex, sex during the menstrual period or the use of sex toys (including dildos and female vibrators) to enhance one's performance. What is essential is that sexual practices are consensual and not harmful. Within the non-Orthodox Jewish world, much the same situation applies. What goes on within the privacy of married couples' lives is their own affair. Non-Orthodox rabbis are unconcerned with such matters. Instead the Jewish non-Orthodox religious establishment stresses the importance of Jewish marriage and the need for children to grow up within the faith. What goes on in the bedrooms of married couples is a private matter.

I am not aware of a massive Jewish industry – parallel to what goes on within Christianity – of books on how to spice up your sex life, nor of Jewish sex toys and Jewish websites with names such as Jewish nymphs, hot Jewish marriage or bettersex4Jews.com. There is, however, a well-known exception: the Orthodox rabbi Shmuley Boteach has written extensively about sex within modern marriages. His book *Kosher Sex* – which contains a chapter about sex toys – explores how deep friendship and passionate sex within marriage are possible within the context of Jewish law. There is also a website for Orthodox Jews that sells sex toys: koshersex.net – it stresses that none of its products violate Jewish law. In any event, perhaps the Jewish community has simply not woken up to the commercial opportunities as the Christian community has done. Certainly the Orthodox would be outraged by such activities, and no doubt some more conservative Jews would recoil with horror. But at the same time there would be many non-Orthodox and secular Jews who would regard such material as harmless.

8

Homosexuality

George

I'd like to start with Dawoud's statement, 'Homosexuality is prohibited in Islam' (Chapter 1). I don't think one can prohibit homosexuality as such, any more than one could prohibit one's sex, ethnicity or any other innate condition. We don't know what makes someone gay rather than straight: it is an orientation, and gay and lesbian people often report that as they grew up they found themselves more attracted to members of the same sex rather than the opposite. The real question, therefore, is what if anything one should do about one's sexual orientation.

Societal homophobia has made gays and lesbians the victims of prejudice and discrimination, even physical violence. So I don't think that Christians, being committed to the fundamental law of love, should perpetrate the idea that homosexuality is a sin, an ailment or a perversion. Some of the mainstream churches acknowledge that homosexuality is a condition but want to outlaw its practice, and some evangelical Christians have even organized projects for 'curing' homosexuals. Quite apart from the prejudice they perpetuate, such programmes do not seem to be effective.

Gay and lesbian sexual relationships do not harm anyone, unlike war and violence, of which Christians (and followers of other faiths, of course) have contributed their fair share. The idea that sexually transmitted diseases, and particularly AIDS, are associated with homosexuality does not meet with wide medical support. Obviously there are risks, just as there are with 'straight sex', but equally there are precautions that sensible partners should take. It seems unduly discriminatory that some church leaders should assert that 'homosexual persons are called to chastity' (*Catechism*

2359), unless of course one takes the view – which is somewhat outmoded, in my opinion – that the sex must leave open the possibility of procreation, which gay sex cannot do.

Dawoud refers to the story of Lot and the destruction of Sodom and Gomorrah (Gen. 19). Earlier in our discussion he appropriately asks Dan how one can reconcile the divine inspiration of Scripture with the making of one's own personal moral judgements. This is a challenging question, which the story of Lot highlights. On the face of it it looks as if the story is about God destroying the two cities because of their sexual depravity. This interpretation is fuelled by our understanding of the English word 'sodomy', which is not only defined as same-sex copulation but also encompasses practices like bestiality.

However, the Christian understanding of Scripture has developed through time and continues to do so. No doubt Dan can shed light on Jewish interpretations of the story, but at least one commentator suggests that the popular interpretation did not enter the Christian tradition until the third century CE and only gained popularity several centuries after.[1]

The story of Lot and the destruction of Sodom and Gomorrah, and the surrounding narrative, has a number of themes. One is genocide: God wipes out two entire civilizations. Another theme is xenophobia: Lot and his family are strangers who have settled in Sodom, and the natives seem to have resented this (Gen. 19.9). Hospitality to strangers is a further theme: Lot offers two male visitors hospitality but this causes the men of the city to demand sex with them (19.5). This is not consensual gay sex, however, which the men could easily have had with each other. So a further topic is rape, for which purpose Lot offers his own two daughters. The story that follows the destruction of the cities becomes even stranger: the two daughters are without partners since all the men of Sodom have been exterminated, and so they get their father drunk and commit incest with him (19.30–6). God does not condemn this, despite having dealt so severely with the Sodomites: it is important for Lot to have progeny and by becoming the father

---

[1] Michael Carden, 'Genesis/Bereshit', in Deryn Guest, Robert E. Goss, Mona West and Thomas Bohache (eds), *The Queer Bible Commentary*, London: SCM Press, 2006, pp. 21–60.

of the Moabites he is by implication an ancestor of Ruth, and hence of the Messiah himself.

What conclusions should we draw from these stories? Which characters are behaving badly and which are behaving well? The problems of interpreting these stories demonstrate the difficulty of using the biblical narrative, particularly difficult passages, to draw conclusions about moral behaviour. The Bible is a book that has to be critically interpreted, using one's reason, with the aid of the wider community of Christian scholars and with progressive understanding. We certainly shouldn't accept the interpretation that God punishes sodomites – less still that today's punishment is AIDS.

Dan

Dawoud brought up the story of Lot, and George has discussed this biblical narrative at length. In recent times there has been an attempt to reinterpret this tale; in the view of these liberal biblical scholars, the passage in Genesis was not originally intended to condemn homosexual activity. Rather, as George has noted, there are other themes with which this narrative is concerned. No doubt there are many Christians today who would agree with George that it has been a mistake for the Church to view gays and lesbians as immoral. Yet it is undeniable that the Hebrew Bible is unconditionally critical of male homosexual conduct. The book of Leviticus states clearly that the act itself is forbidden: 'You shall not lie with a male as with a woman; it is an abomination' (Lev. 18.22). Again, Leviticus 20.13 states: 'If a man lies with a male as with a woman, both of them have committed an abomination; they shall be put to death, their blood is upon them.'

Whatever one makes of the story of Sodom in Genesis, Scripture is adamant that homosexual activity between men is abhorrent. While condemning homosexuality as Scripture demands, the rabbis debated a range of issues connected with this prohibition. In the Mishnah, for example, Rabbi Judah forbids two unmarried males to sleep together in the same bed; the sages, however, permit it. The Talmudic commentary on this Mishnaic text states that the reason why the sages disagree with Rabbi Judah is that

Jews are not suspected of engaging in homosexual practices. The *Code of Jewish Law* records the view of the sages but continues: 'But in these times, when there are many loose-livers about, a man should avoid being alone with another male' (Even Ha-Ezer 24). According to rabbinic tradition, Gentiles too are commanded by the Torah to abstain from male homosexual acts.

Lesbianism, however, appears to be a less clear issue. The Sifra, a rabbinic *midrash*, comments on the verse, 'You shall not do as they do in the land of Egypt, where you dwelt, and you shall not do as they do in the land of Canaan, to which I am bringing you. You shall not walk in their statutes' (Lev. 18.3) that the reference is to sexual practices of the Egyptians and the Canaanites in which they married off a man to a man and a woman to a woman. The Talmud rules that women who perform sex acts with one another are not treated as harlots but only as indulging in lewd acts (Yevamot 76a).

Thus on the basis of biblical and rabbinical legislation, traditional Judaism strongly condemns both homosexual and lesbian behaviour. Yet as I noted in Chapter 1, there has been a revolution in Jewish consciousness. Within the various branches of non-Orthodox Judaism homosexual and gay relations are fully accepted: within these movements there are practising gay rabbis as well as gay congregations. Most non-Orthodox and secular Jews today would agree with George's view that gay and lesbian sexual relationships do not harm anyone and should therefore be accepted. As I noted previously, such a shift in perspective hinges on the way in which both the Bible and the rabbinic tradition are viewed. Dawoud has asked how one can reconcile the divine inspiration of Scripture with the making of one's own personal moral judgements. Let me answer this question by quoting from the Pittsburgh Platform – a statement of Reform Jewish belief formulated at the end of the nineteenth century, which deals directly with this question:

> We recognize in the Bible the record of the consecration of the Jewish people to its mission as priest of the One God, and value it as the most potent instrument of religious and moral instruction. We hold that the modern discoveries of scientific researches

in the domain of nature and history are not antagonistic to the doctrines of Judaism, the Bible reflecting the primitive ideas of its own age and at times clothing its conception of divine providence and justice dealing with men in miraculous narratives. We recognize in the Mosaic legislation a system of training the Jewish people for its mission during its national life in Palestine, and today we accept as binding only the moral laws and maintain only such ceremony as elevate and sanctify our lives, but reject all such as are not adapted to the views and habits of modern civilization ... We hold that all such Mosaic and rabbinic laws as regulate diet, priestly purity and dress originated in ages and under the influence of ideas altogether foreign to our present mental and spiritual state. They fail to impress the modern Jew with a spirit of priestly holiness; their observance in our days is apt rather to obstruct than to further modern spiritual development ... We recognize in Judaism a progressive religion, ever striving to be in accord with the postulates of reason.[2]

Dawoud

I note George's point that it is impossible to prohibit something innate such as homosexuality or same-sex attraction and I realize that I should have worded this more carefully. What I should have said is that Islam prohibits homosexual acts. As I have mentioned before, this is an absolute based on the primary sources and juristic opinion, and there is no toleration in this. Of course, this is not to say that there are no Muslims who are homosexual, but there is no school of thought in Islam of any standing that will recognize the acceptability of homosexual behaviour or its moral equivalence to the heterosexual relationship between husband and wife. Muslim society is for the most part deeply conservative and essentially opposed to any sexual relationship outside lawful marriage.

---

2 Dan Cohn-Sherbok, *Modern Judaism*, Basingstoke and London: Palgrave Macmillan, 1996, pp. 82–3.

HOMOSEXUALITY

Less than ten years ago I supervised an MPhil student from a Muslim country who was writing a thesis on Shari'a punishments. Although this student spoke excellent English and had lived, studied and worked in a western country for a number of years, he had no qualms in expressing without challenge or qualification the juristic position that homosexuals should be executed. He had no sense of the inappropriateness of expressing this in academic writing (or any other forum for that matter), and was surprised when I advised him that writing in this way would expose him to accusations of homophobia and perhaps even incitement to hate crime. As things stand, the current trend in Islam is not towards liberalization but towards adherence to the primary sources and acceptance of a received conservative viewpoint.

Homosexuals in Muslim countries generally maintain a low profile and there is very little of an agenda for recognition or acceptance. Apart from the real danger of persecution, most homosexuals would avoid bringing shame on their families. The same is true to a great extent for homosexual Muslims in western countries. In the popular British soap *EastEnders*, a young British Muslim of Asian origin is in an openly gay relationship with an ethnically English non-Muslim man. While it is a positive thing that the BBC has attempted to deal with this topic, and the immediate reaction of the parents in feeling utterly humiliated and experiencing a sense of bereavement was believable, the denouement has been unrealistic and offensive to many Muslims. The two men are demonstrative in a way that would be considered improper between a married heterosexual couple, and the way in which the family have come to accept the situation is at best improbable.

Although there are some organizations providing support to LGBT people and their families, such as www.imaan.org.uk in Britain, a homosexual Muslim looking for advice and support on the internet is more likely to find websites such as www.gaymuslim.org or www.straightway.sinfree.net/ that appear to offer compassion and understanding but maintain a hard line on homosexual activity and are dedicated to helping Muslims who experience same-sex attraction to overcome this through faith.

Many homosexual Muslims marry and live apparently 'normal'

family lives, accepting that there is no real alternative for them, and they may or may not have a secret life of their own. Not uncommonly, where they have sufficient independence and resources to do so they find ways through networks to find suitable partners who are also homosexual for a marriage of convenience, where they have agreement to live an ostensibly conventional married life, often with children, for the sake of their families and communities, but each being able to make their own relationships and fulfil their sexuality outside the marriage. This existed before the internet but it has been greatly facilitated by dedicated matchmaking websites and message boards, such as those on www.al-jannah.proboards.com/.

What is clear is that a western-style human rights approach towards promoting equality and tolerance of homosexuals in Muslim countries is generally counterproductive as it is perceived by Islamic authorities and by the public as an affront to Islamic law and fundamental values, and a form of western imperial interference in Muslim culture.

9

Polygamy

Dan

George previously mentioned that polygamy has not officially been banned in the Christian faith although it is widely condemned. A similar situation exists in the Jewish world. As you will know, this was not always the case. In the biblical period polygamy was the norm, yet the Torah contains a number of rules regarding this practice. Exodus 21.10, for example, stipulates that multiple marriages should not diminish the status of the first wife (specifically her right to food, clothing and conjugal relations). Deuteronomy 17.17 states that a man must award the inheritance due to a firstborn son to the son who was actually born first even if he hates that son's mother and likes another wife more.

Some traditional scholars have argued that the underlying reason why the Torah allows a man more than one wife at a time – while a woman is permitted only one husband at a time – is biological. Men are able to father children with more than one woman whereas a woman cannot become simultaneously pregnant from more than one man. On this basis the intent of the allowance of polygamy does not imply that monogamous marriage is not ideal but rather the intent of the law is to create a social structure inclusive of the natural process of sexual activity. Since a man may be linked to several women at the same time it is better to consider these multiple relationships legitimate rather than to criminalize them and put them outside the norms of respectability.

In contemporary society, however, polygamy is generally not permitted. Ashkenazi Jews have followed Rabbenu Gershom's ban since the eleventh century. Some Sephardi and Mizrahi Jewish communities – particularly from North Africa, Yemen, Kurdistan and Iran – discontinued polygamy much more recently when they emigrated to countries where it is forbidden. Yet it should be noted that polygamy still occurs infrequently in non-European Jewish communities that exist in countries where it is not forbidden, such as Yemen and the Arab world. Among the very few Karaite Jews (who do not adhere to the rabbinic interpretation of the Torah), polygamy is almost non-existent. Like other Jews, Karaites interpret Leviticus 18.18 to mean that a man can only take a second wife if his first wife gives her consent. Further, they interpret Exodus 21.10 to mean that a man can only take a second wife if he is capable of maintaining the same level of marital duty to his first wife. Because of these two limitations and because most countries outlaw polygamy, the practice is considered highly impractical. In accordance with western moral attitudes, the state of Israel has made polygamy illegal. Nonetheless, provisions have been instituted to allow for existing polygamous families immigrating from countries where the practice was legal. Furthermore, Chief Rabbi Ovadia Yosef came out in favour of legalizing polygamy as well as the practice of *pilegesh* (concubine) by the Israeli government. In this context Tzvi Zohar, a professor from Bar-Ilan University, suggested that based on the opinions of leading halakhic authorities, the concept of concubines may serve as a practical halakhic justification for premarital or non-marital cohabitation.

Perhaps I should note in this regard that a new organization in Israel has recently been seeking to reinstate polygamy into mainstream Orthodox Judaism despite its being against the contemporary norm of Jewish law. This is being promoted as the Jewish solution for the abundance of single women, the Arab demographic threat and the male predicament of seeking extramarital relations. The weekly handout *Shabbat Beshabato* distributed to synagogues quoted a paragraph from Rabbi Ovadia Yosef in which he wrote that it is a mistake for non-Ashkenazim to follow Rabbenu Gershom's ruling in which it is prohibited for a man to marry more than one wife. According to Rabbi Yehezkel Sopher, if a man wants to take another wife the Torah does not object to such a practice. In his view the notion of monogamy is not an essentially Jewish idea. Polygamy, he believes, is acceptable within Judaism and today can serve to solve pressing social problems in the modern world.

George

No doubt you've heard the joke that Muslims believe in one God and four wives while Christians believe in three gods and one wife! The Christian doctrine of the Trinity can no doubt await our discussion in another forum; in the meantime the issue of polygamy is complicated enough.

It's interesting that contrary to popular belief, none of our traditions rules out polygamy completely and that there are issues here with which all three of us are struggling. Quite apart from the recent controversies about polygyny among African Christians, a quick web search reveals a very small number of Christian fundamentalists who favour multiple wives. As I argued earlier (Chapter 4), the Bible does not explicitly condemn polygamy. It appears to be condoned – but neither required nor condemned – in the Old Testament, but many Christians would argue that the practice belongs to the 'old covenant', and the fact that the Bible refers to a custom does not imply that it should be emulated.

In western countries polygamy is illegal and it is therefore not a live issue for the majority of Christians there. Christians have acknowledged an obligation to obey civil authorities: as Paul says, 'Let everyone be subject to the governing authorities, for ... the authorities that exist have been established by God' (Rom. 13.1). While exceptional circumstances may justify civil disobedience, for example if Christians are being required to act against their faith, only a handful of fundamentalist Mormon groups would wish to stand against the state on this issue.

In the missionary heyday, Christians often assumed a stance of superiority not only on matters of religion but on medicine, technology and social mores. However, some of us are now more inclined to ask whether we might be guilty of cultural imperialism in countries that the West colonized, and the African situation has forced us to ask whether monogamy is really a Christian requirement or simply a cultural phenomenon. Conversely, Dawoud mentions the prohibition of polygyny in Islamic countries such as Turkey and Tunisia. I would be interested to hear his reflections on this. Is this progress or is it to be regretted that Turkey has replaced Shari'a law with a secular legal system?

It is interesting that Dan mentions the state of Israel's concessions towards polygamous immigrants from the Yemen and Iran (Chapter 4). It seems that, like the Christians, the Jewish community is trying to strike a balance between upholding monogamy as its preferred social institution and showing love towards women who might be left without due provision if a polygamous husband were required to remain with only one wife.

Dan mentions Rabbi Yehezkel Sopher's view that polygyny 'can serve to solve pressing social problems in the modern world'. But what are these problems? Polygyny can certainly enable one man to father more children than would be possible with one wife. However, we scarcely need more children in a world that is already overpopulated. The size of one's nation no longer determines its military strength – something that is related more to technological advancement. If it is argued that polygyny can provide children where a wife is infertile, this argument could also be used to recommend polyandry to assist infertile men.

Dan also mentions the modern Jewish organization that champions polygyny as 'the Jewish solution for the abundance of single women'. It has sometimes been said that polygyny provides a solution for societies in which the number of women substantially exceeds the number of men. However, according to the 2012 *CIA World Factbook* the proportion of male to female births is remarkably even and consistent worldwide. The ratio of male to female births worldwide lies between 102 and 107 male children to every 100 females. In Israel there is actually a surplus of men: 105 male babies to every 100 female, dropping down slightly to 103:100 in the age range 15–64, and it is only in the over-65 band that women begin to outnumber men (77 men to 100 women).

So where is this abundance of single women? I am conscious in contributing to this book that like Dan and Dawoud I am writing from a male viewpoint, and I can't help wondering if it is simply a male fantasy to suppose that a polygamous husband might help 'surplus women' who might otherwise be impoverished. Polygamy is more a statement of wealth or power than of compassion, and the slight preponderance of men worldwide presents more of a case for polyandry.

Although I can't write from a woman's point of view, I can ask myself what it might be like to be one of several husbands. I'm not keen on the idea. My wife tells me that she would not welcome being one of several wives either.

Dawoud

As George points out, the issue of polygyny is complex. The very notion of polygyny creates a distinction between concepts of what a 'marriage' actually is. Many of us of all faiths would understand a marriage to be a unique bond between two people with absolute commitment to each other and to a shared life plan, who set out on a journey together in the hope of completing it together and sharing all of its experiences. Where another party or parties become involved, the nature of the relationship cannot be the same. Where a woman's entire commitment is to a man but a man's commitment is divided between two, three or four women, it is difficult to avoid the conclusion that there is an inequality in the way they are valued as people and in what they are considered to be entitled to as human beings. A woman in a polygamous marriage may be part of a social structure with clearly defined rights, but she will not have the personal fulfilment of a unique partnership with her husband, nor will she have a full voice in the shaping of their life plan if it has to accommodate someone else. It is nevertheless permitted explicitly by the Qur'an, albeit with certain conditions, and as such it cannot be outlawed. George has asked about the situation in Turkey and Tunisia. While polygyny is prohibited in law, this does not prevent unregistered second marriages that are religiously valid but not legally recognized, thereby leaving second (third or fourth) wives with little legal protection. There is considerable pressure from the religious parties in Tunisia, following the revolution, for polygyny to be permitted in law.

In Muslim societies, attitudes to polygyny have varied historically and across different cultures and social classes. It is difficult to generalize other than to say that in urban and middle-class society monogamy has tended to be the norm. In the generation, culture and social class of my parents (who were born before the fall of the Ottoman Empire), it would have been unthinkable among people of respectable families for a man to insult and humiliate his wife and her family by taking a second wife. It would have been considered improper. Among their peers it did not happen, and the same is true for the generation of my elder siblings born in the 1930s and 40s. It has always existed to some extent among rural populations and in poorer city areas, particularly in communities with stricter segregation of the sexes, but very much less so among the educated professional and urban classes, at least until recent times. There have been social and cultural changes in the last two or three decades, however, that have led to changes in attitude. Whereas until recent years people would talk about taking a second wife in banter or just to tease their wives, the Islamic revival has led to a new acceptance of traditional Islamic values that are supported by the Qur'an as part of a renewed assertion of Islamic identity. On another level, economic factors mean that it is often impossible for young men to marry as they cannot afford to set up home and support a family. This makes it difficult for young women to find suitable husbands and some will prefer to be the second wife of a man who is already married rather than single and living with their parents. Moreover in some of the countries, such as Iran and Iraq, that have suffered enormous losses in conflict in recent decades, polygyny has been actively encouraged as the alternative to a surplus of unmarried women.

Inevitably there are also men who take second wives in the same way that some non-Muslim men take mistresses, even claiming a moral high ground over their non-Muslim counterparts or at least attempting to justify it on the basis that they are creating an 'honourable' relationship rather than simply betraying their wives and exploiting another woman to whom they have no intention of making a life commitment.

Polygyny has become more common in Britain, even among Muslims born and brought up in Britain. While the second marriage is not legally valid, a properly contracted *nikah* is lawful in Islamic terms. Some men take a second wife because they are unfulfilled in an arranged marriage but do not want to hurt their wives, parents, in-laws and children by divorcing. Some will do so simply because they can or because their friends have done so and encourage them to do the same – a kind of peer pressure. Some career women will accept the role of second wife in preference to taking on the full-time commitment of family life. Many different grounds are given, but whatever the reasons, this is an issue that is likely to become more prominent and that the Muslim community will have to look at in the near future.

10

Intermarriage

Dawoud

What do we mean by 'intermarriage'? This is an enormous topic and can only be touched upon fairly generally in our current discussion. The expression may apply to marriage between adherents of different religions but it may also apply to any pairing other than marriage between members of a single denomination and culture.

It is easy to describe the law regarding marriage between Muslims and non-Muslims or between different Islamic denominations, but not so easy to describe the reality because it is so varied and depends as much on culture as religion.

Many Muslim communities are strongly endogamous, and this often remains the case when they no longer live in their country of origin. For some, including many Arab and Asian countries, cousin marriage is the ideal and constitutes a high percentage of all marriages. This is a matter of tradition and it is not difficult to understand how families and communities see it as a way of keeping their children close and reassuring themselves – rightly or wrongly – that they will be happy in a relationship where there is familiarity and mutual understanding, as well as preserving their culture, controlling the transfer of property and cementing family alliances. Suitability to form a family unit that will integrate with the larger community is the principal consideration and is seen as the most important factor in creating and sustaining a marriage in the long term. Closely consanguineous marriage presents certain risks, however. There has been a great deal of research into the risks of preserving recessive genes for serious health problems by cousin marriage over several generations, but programmes to discourage this often meet with considerable resistance.

INTERMARRIAGE

Even in less strongly endogamous communities, many Muslim families will be resistant to allowing their children to marry people of other faiths. For women this is an absolute and many Muslim communities will even be resistant to their daughters marrying Muslims of other ethnic backgrounds. For men there is more leeway, but a wife of a different religion, denomination or ethnicity may not be fully accepted in the same way as one from the same community.

Intermarriage between people of different Muslim denominations, Sunna and Shi'a, is relatively uncommon but it does exist and there is nothing in principle to prevent it. The rift between the denominations runs deep, however, and the problems Sunni–Shi'i couples may face are potentially greater and more destructive than those between Muslims and non-Muslims. Postings on matchmaking websites for Muslims seeking marriage partners invariably specify denomination. Many young Muslims raised in western countries, however, have limited knowledge and understanding of the difference between the sects, only considering themselves to be Muslims, so where Sunni and Shi'i meet and fall in love they are often unaware of the problems they will face if they wish to marry.

The Qur'an is quite clear about the marriage of Muslims to unbelievers. Neither Muslim men nor women may marry outside the three recognized monotheistic faiths, which means they are not allowed to marry Hindus, Sikhs or Buddhists, for example, but Muslim men are permitted to marry women of the 'People of the Book', that is, Christians or Jews, provided that their children are raised as Muslims. Because there is no explicit permission to Muslim women to marry Christian or Jewish men, and because it is assumed that a man will be head of a household, it has been deemed to be prohibited. The reasoning by the jurists is that a non-Muslim man should not have authority or influence over a Muslim woman or children.

Marriages of Muslims to Christians or Jews is much less common in Muslim countries than in the West, and where it does occur it is most often to Christian or Jewish women from non-Muslim countries who have either met their husbands while visiting the country or while the men have been working or studying overseas.

Inevitably much more is heard in the western media about marriages that have failed and the ensuing problems concerning custody of children than about the many successful and enduring marriages. Any marriage requires give and take and a willingness to see things from the perspective of the other person, but in a marriage between people of different backgrounds and beliefs there are much greater obstacles to be overcome, and the success of such a relationship depends on the ability and willingness of the parties to adapt and be flexible, and most of all on trust.

George

Dawoud notes that there are different kinds of mixed marriage. The ones I have come across most frequently are between a Christian – usually the wife – and a spouse who is indifferent to religion. Usually these partnerships seem to work as well as any others. The husband might attend the annual carol service and the occasional social event, but otherwise is never seen – at least not in church.

Dan and Dawoud outline the Jewish and Muslim positions on mixed marriage, and I've already mentioned some of the Christian stances. For would-be marriage partners coming from different religious backgrounds, a number of questions arise. Should the wedding ceremony be Christian or that of the other partner's faith? Which religion will they practise after marriage? What happens to the children?

As you would expect, marriages between Christians of different denominations cause fewer difficulties than marriages between a Christian and a member of another faith. The Orthodox Church does not allow the latter, and anyone who marries outside the Church is barred from receiving the sacrament. For Catholics interfaith marriage is possible, but it cannot be a 'sacramental' one. The Church of England is obliged to conduct the wedding of anyone living within a local parish, so in theory a Jew could marry a Muslim in a parish church. I doubt if this has ever happened because the Church of England's apparent inclusivity does not mean that anything goes. The vicar must follow the prescribed (Christian) order of service, which includes taking vows in the name of the Father, the Son and the Holy Spirit. Although conservative evangelical Protestants take Paul's words to heart, 'Do not be yoked together with unbelievers' (2 Cor. 6.14), there are fewer statutory barriers to interfaith marriage in the Protestant tradition.

Some couples have turned to civil ceremonies. However (at least in Britain), they must not incorporate any religious material whatsoever and therefore the ceremony is non-faith rather than multi-faith. A more adventurous recent alternative has been to have officiants from each tradition to play a key role. The practice is not widespread but there have been interfaith weddings in which a rabbi or an imam has conducted the ceremony, together with a Christian priest. Such weddings must satisfy the requirements of the religious traditions involved and also ensure that the marriage is valid in law. It would be interesting to hear what Dan has to say about this. As a Jewish rabbi, would he be willing to conduct a joint wedding ceremony with a Christian or Muslim officiant, and under what circumstances?

Moving on to children, questions arise about the faith in which they should be brought up. Should they be baptized, circumcised, both or neither? Baptism and circumcision are rites that could be construed as 'claiming' the child for a particular faith and may cause one of the partners to be unhappy about it. Baptism does not require the presence of both parents (although it is usual for the mother and the father to attend), so a baptism involving only one parent is an option.

Do the children get taught about one faith, both faiths or none? Practising Christians would certainly want the Bible's teachings to be passed on to their children as part of their tradition, as well as for religious and moral guidance. Since Jewish Scriptures are part of the Christian heritage, Christians would have no problem with their children being taught about the Old Testament. Islam might be a different matter since the Qur'an is a new Scripture, contradicting the Bible at many points.

Religious festivals require some mention. Because Christmas has become a cultural as well as a religious celebration, many of my Muslim students tell me that they celebrate Christmas, and even send me the odd Christmas card, even without belonging to mixed-faith families. Christians married to Jews or Muslims can therefore decide whether they also want to bring in the Sabbath, commemorate Passover or celebrate Eid. But it's not all fun: there are fasts as well as feasts, and interfaith marriage partners may have to decide whether Lent, Ramadan or the Day of Atonement are on their agenda too.

All these issues are matters of negotiation between marriage partners. As Dawoud says, mixed marriage is an enormous topic. There's lots more material on the internet, and those who want to explore the topic further might look at the Church of England's guidelines on interfaith marriage (www.churchofengland.org/about-us/interfaith/resources.aspx), the website of the Association of Interchurch Families in England, Scotland and Wales (www.interchurchfamilies.org.uk) and the Inter-faith Marriage Network Resource Pack (www.interfaithmarriage.org.uk).

Dan

In Chapter 1 I briefly discussed the issue of intermarriage between a Jew and a non-Jew. Traditionally this has been understood as abhorrent (despite the various instances in Scripture where it occurred). Today Orthodox Judaism is firmly opposed to the marriage of a Jew to a non-Jew. No Orthodox rabbi would ever consider officiating at such a marriage and enormous pressure will be applied on the Jewish partner not to consider taking such a step. All the reasons given by Dawoud – and others as well – are rehearsed: couples are happier in a relationship where there is familiarity and mutual understanding; Jewish culture would be more likely to be preserved; children will have greater stability when both parents are Jewish; there will be a greater sense of identification with the Jewish community. The Jewish person contemplating marrying a non-Jew will be accused of betraying his or her family as well as the Jewish heritage.

Despite such pressures, intermarriage outside of Israel is today a very common occurrence. Of course in Israel, where the majority of the population is Jewish, marriages between two Jews are common. But in the diaspora the majority of all marriages of Jews are to non-Jews. Faced with this threat to Jewish life, the non-

INTERMARRIAGE

Orthodox community has taken dramatic steps to include non-Jews within the fold. Some Reform rabbis, for example, officiate at intermarriage ceremonies as long as the couple is willing to join the synagogue and rear their children as Jews. In general, non-Jewish spouses are allowed to be full members of the synagogue, paying ordinary dues. In some cases they are restricted from participating in various activities (such as reading the blessing over the Torah on the Sabbath or serving as an officer of the synagogue). There are some – though not many – rabbis who are willing to officiate with ministers or priests in a synagogue or church service for an intermarried couple. In general rabbis who officiate at intermarriages do so in the hope that the non-Jewish spouse will eventually convert to Judaism and that the children of such a marriage will be raised as Jews. Their justification for abandoning traditional attitudes is the determination to ensure the survival of the Jewish people and the Jewish faith.

George has asked if I myself would consider officiating at a marriage between a Jew and a Muslim. I have never been asked to do so but I have participated in marriage services with a Christian officiant. Some years ago the chaplain at Trinity College, Cambridge and I conducted a wedding service in the chapel for the Jewish daughter of one of the Fellows and her non-Jewish partner. Similarly, together with a Methodist minister I conducted a wedding service for a Jewish man and his non-Jewish partner in a small chapel in Wales. In both cases the Christian clergyman and I constructed a service that would be acceptable to both Jews and Christians; we were careful to exclude any Christological references or prayers that Jews would find objectionable. What we sought instead was an inclusive liturgy. I participated in such services because as a rabbi I believe it is my duty to help Jews in their personal lives and to present Judaism to Gentiles in as positive a light as possible. Of course, there are many Reform rabbis who would disagree with this approach, and I respect their opinions though I do not share their reservations.

Elsewhere in our book we have discussed the issue of homosexuality. I should note that within Reform Judaism and other non-Orthodox branches of Judaism it is widely accepted that marriage may take place between two Jewish men or two Jewish women. Some of my rabbinical friends officiate at such gay wedding services. But they refuse to officiate at the marriage of two gay men or two lesbians if one of them is a non-Jew. So the situation is as follows: in their view, marriage between two Jews – regardless of gender – is acceptable but an intermarriage is invalid. Defending such a stance, one of my rabbinical friends declared that he is prepared to be liberal about most things (such as violating Sabbath law or eating non-kosher food or marrying two gay or lesbian Jews), but there are things that the tradition simply won't allow him to do – such as perform an intermarriage. In my view this is misguided. But he is entitled to his opinion.

11

Abortion

George

When we let our students choose a moral issue to write about, abortion and euthanasia are favourites. They are very hot issues, but students soon find how difficult it is to come up with reasoned arguments and reach definite conclusions.

Abortion is a problematic topic because there is no certain way of establishing when the soul enters a body (if indeed there is a soul distinct from the body), whether we should place different values on different stages of embryonic life and, if so, for what reasons. Does life begin when we become conscious, when we are capable of feeling pain or when an embryo develops recognizably human features such as hands and feet – or what? These issues are more than paragraphs in student essays. Many women – and sometimes their partners – cannot avoid having to answer them in real life.

It is sometimes thought that abortion is an issue that divides different Christian denominations – a view encouraged by media reports of young women leaving Southern Ireland to have abortions in Britain, where Protestantism is the dominant form of the religion. The expression 'a woman's right to choose' is frequently heard in the context of the abortion debate, but those who want abortion on demand tend to be secularists rather than religious people. Although many Christians would accept that abortion should be a legal right, Christians certainly do not hold that prenatal life is expendable and can be terminated simply for the convenience of the parents. The 'inalienable right to life' must take precedence over any presumed right to choose.

Yet there are situations that present a strong case for justifying an abortion. We have still to hear Dawoud's views on the topic but I think the vast majority of Christians, including Roman Catholics, would agree with Dan that abortion may be justified where it saves the life of the mother. However, once we allow exceptions we seem to be on a slippery slope. What if the expectant mother is a victim of rape or of incest? (The Southern Baptist Convention, in common with many other Christians, acknowledges that these are exceptions too.) Rape victims find the experience traumatic enough without having the added trauma of carrying the baby of (perhaps) a violent attacker and a child as a living reminder of the incident and its perpetrator. Again, what about the young teenager who gets pregnant and is not able to look after her baby?

The likelihood of giving birth to a seriously deformed child is another scenario presenting a case for abortion. How might I feel if my child were likely to have spina bifida or Down's syndrome? We can now detect such conditions prenatally, so the mother cannot simply hope that her baby will be normal. But to terminate a pregnancy in such circumstances is to decide that some human lives are simply not worth living – and that's a very slippery slope indeed. Might we not use similar arguments for terminating the life of an elderly person who has a chronic and seriously debilitating illness? Children with spina bifida or Down's syndrome are not 'write-offs' from humanity. Many can be treated and they have a right to treatment, and their parents are frequently able to love and cherish them with the same affection as other parents.

A greyer area exists where foetal matter is so seriously deformed that it is debatable whether it should be classified as human. In anencephaly the foetus has no brain or spinal cord, and if the pregnancy runs to full term the likelihood is that the baby will be stillborn or only live for a few hours, although occasionally anencephalic babies live longer: an anencephalic girl in Brazil lived for two weeks some years ago. Her parents said they never considered abortion and were thankful for the small window of life God gave her. Some Christians may believe that God has put them in such situations as part of a divine purpose, while others might hold that we ought to let God-given reason direct our decisions.

Again, I'm conscious that I'm writing as a man and that it is women who have abortions. However, men are by no means exempt from these life-and-death decisions. Apart from sometimes being party to the decision about whether to abort, those who 'formally co-operate' – doctors, nurses and ancillary staff in hospitals and clinics – have to be able to reconcile what they do with what their religion teaches.

I've raised quite a few questions but don't have so many firm answers. Maybe Dan and Dawoud can offer firmer conclusions.

Dan

George is right that the issue of abortion revolves around the understanding of the foetus. In traditional Judaism the various views on abortion are based on the legal and ethical teaching of the Hebrew Bible, the Talmud and later response literature. Scripture says little about the matter – there is only one passage that establishes the rule about the killing of an embryo or foetus:

> When men strive together, and hurt a woman with child, so that there is a miscarriage, and yet no harm follows, the one who hurt her shall be fined, according as the woman's husband shall lay upon him. (Exod. 21.22)

On the basis of this passage, abortion is not viewed as murder since the person who committed this offence did not forfeit his life as a punishment. A core text in rabbinic law crystallizes the status of the foetus. The Mishnah explicitly indicates that one must abort a foetus if the continuation of the pregnancy might imperil the life of the mother:

> If a woman is in hard travail, one cuts up the offspring in her womb and brings it forth member by member, because her life comes before the life of the foetus. But if the greater part has proceeded forth, one may not set aside one person for the sake of saving another.

In Talmudic law an embryo is not deemed a fully viable person. After the Talmudic period, Jewish views on abortion became more refined. The twelfth-century Jewish philosopher Moses

Maimonides, for example, justified the requirement to abort a pregnancy that threatens the woman's life not because the foetus is less than a human being but through the principle of the *rodef* or pursuer (pursuing her to kill her).

In the *Code of Jewish Law* therapeutic abortion is permitted. The scope of therapeutic abortion is not narrowly defined and there are many debates in this area of the *halakah*. Maimonides seems to have confined therapeutic abortion to cases where the foetus poses a direct and immediate threat to the physical and mental health of the mother. Abortions of pregnancies resulting from rape or that would result in the mother's loss of sight or hearing have also been considered justified in Jewish law. Opinions are divided regarding the abortion of the foetus of a mother who contracted rubella during pregnancy and in relation to severe disorders that may be detected by genetic analysis during the early part of the pregnancy. With regard to the abortion of defective foetuses, the lenient school permits abortion until the seventh month. The issues of foetal reduction in artificial reproductive procedures and of the use of foetal tissue for research and therapeutic purposes have generally been treated in a permissive fashion in Jewish law.

Turning to non-Orthodox Judaism, attitudes have been more lenient. The Rabbinic Assembly of the Conservative movement has ruled that abortion is justifiable if a continuation of pregnancy might cause the woman severe physical or psychological harm or when the foetus is judged by competent medical opinion as severely defective. Before reaching her final decision, Conservative Judaism stresses that the woman should consult with the biological father, other members of the family, her physician, her rabbi and any other person who might be able to help her.

Reform Judaism permits abortion not only when the woman's life is at stake but also when a pregnancy is a result of rape or incest, when through genetic testing it is determined that the child to be born will have a disease that will cause death or severe disability, when the parents believe that the impending birth will be an impossible situation for them, and for several other reasons as well. As a consequence of its view, the Reform movement has opposed legislation that would restrict the right of a woman to choose to abort a foetus, especially in situations in which the health of the woman is endangered by continued pregnancy. Such a position is linked to the Reform movement's commitment to personal autonomy in moral matters.

Among secular Jews liberal attitudes are dominant, and a considerable number of Jewish women have been active in the pro-choice movement. These reproductive rights activists include Betty Friedan and Gloria Steinem. In addition there are a number of Jewish groups that promote pro-choice issues. It is clear then that the Jewish tradition – even in its most Orthodox form – is far more flexible than Christianity, which has through the ages stressed the inviolable rights of the unborn child.

Dawoud

The majority opinion in Islam is that abortion is forbidden. There is an underlying notion that there should be no sex outside marriage and therefore no pregnancy outside marriage. As one of the main purposes of marriage is procreation, within marriage it should be accepted that all children are a gift from God and should be wanted. The idea that a foetus might be aborted simply because it is conceived at a time that is inconvenient for the parents or because they believe that they cannot afford to raise a child is unacceptable. The Qur'an says: 'Do not kill your children for fear of poverty. We provide for them and for you. Surely, the killing of them is a great sin.'

The scholars argue that only God can decide who is born and who dies, and that to attempt to interfere in this process is a sin. Up until the point where it is believed that the soul is breathed into the foetus, which according to most scholars is at 120 days, abortion is considered sinful but there is no prescribed punishment. After this point, however, it is considered equivalent to killing a child and subject to the same penalties.

If a person injures a pregnant woman thereby causing a miscarriage, he or she will be liable to pay the *diyya* or blood money to the family of the child. If a woman procures an abortion herself without the consent of her husband, then – notwithstanding any other consequences – she will be liable to pay *diyya* to her husband.

Most scholars and most Islamic countries prohibit abortion in almost all circumstances, with only very limited exceptions. If the life or health of the mother is in danger then abortion is permitted even after 120 days as her existing life outweighs the potential life of the foetus. A foetus may not be aborted due to a potential birth defect, however.

As in so many spheres, however, the black and white principles do not always correspond with the realities of people's lives. This does not mean that abortion does not take place in Muslim countries, but the options available to women depend very much on their social and economic circumstances. While well-off women may be able to seek an abortion privately and discreetly through a private practitioner, usually under the guise of another gynaecological procedure or treatment or by travelling abroad, poorer women will not have this option and may be forced to go to unqualified abortionists or traditional midwives and risk their lives in unsafe and unsanitary conditions. In such cases the reasons given are usually that they already have too many children and are unable to cope physically and financially with more.

Where a pregnancy occurs in the case of adultery or fornication, most jurists are of the opinion that abortion is unlawful because the child is innocent of the sin. For a majority of Shari'a jurists it is not permissible even for a woman who has been a victim of rape or incest to obtain an abortion. In some recent conflicts there have been cases or accusations of rape as a form of terrorism against populations, such as the rape of Kuwaiti women by Iraqi soldiers in the first Gulf War and of Kosovan women by Serbian forces in the late 1990s. In these cases the women faced not only the disgrace and stigma of the rape and rejection by their husbands or annihilation of their marriage prospects, but on top of this many were forced to carry and give birth to the offspring of their attackers. The tragic consequence of this was that many children were rejected and abandoned in orphanages and others were brought up unloved and unwanted by their unwilling mothers. The scholars were mostly of the opinion that even in such cases abortion is unlawful as the child is innocent in the same way as the child born out of wedlock. In a rare exception to this the Grand Mufti of the Palestinian Authority in 1999 issued a fatwa

ABORTION

permitting the taking of drugs to induce an early abortion for women raped in Kosovo, on the grounds that Muslim women should not carry Serb children who might later be recruited by the enemy.

12

Assisted Reproduction and Adoption

Dan

I have a particular interest in the issue of artificial insemination because I was one of the first children in the United States to have been born using this procedure. My father was an orthopaedic surgeon. When he and my mother discovered that they could not have children, they arranged for my conception to take place at the University of Chicago. I have no idea who my real father is. As far as Jewish law is concerned, most traditional rabbinic authorities have no objection to the procedure if the husband's sperm is used (AIH – artificial insemination from the husband). Some scholars, however, are concerned about the means by which the husband's sperm is obtained. To ensure that no destruction of the seed in vain takes place (which would be a violation of Gen. 38.9), these rabbis advocate collecting it from the vaginal cavity after intercourse. Other scholars, however, permit the husband to use a condom.

However, artificial insemination using a donor's sperm (AID) is a different matter. In this case a married woman is being inseminated with the sperm of a man other than her husband; in the view of some rabbinic authorities such an act is adultery. This would make any child born in this way illegitimate (a *mamzer*) – such a person and his or her descendants would not be permitted to marry a Jew for ten generations. Other authorities, however, maintain that AID is not in fact adultery since the wife has in no sense cheated on her husband by having sexual intercourse with another man.

Turning to IVF (*in vitro* fertilization), there are three different halakhic opinions:

- IVF may not be permitted since it violates Torah prohibitions, in particular the prohibition against wasting of a man's seed.
- IVF may be permitted, but all physical components – sperm, eggs, serums, uterus, related medications – must be only of the married couple themselves. The entire fertilization process must be strictly supervised by a third-party Jewish person who has undergone training.
- IVF may be permitted even though physical components – sperm and eggs – are from a non-Jewish source. By using non-Jewish semen, if a boy is born he is not a Kohen or a Levite (even if the husband is). If a girl is born she may not marry a Kohen because her biological father is non-Jewish. By using a non-Jewish woman's eggs, the resulting child will have two mothers: one mother who provided the genetic material (the non-Jewish egg donor) and one who is the birth mother (the Jewish mother who carried the pregnancy). The dual mother situation renders the child part Jewish and part non-Jewish. In such a case the child must therefore be properly converted.

It should be noted, however, that among the non-Orthodox these halakhic issues have no relevance. IVF is generally viewed with favour as a means by which parents are able to have children of their own.

With regard to adoption, there are certain Jewish laws that are relevant if a child is raised by someone other than the parents. The Talmud declares that a person who raises someone else's child is regarded as if he had actually brought him into the world. For those who cannot have children of their own, raising adoptive children satisfies the obligation to be fruitful and multiply. Yet the issue of status is particularly important in the case of non-Jewish children adopted by Jews. According to traditional Jewish law, children born of non-Jewish parents are not Jewish unless they are converted, regardless of how they have been raised. Hence if Jewish parents adopt a non-Jewish child, the child must be converted. Such a conversion must be approved by a Bet Din. In non-Orthodox circles, however, conversion is generally not required.

George

Dan has given an informative account of Jewish views on assisted reproduction, drawing on his own personal situation. It is interesting that he has no idea who his biological father is. I have already mentioned the official Roman Catholic position that a child has the right to know who his or her natural parents are (Chapter 3). When having a health check, a typical question is whether one's parents have suffered from specific medical conditions, since such information is relevant to health care, and children who do not know their natural parents' identity are therefore at some disadvantage. There are also emotional considerations. Many adopted children feel a very strong urge to trace their biological parents and meet them, in an attempt to discover their own real identity.

I have already outlined the Catholic and Protestant views on assisted reproduction. Orthodoxy takes much the same view as Roman Catholicism, affirming that sexual intercourse and reproduction must be linked, and viewing attempts to separate the two as 'desacralizing' men and women and treating humans like pieces of equipment for producing children.

Occasionally I go to an acupuncturist. On arriving for my appointment recently I was informed that Rachel – my regular therapist – was taking maternity leave, and would I be happy for Lisa to treat me instead? (Names and some details have been changed to maintain confidentiality.) On talking to Lisa it transpired that Rachel was not taking normal maternity leave. She had agreed to be a surrogate mother for another couple. From previous conversations with Rachel, I had learned that she belonged to the Church of England, so presumably she had no problems reconciling surrogate motherhood with her faith. Lisa, however, did not seem so sure that her decision was a good idea. How would it feel, she asked, to undergo all the stages of pregnancy and childbirth and then not keep the child? How would she explain to her other children – she has two of her own – that another baby was on the way but would not be a new brother or sister for them? We presumed that Rachel was being paid for her surrogate pregnancy, and this raises issues about commodifying one's body. Was she in effect 'renting out' her womb to another couple? If so, is it significantly different from offering any other service associated with child-rearing, such as wet-nursing or child minding?

Christians in the Protestant and Anglican traditions engage in much the same moral deliberation as those who profess no faith. This in itself should be no cause for concern, for as I pointed out in Chapter 1, Christians have not sought to stand out as markedly different from others but rather to interact with what is happening in the world, politically, socially and scientifically. Over the years the Church of England has done precisely this by producing several reports, some of which are independent and some responses to secular bodies. Contrary to the opinions of the 'new atheists' such as Richard Dawkins, the Church is not in the business of retarding scientific progress. Apart from 'creationists' who oppose Darwin's evolutionism, Christianity has generally welcomed scientific advance, and the Church of England has explicitly stated that this includes embryo research.

Protestants and Anglicans acknowledge that there are uncertainties. We cannot say definitely when a human life begins and it is hard to decide the extent to which differences between a sperm, an embryo and a foetus are morally significant. The Church of England's recent response to the Nuffield Council on Bioethics Consultation on Donor Conception (May 2012) offers a number of recommendations that anyone contemplating surrogate parenting or sperm donation might profitably consider. Donor-conceived children have a right to be informed of their mode of conception, and some basic information might profitably be made available to the child (for example, about the donor's education, financial status, whether he or she has a criminal record). Reciprocally, the donor may want to know about the child's sex, state of health, or subsequent academic or sporting achievements. However, the report underlines the point that a 'donor' is literally someone who makes a gift, and that a gift should not have strings attached to it. A donor is not a remote parent.

Religion cannot always offer definitive solutions to the problems raised by advancing technology, but it can contribute to societal debate on such matters. I look forward to hearing how Dawoud does this on behalf of Islam.

Dawoud

Muslims are enjoined to marry and to multiply in the Qur'an, but it is made clear that ultimately fertility is in God's hands.

> To Allah belongs the dominion of the heavens and the earth. He creates what He wills. He bestows (children) male or female according to His will. Or He bestows both males and females, and He leaves barren whom He wills; for he is full of knowledge and power. (Sura 42.49–50)

This does not mean, however, that there should be no assisted reproduction, nor that it should be seen as challenging God's will. Most scholars agree that it is permissible to assist reproduction in the ways that are permissible and that advancements in medical science should be encouraged as a means of promoting family life and procreation.

The essential principles for Sunni Muslims were set out in 1980 by Gad El-Hak Ali Gad El-Hak, Sheikh of Al-Azhar in Egypt, which is recognized as one of the most authoritative sources of Sunni doctrine and law. He issued a fatwa that in summary stated that artificial insemination and *in vitro* fertilization were legitimate for married couples provided there was no involvement of any third-party donor. He reasoned that any third-party involvement in the reproductive process, whether by donation of eggs, sperm, embryos or surrogacy, is tantamount to adultery and therefore unlawful. Moreover, such procedures lead to confusion of lineage, which is held to be of great importance in Islam. Any assisted procedure should only take place during the valid marriage contract; no implantation of embryos or insemination may take place after divorce or death of the husband.

Embryos not used in a cycle of treatment may be frozen and used at a later date provided they are only used by the couple who produced them within the duration of a valid marriage. They may not be donated to another couple. In the case of multiple foetuses, reduction or selective abortion may only take place if the continuation of the multiple pregnancy threatens the life or health of the mother or if the multiple pregnancy is determined not to be viable but more likely to result in a live birth with a smaller number of embryos.

Any procedure should only be carried out by a medical practitioner, and any doctor who carries out a procedure in contravention of these principles is considered to be guilty of an unlawful act. These principles have been broadly accepted throughout the Sunni world.

In 1999 Ayatollah Khamanei of Iran, whose opinions are considered authoritative for many Shi'i Muslims, issued a fatwa stating that recourse to third-party donations may be legitimate, although other scholars disagree. There are numerous and complex arguments too lengthy to discuss here, but other considerations come into the argument, such as the ruling that inheritance rules will apply between an egg donor and the child resulting from the donation but not between the child and the mother who carries him or her. The institution of *mut'a* marriage has also been used to make the donation of eggs and their recovery and fertilization by the husband and implantation in his wife legitimate during the term of a *mut'a* marriage. This is seen as valid under the laws of polygyny, but many scholars consider sperm donation unlawful as a woman may not have two husbands. Embryo donation from one married couple to another is permitted, however, as all parties are legitimately married.

There is a perception that Islam does not permit adoption, but in fact the taking in and rearing of orphans or foundling children within a family that is not their birth family is not only permitted but actively encouraged. The Prophet Muhammad's father died before he was born and his mother died when he was about six years old. He was raised by his grandfather and uncle and he in turn adopted a son, Zaid. Islam encourages the nurturing of adopted or fostered children within a loving family but only prohibits the ascription of the lineage of the adoptive parents to the child and the ascription of mutual inheritance rights. Sura 33.4–5 says:

> And he has not made your adopted sons your [true] sons. That is [merely] your saying by your mouths, but Allah says the truth, and He guides to the [right] way. Call them by [the names

of] their fathers; it is more just in the sight of Allah. But if you do not know their fathers – then they are [still] your brothers in religion and those entrusted to you. And there is no blame upon you for that in which you have erred but [only for] what your hearts intended.

Inheritance laws allow bequests of up to a third of the total estate before the distribution of statutory shares, however, so adopted children need not be excluded from inheritance and may in fact receive a greater share of an estate than they might have done as a biological child.

13

Family Life

Dan

In Chapter 3 I described Jewish family life in its various forms. Throughout, I stressed that traditional Judaism regards the home as fundamental. The Ten Commandments emphasize that children are to honour and respect their parents, and rabbinic sages explained in detail how this should be done. As I pointed out, among the Orthodox the roles of men and women are very different: because of her domestic chores, a wife is not expected to perform all the positive time-bound commandments as outlined in Scripture and later defined by rabbinic sages. Her duties are essentially to care for the material needs of her family. The Jewish tradition also stresses that women must be modest in dress and demeanour. Further, the *Code of Jewish Law* lays down rules for sexual contact between husbands and wives and ensures that women observe the manifold regulations regarding spiritual uncleanliness.

It should not be assumed, however, that these complex rules are followed in the same way as they were in previous centuries. Rather, Jewish life has fundamentally changed for the vast majority of Jews. Let me begin with the subject of marriage. As I noted in previous chapters, Judaism teaches that Jewish men must marry Jewish women: only in this way, it is argued, will the Jewish people survive. Yet despite the views of the Jewish establishment, intermarriage between Jews and Gentiles is widespread. In addition there are a sizeable number of Jewish men and women who live in a same-sex relationship. Such a situation is far removed from the pattern of married life in the past. Further, many home ceremonies dealing with family life that I described in detail have been abandoned. Today, for example, it is rare for Jewish wives to go to the *mikveh* – only the strictly Orthodox continue to observe the manifold regulations regarding menstruation. The same applies to regulations specifying that women must cover their hair in public – most Jewish women today do not feel compelled to wear wigs or some form of head covering. Nor do most Jewish men wear skullcaps outside of synagogues. Again, it is only the strictly Orthodox who wear fringed undergarments in accordance with rabbinic law.

Yet arguably the greatest transformation of family life concerns the place of women in the community. As I noted previously, many Jewish women today are unhappy with this traditional role. They believe that this pattern has been imposed on them by men and wish to make their mark beyond the home. In the various non-Orthodox movements, women are ordained as rabbis and are permitted to lead religious services as cantors. In the secular sphere most parents are anxious that their daughters as well as sons should achieve the highest educational standards. In the diaspora young people are marrying late; in addition there are many single people who prefer to live alone.

At the same time, the community is wistful about the old ways. Secular Jews often look to the family lives of the strictly Orthodox with their clearly demarcated areas of responsibility and their large numbers of children with a mixture of awe, disapproval and envy. As the modern secular husband examines his high-powered working wife and his one or two difficult adolescent children, traditional Jewish values can seem attractive. Nonetheless, for most they are unattainable. It would be nice to be honoured by one's offspring, to have a son who, as the Talmud puts it, does not contradict his father's words nor decides against his opinions. Regrettably such a relationship goes against all modern ideas of child-rearing.

Other Jewish attitudes are also admired by the non-Orthodox. The law insists on integrity in business as the mark of an upright man. The relationship between employer and employee must be one of mutual co-operation, fairness and trust. All Jews have a duty to support the poor and needy and give generously and regularly to charity. This is still taken seriously and Orthodox

Jewish welfare organizations are, in general, efficiently run and well supported. Hospitality to the stranger is another obligation, and most traditional Jewish households entertain regularly, particularly on the festivals and for Sabbath dinner on Friday night. Judaism teaches that the upright person will speak the truth at all times; gossip and slander are to be deplored; animals must be treated with kindness and compassion and honest labour is to be commended. It is obvious that all is not as it should be in the world. The duty of the pious Jew is to start the work of repair and restore again the peace created by God. At its best, the traditional Jewish family is a microcosm of that ideal harmony that should exist in the world.

George

Dan has drawn attention to the way in which the Jewish faith has changed in the past couple of generations. Christianity has also witnessed change over the past half century or so. I too was taught to obey my parents and never to contradict them – at least in public. However, Kahlil Gibran points out that there comes a point in the parent–child relationship where we have to recognize that 'your children are not your children', that they have independent lives and that one can even learn from them. It's actually very rewarding to have a daughter who has done postgraduate work and with whom one can intellectually debate things. She even suggested an opening for a conference paper I was giving recently! So I certainly would not want a return to the days when she had to accept what her parents said.

Dan also mentions the way attitudes to religious dress have changed over the years. I quoted the Letter to Diognetus earlier (Chapter 1), in which the anonymous author makes the point that Christians don't seek to stand out by their distinctive dress but try to blend in with the prevailing culture. Although some Christians choose to wear crosses or fish symbols, this is a preference rather than a religious requirement. (The fish symbol, incidentally, derives from the Greek word ICHTHUS meaning fish, which is an acronym for 'Jesus Christ Son of God Saviour.) In my childhood we were expected to wear our 'Sunday best' to church, and men were required to remove headgear inside. In some denominations, such as some Pentecostal churches, these standards prevail, but casual clothing is now the norm, and baseball caps seem to have become exempt from the 'hats off' rule.

In Islam the wearing of distinctive dress seems to have gone in a more conservative direction. Dawoud hasn't yet commented on the increasing practice of Muslim women wearing the veil in the West. When I first came to the English Midlands 20 years ago no one seemed to do this, but increasingly fully veiled women are a common sight. The practice has been much criticized as being repressive and for implying that exposing parts of the female body attract male lust. Perhaps the West needs to reappraise its lack of modesty regarding the female body and the way sex is flaunted in the media. However, isn't the practice of veiling going to the opposite extreme?

The custom seems to derive from a time when women largely stayed in the home and were not normally seen by men outside the family. As Dan points out, however, women now have educational and career aspirations, and this is true of all three religions. Such ambitions mean no longer being confined to domestic chores, and to a non-Muslim like myself the practice of veiling seems something of a contradiction. The female Muslim students whom I meet seem to want to break away from traditional roles, but revert to a very conservative practice that seems more appropriate to the woman as the home-dweller.

The *hijab*, which covers the head and neck, can look very attractive, but many westerners find that the *niqab* (face veil, revealing only the eyes) presents a barrier to communication and gives rise to problems such as the increased ease of impersonation. Facial gestures are important in giving oral presentations, and one can understand parents' reluctance for their child to be taught by someone whose face is hidden. A few Muslim students were loath to have photographs taken for their university ID cards. When there is so much Islamophobia around, would it not be better – as the writer to Diognetus describes – to blend in with the society in which they live rather than stand apart visibly and incur criticism?

Although the issue of veiling has hit the headlines, I think all three religions share similar problems. How do we move with the times without totally abandoning our traditions? While Christians tend to blend in with their environment, this policy carries the risk that we totally succumb to secular values. The challenge for our various faiths in the modern world is whether we accommodate these or whether we practise our faiths with renewed vigour.

Dawoud

A few years ago I took a group of undergraduate and postgraduate students to Cairo on a field trip. They were taking various courses in religious and Islamic studies and they had various academic objectives, but at the same time I believed it would be valuable for them to see ordinary everyday life in a Muslim country. It was therefore a priceless moment when I overheard one of the mature students at the back of the bus commenting to his neighbour with some surprise, 'They look quite happy really, don't they!'

The lives of Muslims in different parts of the world are diverse and it is difficult to generalize about them. In some parts of the Muslim world there have been enormous improvements in the position of women and opportunities available to them over the course of the last century. Yet in some areas there seems to be little hope of reform, and in some cases there have been retrograde steps. In the news media we hear regularly of abuses of women both at home and abroad. It is not uncommon to hear reports of British-born teenagers taken abroad to be married or younger children to undergo genital mutilation. There are reports of honour killings in other countries and sometimes in Britain, the prevention of education for girls (or simple disregard for its importance), punishment of the victims of rape, the enforcement of the *burqa* and the many other aspects of the powerlessness of women in many Muslim communities. It is impossible to reconcile the position of oppressed women in some of the poorer, troubled areas of the Muslim world with, for example, the worldview portrayed by *emel*, the British-Muslim lifestyle magazine that presents positive images of the life of ordinary Muslims with features on food, shopping, culture, design, politics, gardening and the life of moderate, thoughtful Muslims living in harmony with their non-Muslim neighbours, colleagues and friends in Britain and other western countries. The magazine has regular features on marriage and family life and profiles of couples of all backgrounds, who talk about their marriages, the way they met and married, their lives together, the way they negotiate cultural differences, what they appreciate about each other, how they resolve their problems and how their faith gives them a shared meaning in life – something bigger than themselves. Among these features are couples who had arranged marriages and only met on their wedding day, couples who met through friends, at work, via introductions or online. Some have been married for 40 years and some are relatively newly wed. Some of the women are home makers but others have high-flying professional careers. Neither of these perspectives is the whole picture, and the lives of the majority of Muslims in the world are somewhere on the spectrum in between.

George has asked about veiling. I mentioned it briefly in Chapter 1, and George is quite correct in his observation that there has been a marked increase in the wearing of the *hijab* in Britain and other European countries. There are many factors involved, including the growth in the Muslim population through immigration from many different countries where the veil is customarily worn, a global resurgence of Islam and a cultural confidence encouraged by a general acceptance of diversity and multiculturalism. Although it should be a personal choice, it has reached, in effect, critical mass, so that it has become an expectation among Muslim communities for women to wear the *hijab*, although those who wear the *niqab*, the full veil, are still a small minority. Among young women in schools and universities there is a degree of peer pressure. Young women will naturally want to fit in with their friends but they may also have a sense that they will be regarded with less respect by their communities if they do not wear the *hijab*. Many will argue that the *hijab* gives them freedom to be treated as an individual on personal or professional merit and not to be judged by their hair, make-up, dress size or fashion sense. It may make them feel more protected from pressure to conform to conventions of fashion and behaviour in what they perceive to be an increasingly sexualized society. Like many distinctive forms of dress, however, it makes a statement about the wearer that inevitably leads to some prejudgement.

14

Divorce

George

I think our dialogues have enabled us to identify many points in common on the themes of sex and marriage, while our points of difference can cause us to reflect on whether our own traditions might learn something from each other. I believe this is particularly the case when it comes to divorce.

We all seem to agree that marriage is a desirable state of affairs and that divorce is not. However, all three of us acknowledge that relationships can become problematic over the years, causing partners to reappraise their marriage commitments. We are also agreed that appropriate financial arrangements should be made so that neither party has insuperable financial problems, and that suitable custody arrangements should be made for any children who are involved. The Church of England's marriage ceremony contains the words, 'all that I am I give to you, and all that I have I share with you', which both partners affirm. Hence at least in theory, property is owned in common by both marriage partners, and in the event of a divorce it would be normal practice to split one's joint assets equally. However, apportioning one's wealth would be a civil rather than a religious matter, since the Church does not have a role in divorce proceedings.

All three of us place marriage within our religious framework – the ceremonies take place in the synagogue, church or mosque – but it seems that it is only the Christian who is reluctant to give divorce a place within the context of religion. The Christian vows that the partnership exists 'till death us do part', but about a third of marriages in which this vow has been invoked have broken down. It seems as if the Jewish and Islamic traditions acknowledge at the outset that marital breakdown is a possibility – something that Christians are reluctant to do. I suspect that we may have something to learn from Judaism and Islam in this regard, and I think the introduction of Christian divorce ceremonies is a start. Christians seek to place marriage within the context of the Church, but if a marriage is not working out the couple need to turn to civil law if they decide to divorce. However, once divorce gains official recognition in the Church's liturgy, it rather militates against the lifelong commitment that the marriage ceremony involves. I would be interested to know what Dan and Dawoud think of this. Do your marriage ceremonies explicitly require a lifelong commitment and, if not, does this imply that a marriage partnership is to some degree disposable?

However, one possible benefit of the Church's non-involvement in divorce is that men and women are on an equal footing. From what each of you says, it looks as if it is easier for the husband to initiate divorce proceedings rather than the wife – although it's interesting to learn that it is possible for women to do this. I wonder if you think there remains a gender imbalance here. From what Dan says there is still a problem for women who are unable to receive a *get* from their husbands, and Dawoud acknowledges that women have fewer avenues than men by which to seek divorce. I wonder if this is an area in which either of you would like to see change.

There is a further issue on which none of us has made substantial comment: remarriage. For many Christians, annulment of a marriage and separation from one's partner are acceptable. However, divorce ensures that remarriage is permitted, at least in law. For Protestants this is not a problem, but in the Roman Catholic and Orthodox traditions, entering into a sexual relationship with another partner is tantamount to adultery and hence attracts strong disapproval. In the Church of England, to have a church wedding for a second marriage requires presenting one's case to the vicar, and remarriage can sometimes be a barrier to holding office within the denomination.

One final comment on divorce: in all our three traditions, divorce seems to be surrounded by a web of legal requirements. Are we all perhaps somewhat legalistic in this regard? Should we not simply acknowledge that while marriage is intended to be for life, relationships sometimes go wrong and, if they do, divorce is the humane remedy, as the Divorce Hope website, which I quoted earlier, suggests (Chapter 4)?

Dawoud

George is right that divorce is recognized and regulated by Islamic law, but this does not mean that for the majority of people it is treated any more lightly than in any other culture. As I mentioned, there is a much quoted *hadith* indicating that of all the things permitted by God, divorce is the most detested.

Leaving aside *mut'a* and travelling marriage, which are rare and not accepted by the majority of Muslims, marriage is to be entered into with the intention that it be for life, and in many Muslim countries the law states that any clause included in a contract to indicate that a marriage is temporary will be void although the marriage itself will be valid.

Marriage is not, however, a sacrament or a holy union but a contract that is in almost every respect like any other. It is regulated according to the Shari'a but there is no religious ceremony as such. While most Muslims arrange for a *Ma'zun* to oversee the conclusion of the contract, this is not a legal requirement; there are no vows, which means that there is no sin involved in ending it where all possibility of its continuation has been exhausted. There is therefore no religious barrier to remarriage; in fact the format of any Islamic marriage contract requires it to be stated whether the bride is a virgin or previously married.

Earlier I discussed the procedure of *khul'* by which a woman may ransom herself from an irretrievable marriage by returning her dower and relinquishing other financial rights. An unexpected consequence of the incorporation of this into Egyptian law has been to offer a remedy to some non-Muslim women. Christians constitute a substantial minority in Egypt. Most are Coptic Orthodox but there are also significant Armenian, Greek and Syrian Orthodox communities as well as Coptic, Armenian, Chaldean, Greek, Maronite, Roman and Syrian Catholics. Strictly speaking none of the churches countenances divorce for any but the gravest of reasons. The Catholic churches forbid divorce and the Coptic Church only permits it in the case of adultery, bigamy or other extreme circumstances. Under the Unified Courts system that replaced the denominational courts in 1955, the law stipulates that in the case of a personal status dispute between non-Muslim Egyptians who are of a single denomination that has a regulated corpus of rules in place at the time of enactment of the law, ruling will be given in accordance with their denominational code, defined by the Court of Cassation as everything that had been applicable under the denominational courts prior to their abolition. Where the parties are of different Christian denominations, however, no single denominational law can be enforced and the case will be subject to 'public guardianship', which in effect means Islamic personal status law. The extrapolation of this is the potential for application of the *khul'* provisions enacted in Law 1 of 2000. This would have been inconceivable prior to the enactment of this law, but some Christian women have used it to obtain a divorce where they have no other access to relief or where the only other option is a protracted process of separation. Some have even resorted to being baptized into another Christian denomination. This came to public attention in the case of a prominent Egyptian actress who obtained a divorce by *khul'* after she converted to Syrian Orthodoxy.

Divorce can never be an easy option, but the notion that a person entering marriage with the best of intentions, perhaps when still very young, could be sentenced for life if things go wrong through no fault of their own seems tragic, and I understand why George suggests that divorce may be the humane remedy. That is not to say, however, that even where divorce is permitted in law, people are not imprisoned by culture and family and societal expectation.

Dan

According to tradition, when a Jewish couple gets married their souls become one. It is equivalent to a spiritual operation that fuses their souls into a new whole. The Jewish divorce ceremony does the reverse: it is like a spiritual amputation that severs one part of the united soul from the other. As such, divorce is viewed as a tragedy. In this respect Judaism's view is parallel to those of Christianity and Islam. Yet unlike traditional Christianity, it is not perceived as a violation of God's will. On the contrary, as we have seen, biblical and rabbinic Judaism provides a framework for such a separation to take place. To expand the analogy: when a limb becomes so diseased that it endangers the rest of the body, a patient is faced with a choice – to face the pain of amputation or risk worse suffering by leaving things as they are. If the future risks are sufficiently high to outweigh the pain, it is only right to cut off the limb. Similarly, divorce is painful for all those involved but it is the right choice if remaining in an unhealthy relationship will only cause more damage and suffering. Nonetheless, divorce should be seen as a last resort. Traditionally everything should be done to avoid such a situation. If there is a remote chance that the marital bond can be salvaged, even with great effort, expense and expertise, an attempt should be made.

As we noted, when a divorce takes place, the marriage contract is destroyed, thereby severing both the spiritual and physical connections between husband and wife. According to traditional Judaism, divorce must be in accord with various rules:

> A man may not divorce his wife concerning whom he has published an evil report (about her unchastity) before marriage. ('And they shall fine him a hundred shekels of silver, and give them to the father of the woman, because he has brought an evil name upon a virgin of Israel; and she shall be his wife; he may not divorce her all his days.') (Deut. 22.19)

A divorce must be enacted by a formal written document.

> When a man takes a wife, and marries her, then it comes to pass that she does not find favour in his eyes, because he has found something unseemly in her, then he writes her a bill of divorce, and gives it in her hand, and sends her out of his house. (Deut. 24.1)

A man who has divorced his wife shall not remarry her if she married another man after the divorce.

Her former husband, who sent her away, may not take her again to be his wife. After that she is defiled, for that is an abomination before the LORD, and thou shall not cause sin in the land which the LORD thy God gives you as an inheritance. (Deut. 24.4)

As I said previously, the power of divorcing a wife rests solely with the husband. In modern times, such discrimination has been challenged in various ways. Jewish feminists in particular have voiced their criticism of the tradition. In the 1960s and 70s, far-reaching changes in women's roles and identities in both the personal and public sphere took place in the Jewish community. One of the most pressing concerns has been the inequality in Jewish divorce law. Within the Orthodox movement, changes in women's roles have been slower due to the view that Jewish law is of divine origin. Within non-Orthodox Judaism, on the other hand, it is universally accepted that the traditional attitudes to divorce are now outmoded.

Here as elsewhere it is clear that our three traditions share much in common: Judaism, Christianity and Islam constitute what is referred to in Islamic thought as the Abrahamic *ummah*. Yet as we have seen throughout the final part of our book, our three faiths have interpreted God's will in different ways. In our discussion, George and I have frequently stressed the many ways in which Judaism and Christianity have undergone significant development in recent times. The Enlightenment has deeply affected the Jewish and Christian understanding of love, sex and marriage. This, however, does not appear to be so in the case of Islam. As yet there has not been a fundamental alteration in the Muslim perception of the role of the founder of the faith and God's revelation to his people. As a Jew I would hope that my Islamic brothers and sisters will perceive the need for a substantial reorientation of perspective so that, like Judaism and Christianity, modern believers will be able to embrace the essentials of the faith while at the same time opening themselves to the insights of the contemporary world.

Glossary

Judaism

Av	fifth month of the Jewish year
Agunah	tied woman
Badeken	veiling ceremony
Bar mitzvah	son of the commandment
Berit milah	circumcision
Bet din	rabbinical court
Birkat hamazon	grace after meals
Erusin	betrothal
Get	bill of divorce
Hanukkah	festival of lights
Haroset	paste made of fruit, spices, wine and matzah for the Passover meal
Havdalah	ceremony marking the end of the Sabbath
Hazzan	cantor
Heter meah rabbanim	permission by 100 rabbis
Horah	Israeli dance
Huppah	wedding canopy
Kabbalah	mystical Judaism
Kaddish	prayer for the dead
Kashrut	ritual food law

Ketubah	marriage document
Kiddush	prayer recited over a cup of wine to consecrate the Sabbath or a festival
Kiddushin	stage in betrothal
Krenzel	traditional dance in which the bride's mother is crowned
Mamzer	bastard
Matzot	unleavened bread
Mazel tov	congratulations
Mezuzah	parchment scroll placed in a container and fixed to the doorpost
Mikveh	ritual bath
Minyan	quorum
Mitzvah tantz	dance in which family members and honoured rabbis are invited to dance
Mizinke	dance for parents of the bride or groom
Mohar	payment by the groom
Mohel	circumciser
Nisan	first month of the Jewish year
Nissuin	second stage in the marriage procedure
Noachide laws	seven moral laws obligatory on all human beings
Sandak	person responsible for holding a child during a circumcision
Seder	Passover meal
Sefer Torah	scroll of the Five Books of Moses
Sheitel	wig
Shema	central prayer of the Jewish liturgy
Shetar pesikta	document detailing financial obligations
Sheva berachot	seven blessings

Shiddukhin	financial obligations
Shivah	seven-day period of mourning
Sofer	scribe
Tallit katan	fringed undergarment
Tikkun olam	healing of the world
Tzitzit	fringes
Vort	verbal understanding
Yeshivah	Jewish higher educational institution
Yetzer ha-ra	evil inclination
Yetzer ha-tov	good inclination
Yichud	togetherness
Zohar	medieval work of mystical Judaism

Christianity

Adventism	denomination whose followers expect an imminent return of Jesus Christ
Canon	rule, standard, piece of ecclesiastical legislation or defined body of Scripture
Counter-Reformation	Reform movements within the Roman Catholic Church in Europe, as a response to the Protestant Reformation
Encyclical	general letter written by the Pope to the entire Church
Eucharist	sacrament commemorating Jesus' last meal, also known as holy communion and sometimes as the Lord's Supper
Fundamentalism	movement whose key tenets include the inerrancy of the Bible
Gospel	(1) Christian faith's key proclamation of Christ's coming and his redeeming work

	(2) first four books in the New Testament (Matthew, Mark, Luke and John)
Grace	undeserved favour from God
Great Schism	split between Eastern and Western Christianity in 1054 CE
Magisterium	Roman Catholic ecclesiastical hierarchy, consisting of bishops, archbishops and cardinals
Orthodox churches	Eastern churches that split away from Western Christianity in 1054, rejecting the authority of Rome
Puritans	groups of sixteenth- and seventeenth-century English Protestants, opposed to elaborate liturgy, seeking an austere lifestyle
Sacraments	outward signs of inner grace, manifested particularly in the Church's rites of baptism and the Eucharist
Southern Baptists	largest Protestant denomination in the United States, affirms the inerrancy of the Bible
Thirty-Nine Articles	summary of the official teaching of the Church of England, drawn up in 1553
Unitarians	non-mainstream denomination that questioned the doctrine of the Trinity

Islam

'Aqd al-Zawaj / 'Aqd al-Nikah	marriage contract
'Idda	waiting period following divorce or widowhood during which a woman may not remarry
'Urf	custom

GLOSSARY

Bikr	virgin
Hadd	prescribed punishment for certain serious crimes including murder, robbery, theft, adultery and false accusation of adultery – prescribed in the Qur'an
Hadith	reports of the words, deeds and tacit approval of the Prophet Muhammad – this is the second main textual source of law in Islam
Hijab	head veil covering a woman's hair and neck – in general terms it may refer to the complete form of dress covering a woman's head and body
Ijab	offer of contract
Khul'	procedure by which a woman may ransom herself from an unhappy marriage by repaying her dower
Khutba	betrothal or engagement
Mahr / Sadaq	dower or bride price required in the marriage contract and the absolute property of the wife
Mubara'a	similar to khul' – divorce by financial agreement
Muhajjaba	wearing the veil / woman who wears the veil
Muharramat (min al-nisa')	women forbidden to a man in marriage
Musahara	'in-law' relationship which is an impediment to marriage
Nikah	marriage
Niqab	complete veil covering a woman's head and face leaving only a gap for the eyes
Qadi	judge
Qubul	acceptance of contract

Qur'an	Islam's holy book, believed to be the literal word of God revealed to the Prophet Muhammad between 610 and 632 CE
Shahid – Shuhud	witness(es)
Shari'a	Islamic Law – which governs all aspects of the life of a Muslim including worship, personal relationships, business and finance, crime and punishment, war and politics
Sunna	custom or way of life, used specifically to refer to the custom of the Prophet Muhammad, which is the model for the behaviour of all Muslims – recorded in the *Sira*, the biography of the Prophet, and individual reports or *hadith* (see above)
Ta'zir	discretionary punishments for lesser offences not prescribed in the Qur'an but determined by the Qadi
Talaq ba'in baynuna kubra	greater irrevocable divorce (where the parties may not remarry)
Talaq ba'in baynuna sughra	lesser irrevocable divorce (where the parties may remarry with a new contract and dower)
Talaq raja'i	revocable divorce
Talaq	divorce
Thayyib	woman who has been previously married and divorced or widowed
Wilaya, Wali	marriage guardian who represents a woman in the marriage contract
Zawaj al-Misyar	traveller's marriage – contracted by men away from home. This does not involve setting up home. The man usually visits the woman at her home or her family's home
Zawaj al-Mut'a	form of fixed-term marriage in return for payment
Zawaj	marriage

Further Reading

Judaism

Abrams, Nathan (ed.) (2008), *Jews and Sex*, Nottingham: Five Leaves Publications.

Berg, Yehudi (2006), *The Kabbalah Book of Sex and Other Mysteries of the Universe*, Toronto: Research Centre of Kabbalah.

Boteach, Shmuley (2000), *Kosher Sex: A Recipe for Passion and Intimacy*, New York: Three Rivers Press.

Broyde, Michael J. and Michael Ausubel (eds) (2005), *Marriage, Sex, and Family in Judaism: The Past, Present, and Future*, Lanham, MD: Rowman and Littlefield Publishers.

Cowan, Paul and Rachel Cowan (1987), *Mixed Blessings: Marriage Between Jews and Christians*, New York: Doubleday.

Epstein, Louis M. (1981), *Sex Laws and Customs in Judaism*, Jersey City, NJ: Ktav.

Fuchs-Kreimer, Nancy and Nancy H. Wiener (2005), *Judaism for Two: A Spiritual Guide for Strengthening and Celebrating Your Loving Relationship*, Woodstock, VT: Jewish Lights.

Glasner, Samuel (1961), *Judaism and Sex*, New York: Hawthorn Books.

Gordis, Robert (1988), *Love and Sex*, New York: Hippocrene Books.

Gross, David C. and Esther R. Gross (1996), *Under the Wedding Canopy: Love and Marriage in Judaism*, New York: Hippocrene Books.

Lamm, Maurice (2008), *The Jewish Way in Love and Marriage*, New York: Jonathan David Publishers.

Lewis, Mendell (1994), *Jewish Marriage: Rabbinic Law, Legend and Custom*, New York: Jason Bronson.

Olitzky, Kerry and Joan Peterson Littman (2003), *Making a Successful Jewish Interfaith Marriage*, Woodstock, VT: Jewish Lights.

Ruttenberg, Danya (2009), *The Passionate Torah: Sex and Judaism*, New York: New York University Press.

Shoulson, Abraham B. (1959), *Marriage and Family Life: A Jewish View*, New York: Twayne.

Waskow, Arthur (1995), *Down-to-Earth Judaism: Food, Money, Sex, and the Rest of Life*, New York: William Morrow and Co.

Wertheimer, Ruth and Jonathan Mark (1996), *Heavenly Sex: Sex and the Jewish Tradition*, New York: New York University Press.

Christianity

Augustine (1957), *City of God*, trans. John Haley; 2 vols, London: Dent.

Call, Vaughn R. A. and Tim B. Heaton (1997), 'Religious Influence on Marital Stability', *Journal for the Scientific Study of Religion* 3(2), pp. 382–92.

Chryssides, George D. (2010), *Christianity Today*, London: Continuum.

Chryssides, George D. and M. Z. Wilkins (2011), *Christians in the Twenty-first Century*, London: Equinox.

Fletcher, Joseph (1966), *Situation Ethics: The New Morality*, London: SCM Press.

Church of England (1662, 1968), *Book of Common Prayer*, Glasgow: Collins.

Church of Scotland (1940, 1965), *Book of Common Order of the Church of Scotland*, London: Oxford University Press.

Lewis, C. S. (1963), *The Four Loves*, London: Fontana.

Vatican (1994), *Catechism of the Catholic Church*, London: Geoffrey Chapman.

Westminster Confession of Faith (1647, 1969), Edinburgh: William Blackwood and Sons.

Websites

Pope Pius XI (1930), *Casti Connubii* ('Of Chaste Marriage'). Accessible at www.vatican.va/holy_father/pius_xi/encyclicals/documents/hf_p-xi_enc_31121930_casti-connubii_en.html. Accessed 6 October 2012.

Pope Paul VI (1968), *Humanae Vitae* ('Of Human Life'). Accessible at www.vatican.va/holy_father/paul_vi/encyclicals/documents/hf_p-vi_enc_25071968_humanae-vitae_en.html. Accessed 6 October 2012.

Islam

Abu-Lughod, L. (ed.) (1998), *Remaking Women: Feminism and Modernity in the Middle East*, New Jersey: Princeton University Press.

FURTHER READING

El-Alami, D. S. (1996), *The Marriage Contract in Islamic Law: In the Shari'ah and Personal Status Laws of Egypt and Morocco*, London: Graham & Trotman.

Esposito, J. L. (1992), *Women in Muslim Family Law*, Syracuse, NY: Syracuse University Press.

Haeri, S. (1990), *The Law of Desire: Temporary Marriage in Islam*, London: I. B. Tauris.

Mernissi, F. (1991), *Women and Islam*, trans. Mary Jo Lakeland, Oxford: Basil Blackwell.

Mir-Hosseini, Z. (1993), *Marriage on Trial*, London: I. B. Tauris.

Nasir, J. (1994), *The Status of Women Under Islamic Law*, London: Graham & Trotman.

Roald, A. S. (2001), *Women in Islam: The Western Experience*, London: Routledge.

Sherif, Faruq (1988), *A Guide to the Contents of the Qur'an*, Reading: Garnet Publishing.

Welchman, L. (ed.) (2004), *Women's Rights and Islamic Family Law: Perspectives on Reform*, London: Zed Books.

Yamani, M. (ed.) (1996), *Feminism and Islam: Legal and Literary Perspectives*, Reading: Ithaca Press.

Yusuf Ali, Abdullah, *The Holy Qur'an; Arabic Text with English Translation*, Kitab Bhavan and various editions.

Index of Names and Subjects

abortion 29, 31, 91, 108, 114, 127, 219–225, 230
Abraham xii, xvi, xx, 48, 92, 105, 115
abstinence 36, 116, 121, 187, 193, 195
Adam and Eve xii, 16, 34, 48, 47, 75, 91, 105, 108, 109, 117, 159
Adventism 22
adoption 81, 112, 227, 228, 231–2
Africa xx, xxi, 76, 129, 158–60, 205, 207
agunah 51, 140–5
AIDS 112, 198, 200
Aisha 38, 119–20, 126
Al-Azhar xix, 230
Al-Shaarawi, Hoda 42
anencephaly 210, 220
angels xx, 10, 34, 111, 113, 118, 127
animals 11–2, 46–7, 97, 101, 131, 191, 235
Anglicanism viii, 20, 74, 76, 106, 110, 116, 157, 160, 229
annulment 21, 40, 44, 14–2, 145, 148–9, 153, 240

anti-Semitism 96
apostasy 83, 124, 140, 188
arranged marriages 7, 48, 68, 80, 95, 210, 238
artificial insemination 113–4, 222, 226, 230
asceticism 3, 4, 6, 193
Ashkenazim 48, 55, 57, 135, 137, 140, 205
assisted reproduction 226–31
Augustine xv, 27, 28, 108, 110

baptism xvi, 65, 69, 106, 109, 110–1, 116, 153, 154, 157, 158, 177, 215, 242
bar mitzvah vii, 92, 93–4, 99
Barna, George 150
bat mitzvah 94
Bet Din 52, 53, 136, 139, 144, 145, 227
betrothal, *see also* engagement
betrothal ceremony 49–50, 55, 56
Bible (in general) xvii, 19, 21–2, 31, 67–8, 71, 73, 104, 105, 112–3, 117, 156, 159, 200, 215
see also Hebrew bible, New Testament, scripture

255

birth 44, 70, 91–2, 103, 108, 112, 114, 121, 128, 130, 167, 168, 222, 227, 228
Bleich, David 134
blessing 4, 8, 50, 56–7, 75, 76, 92, 93, 99, 102, 107, 179, 217
Boteach, Shmuley 197
buggery 6, 11–12
Bultman, Rudolf 23
burqa 42, 237

Calvin, John 19, 64
canon law 19, 22, 24
Caro, Joseph xiv, 6
Casti Connubii 19
Catechism of the Catholic Church 20, 24, 108, 120, 146, 153
Central Conference of American Rabbis 16, 58, 59
Chabad-Lubavitch 60
chaperones 40, 189
chastity 7, 19, 28, 37, 38, 39, 47, 73, 87, 124, 169, 198
Church of England viii, xv, 20, 27, 93, 76, 116, 148, 177, 193, 214, 216, 228, 229, 239, 240
Church of Scotland viii, 20, 109
circumcision 92–3, 128–9, 215
civil marriage 16, 61–2, 64–5, 74, 149, 152, 154, 215
civil partnership 44, 74–5
Code of Jewish Law xiv, 6–8, 10–12, 15, 138, 179, 184, 195, 201, 222, 233

communal life xiii, 109, 143
confirmation 5, 106
conscience 23–5, 30, 59, 71, 114, 195
Conservative Judaism xiv, 15, 16, 51, 52, 60, 61, 63, 79, 101, 144, 145, 180, 197, 212, 222
contraception 14, 29–30, 104, 126–7, 192
conversion xiv, 58, 60, 79, 88, 110, 141, 157, 158–9, 160, 217, 227, 242
cosmetics 10, 42
custody 135, 136, 155, 168, 171–2, 214, 239

dating 69, 96, 118, 180
death 3, 10, 11–12, 27, 37, 40, 45, 46, 47, 51, 63, 85, 90. 106, 116, 119, 122, 126, 127, 141, 146, 147, 155, 186, 200, 222, 230, 239
diaspora xiii, xv, 96, 97, 136, 140, 143, 216, 234
diet 22, 202
Diognetus 18, 235, 236
disability 146, 221
divorce xx, 3, 31, 49, 51, 55, 58, 78, 81, 83, 85, 88–90, 96, 117, 121, 123, 132–73, 186–8, 230, 239–244
divorce ceremony 155–7, 242
dower 47, 79, 83–5, 124, 162, 165, 169–70, 189, 241
dress 10, 18, 41–3, 67, 100, 202, 233, 235–6, 238

INDEX OF NAMES AND SUBJECTS

education 26, 31, 40, 66, 69, 86, 94–7, 109–11, 123, 130, 150, 152, 171, 210, 229, 234, 236, 237
Egypt ix, xxi, 4, 42–3, 46, 47, 89, 99, 102, 129, 166, 182, 185–6, 188, 191, 201, 230, 241–2
Eibeschutz, Jonathan 9
emel 237
embryo 124, 219, 221, 229, 230–1
engagement 48, 77, 78, 180
Enlightenment xvii, 244
ethics xx, 14, 17–20, 21, 25, 113, 177, 221, 229
ethnicity 35–6, 86, 150, 188, 198, 203, 213
eucharist xiv, 65, 116, 152, 156, 158

Falk, Zev 133
fasting 36, 44, 131, 167, 216
fatwa 224, 230, 231
feminism 17, 64, 66, 68, 92, 96, 244
festivals xvi, 92, 97, 101–3, 131, 215, 235
Fletcher, Joseph 25
foetus 127, 222–4, 229, 230
fornication 31, 37–8, 45, 90, 142, 177, 178, 181–2, 224
fundamentalism viii, xvii, 15, 21, 66–7, 72, 74, 207

gender 17, 28, 29, 46, 62, 76, 110, 130, 218, 240
Gershom, Rebbenu 48, 137, 139–40, 205, 206

get 51, 55, 57, 132–3, 135–45, 240
Gibran, Kahlil 235
godparents 110–1, 153
grace xvii, 18, 20, 22, 65, 108, 109
guardianship 79, 86–7, 168, 171–2, 242

HaCohen, Menahem 143
hadith xxi, 34–7, 45, 46, 47, 78, 83, 84, 86, 88, 119, 121, 124, 126, 129, 160, 165, 171, 191, 241
halakah 31, 133, 139, 141, 142, 143, 206, 222, 226–7
Hanafi school 35, 45, 46, 121, 173
Hanbali school 35
Ha-Nasi, Judah xiii, 9, 200
Hanukkah 103
Haredim 180
Hebrew Bible xii, 3, 6, 9, 12–3, 15, 29, 31, 48, 49, 55–6, 57–8, 99, 101, 105, 132, 135, 145, 181, 183, 196, 200, 201–2, 205, 207, 215, 221, 243
hijab 41, 43, 191, 236, 238
Hillel 25, 132–3
Holocaust xv, 94
Holy Spirit xvi, 71, 215
homophobia 198, 203
homosexuality 3, 5, 13, 16, 44–6, 61–3, 72–6, 180, 187, 198–204, 217–8
honour killing 185, 237
hospitality 97, 199, 235

Humanae Vitae 19, 30
Humanistic Judaism 15, 17, 97, 180,
Huna, R. 13
huppah 55, 57, 179

illegitimacy 181, 226
incest 95, 199, 220, 222, 224
infertility 88, 112–4, 208
inheritance xx, 64, 89, 118, 121, 122, 186, 205, 231–2, 244
intercourse 3, 7–8, 13, 18, 29, 37, 43–4, 46, 50, 59, 71, 77, 121–2, 134, 162, 163, 167, 180, 191, 193, 195, 196, 226, 228
intermarriage 57–61, 96, 212–8
internet 69, 155, 192, 193, 203, 204, 216
in vitro fertilisation 113, 114, 226–7, 230
Iran 46, 137, 178, 182, 189, 206, 208, 210, 231
Ishmael, R. 13
Israel xiii, xv, 50, 56, 57, 93, 94, 96, 135–7, 143, 144, 206, 208, 216, 243

Jehovah's Witnesses 22
Jesus xvi, 20, 22–3, 25, 26, 27, 29, 31, 33, 65, 48, 70, 73, 105, 107, 111, 115, 147, 150, 152, 153, 155, 159, 235
Johanna, R. 13
John Paul II 31

Judah b. Illai, R. 12

Kabbalah xiv, 5
Karaites 206
kashrut 100–1
ketubah 49, 51–5, 144, 145, 179
Khadija 118, 119, 126
Khamanei, Ayatollah 231
khul' 165–6, 241–2
Kotb, Heba 191–2

lesbianism 13, 16, 61–3, 72–6, 114, 180, 195, 198, 200–1, 218
Lewis, C.S. 25, 167
liberalism 18, 22–3, 30, 32, 33, 58, 68, 71, 73, 76, 144, 178, 179, 180, 182, 184, 200, 203, 218, 223
Liberal Judaism 15
Liberman clause 52–3, 144
Lot 45, 199–200
love, types of 25–6, 187–8
Luther, Martin xv, xvii, 19, 64, 71
Lutheranism 23, 32

Magisterium 19
Maimonides, Moses 5, 13, 222
maintenance 88, 89, 122–5, 135, 165, 166, 169
Maliki school 35, 45, 46, 78, 123
marriage 48–90, 184–197, 212–8

INDEX OF NAMES AND SUBJECTS

arranged marriage 7, 48, 68, 80, 95, 210, 238
marriage contract ix, 48, 51, 77–81, 83–7, 89–90, 119, 120–1, 124, 146, 151, 162, 164–5, 170, 210, 230, 241, 243
cousin marriage 42, 81, 172, 212
covenant marriage 151–2
misyar marriage 89–90, 185, 186, 87, 241
mut'a marriage 89, 182, 185, 186–7, 189, 231, 241
marriage preparation 151
same-sex marriage 16, 44, 61–3, 72, 73, 74–5, 78, 79, 105, 159, 244
masturbation 5, 11, 13, 31–2, 47
media 71, 185, 193, 214, 219, 236, 237
Mendelssohn, Moses xiv
menstruation 21, 22, 32, 43–4, 70, 98, 121, 162, 163, 168, 193, 196, 234
Methodism 76, 156, 217
Metropolitan Community Church 74, 75
mezuzah 99–100
Middle Ages 5, 10, 93, 140
mikveh 98–9, 234
Mishnah xi, xiii, 50, 133, 200, 221
missionaries xviii, 158, 159, 207
misyar marriage 89–90, 185, 186, 87, 241

Mizrahim 137, 205
modesty 9–11, 41–3, 100, 185, 236
mohar 48–9, 51
monasticism xvii, 36, 116, 195
monogamy 125, 147, 157, 158–60, 206, 207, 208, 209
Moses xii, 15, 20, 22, 50, 54, 56, 93, 115, 147, 181, 202
Muhammad xviii, xx–xxi, 34–8, 45, 46, 78, 84, 86, 88, 115, 118–20, 124, 126, 128, 130, 160, 165, 171, 178, 188, 191, 231
mut'a marriage 89, 182, 185, 186–7, 189, 231, 241
mysticism 5, 13, 115, 195

New Testament 27, 105, 106, 107, 109, 115
niqab 42, 236, 238
Noachide Laws 12

Orthodoxy (Christian) xviii, 20, 28, 31, 65, 70, 106, 110, 116, 214, 228, 241–2
Orthodoxy (Jewish) vii, 6–7, 9, 15–7, 51–3, 59–60, 61, 91–4, 96, 98–101, 103–4, 134, 136, 144, 145, 179, 181, 184, 185, 191, 195–7, 201, 206, 216–7, 223, 233–4, 244

Passover 102–3, 216
patriarchy 3, 17, 68, 92

Paul xv, xvi, 18, 21–2, 24, 26, 27, 67, 68, 71, 72–3, 113, 115, 154, 207, 215
Pauline privilege 154
People of the Book xiii, 82–3, 213
Petrine privilege 154–5
phylactaries 96, 99–100
Plato 26, 27, 28, 188
Polycarp 64
polygamy 205–11
  in African Christianity 157–60, 207
  in Islam 87–9, 125, 207, 209–10, 231
  in Judaism 137, 205–6, 208
polygyny, see polygamy
pornography 30, 31, 32, 70, 187, 194
prayer 25, 28, 36, 44, 47, 49, 55, 57, 73, 92, 93, 94, 99, 1102, 103, 109, 111, 113, 126, 128, 129, 130, 156, 217
pregnancy 14, 25, 29, 31, 32, 43, 112, 113–4, 117, 133, 168, 170, 177, 179, 205, 220–4, 227, 228, 230
procreation 13, 14, 26, 27, 29, 64, 66, 71, 72, 104, 108, 121, 184, 191, 191, 193, 196, 199, 223, 230
prohibited relationships 42, 78, 80–2, 163
prostitution 5–6, 10, 13, 30–1, 158, 185, 187
Protestantism xvii, 19–21, 24, 28, 30, 31, 64–5, 67, 68, 71–2, 106, 108, 110, 114, 116, 149–51, 193, 215, 219, 228–9, 240

Quiverfull 108
Qur'an xx, xxi, 34, 36–9, 41, 43–4, 47, 77, 80, 82–4, 87, 88, 120–3, 126, 127, 129–30, 161–3, 165–71, 179, 181, 183, 188, 191, 209–10, 213, 215, 223, 230

Rabinowitz, Mayer 144
Ramadan 44, 131, 216
rape 3, 5, 6, 31, 47, 121, 127, 132, 199, 220, 221, 222, 224–5, 237
Reconstructionist Judaism 15, 16, 58, 61–2, 97, 101, 180
redemption of the firstborn 93
Reform Judaism vii, xiv, 15, 16, 52, 54, 58, 59, 61, 62, 97, 99, 101, 179–80, 201, 217, 222–3
Reformation xvii, 20, 21, 64, 116
remarriage 147, 152, 173, 240, 241
resurrection 27, 28, 68, 128
Risikoff, Menachem 145
Robinson, Gene 74, 156–7
Robinson, John A. T. 178
Roman Catholicism xvi, xviii, 19–20, 24, 29, 31, 64–5, 68, 70–3, 75, 106, 108, 110, 113, 116, 145, 148, 150, 152–5, 194, 214, 220, 228, 240, 242

INDEX OF NAMES AND SUBJECTS

Sabbath xvi, 22, 92, 93, 97, 101–2, 216, 217, 218, 235
sacraments 65, 73, 75, 106, 110, 116, 146, 148–9, 151, 153–4, 158, 160, 214, 241
same-sex marriage 16, 44, 61–3, 72, 73, 74–5, 78, 79, 105, 159, 244
Satan 6, 33
Saudi Arabia 40, 164, 187
science xvii, xxi, 146, 230
scripture: *see also* Hebrew Bibke, New Testament, Qur'an
  inerrancy of xvii, 15, 21, 34, 123, 188
  sola scriptura 19
Second Temple 16, 48
secularism 239
segregation of sexes 42, 116, 210
Sephardim 48, 55, 56, 57, 137, 140, 205
sex toys 70, 193–4, 196–7
Shafi'i school 35, 45, 47, 123
shame 41, 47, 155, 172, 189, 203, 224
Shammai 132
Shari'a ix, 34, 36, 37, 79, 85, 86, 121, 122, 163, 164, 166, 167, 170, 173, 180, 182, 189, 203, 207, 224, 241
Shema 99
Shi'a Muslims xx, 35, 89, 182, 185, 213
shiva 103–4
sin xvi, 3, 9–11, 14, 21, 23, 32, 36, 37, 38, 45, 70, 74, 80, 105, 142, 149, 154, 158, 160, 170, 177, 191, 196, 198, 223, 241, 244
singleness 36, 69, 91, 97, 105, 114, 115, 117–8, 172, 195, 206, 208, 210, 234
slander 38–9, 97, 166, 167, 189, 235
sodomy 12–3, 43, 44, 199–200
Sopher, Yehezkel 206, 208
Southern Baptist Convention 66, 67, 200, 213
sperm donation 229, 231
Sunna xx, 34, 130
Sunni Muslims xxi, 34, 35, 89, 189, 213, 230, 231
surrogacy 113–4, 228–9, 230

talaq 160–4, 170, 173
Talmud xiii, 4, 6, 12, 14, 48, 56, 58, 94, 97, 98, 133, 139, 141, 142, 144, 145, 195, 200, 201, 221, 227, 234
Tam, Jacob 139, 140
technology 32, 33, 66, 113, 207, 229
theology xx, 4, 21, 27, 107, 111, 153, 159, 178, 186
Toledo, Yaakov Moshe 145, 224
Torah xii, xiii, 6, 7, 11, 15, 23, 37, 39, 92, 93–4, 99, 100, 142, 195, 201, 205, 206, 217

transgender issues 46, 74, 75
Tunisia 89, 207, 209
Turkey xxi, 89, 207, 209

Umar ibn al-Khattab 83, 121, 126
Union of American Hebrew Congregations 16, 62
Union of Orthodox Jewish Congregations of America 61
Unitarians 75, 147, 156
United Church of Christ 32, 156
United Kingdom xii, ix, 30, 57, 64
United Methodist Church 76, 156
United States vii, xiv, xviii, 32, 57, 61, 64, 75, 94, 112, 143, 148, 150, 154, 177, 179, 188, 226

veiling 9, 40, 41–3, 55, 185, 236, 238
virginity 39–40, 83, 85, 86–7, 132, 184–5, 187, 241, 244

wedding 49, 54–7, 59, 61, 62–3, 64–5, 68, 75–6, 77, 86, 98, 148, 151, 157, 177, 179–80, 186, 214–5, 217–8, 238, 240
Wegner, Judith Romney 133
wet nurses 82, 129, 229
Wilcox, Brad 150
witnesses 37–9, 45, 47, 54–6, 64, 68, 85–6, 89, 110, 133, 138–9, 140, 142, 154
World Council of Churches xv, xvii, 18, 160
Wright, Bradley 150

yeshivah 94
Yosef, Ovadia 206

Zahiri school 35, 46
Zionism xii, xiv
Zohar 13
Zohar, Tsvi 206

www.ingramcontent.com/pod-product-compliance
Lightning Source LLC
Chambersburg PA
CBHW051352290426
44108CB00015B/1977